Big Business, Poor Peoples
The Impact of Transnational Corporations on the World's Poor

John Madeley

Zed Books
LONDON AND NEW YORK

Big Business, Poor Peoples: The impact of transnational corporations on the world's poor was first published by Zed Books Ltd, 7 Cynthia Street, London N1 9JF, UK and Room 400, 175 Fifth Avenue, New York, NY 10010, USA in 1999.

Distributed exclusively in the USA by St Martin's Press, Inc., 175 Fifth Avenue, New York, NY 10010, USA.

Cover designed by Andrew Corbett
Set in Monotype Dante by Ewan Smith
Printed and bound in the United Kingdom by Biddles Ltd, Guildford and King's Lynn

A catalogue record for this book is available from the British Library

Library of Congress Cataloging-in Publication Data
Madeley, John.
    Big business, poor peoples: the impact of transnational corporations in the world's poor / John Madeley.
        p.   cm.
    Includes bibliographical references and index.
    ISBN 1-85649-671-6 (hardcover). — ISBN 1-85649-672-4 (pbk)
    1. International business enterprises—Social aspects– –Developing countries.   2. Poor—Developing countries. 3. Developing countries—Economic conditions.   I. Title.
HD2932.M3   1999
305.569–dc21   99-17549
                                                    CIP

ISBN 1 85649 671 6 cased
ISBN 1 85649 672 4 limp

About the Author

John Madeley has been a writer and broadcaster specialising in Third World development and environmental issues for the past twenty years. From 1983 to 1998, he was editor of the renowned magazine, *International Agricultural Development*. A contributor to leading British papers including the *Observer*, the *Financial Times* and the *Independent on Sunday*, he has also written for many NGOs, including Christian Aid, the Panos Institute, and the Catholic Institute for International Relations. He is the author of several books:

When Aid is No Help: How Projects Fail and How They Could Succeed;
Trade and the Poor: The Impact of International Trade on Developing Countries;
Land is Life: Land Reform and Sustainable Agriculture (co-editor).

About this book

'A searing indictment of contemporary corporate plunder, this book constructs an airtight case for international regulation of TNCs.' *Walden Bello, Co-Director, Focus on the Global South*

'Authoritative and highly readable. Madeley names the names and tells the stories to provide a clear answer to those who cling to the myth that foreign investment, transnational corporations, the IMF, the World Bank and UNDP are an answer to the prayers of the poor. An excellent book that should be read by everyone committed to ending global poverty.' *David C. Korten, The People-Centered Development Forum*

'At last, a lucid account of how transnational corporations which should be accountable are destroying the lives of the world's poor. Read it, and understand how we can regain control over the powerful forces that are shaping our future.' *Barry Coates, Director, World Development Movement*

Zed Titles on Multinational Corporations and Globalization

Globalization is the current term used to characterize what is happening in the world economy at the turn of the twentieth century. Integral to this process is the ever more dominant position of very large transnational corporations. Zed Books has published a distinguished list of titles examining these phenomena in all their variety and complexity.

Samir Amin, *Capitalism in the Age of Globalization: The management of contemporary society*

Ricardo Carrere and Larry Lohmann, *Pulping the South: Industrial tree plantations and the world paper economy*

Michel Chossudovsky, *The Globalization of Poverty: Impacts of IMF and World Bank reforms*

Jacques B. Gelinas, *Freedom from Debt: The reappropriation of development through financial self-reliance*

Terence Hopkins, Immanuel Wallerstein et al., *The Age of Transition: Trajectory of the world-system, 1945–2025*

Serge Latouche, *In the Wake of the Affluent Society: An exploration of post-development*

Hans-Peter Martin and Harald Schumann, *The Global Trap: Globalization and the assault on democracy and prosperity*

Stephen Riley, *Stealing from the Poor: Corruption, development and poverty in the South*

Harry Shutt, *The Trouble with Capitalism: An inquiry into the causes of global economic failure*

Kavaljit Singh, *The Globalization of Finance: A citizen's guide*

Henk Thomas (ed.), *Globalization and Third World Trade Unions*

For full details of this list and Zed's other subject and general catalogues, please write to:

The Marketing Department, Zed Books, 7 Cynthia Street, London N1 9JF, UK or email: sales@zedbooks.demon.co.uk

Visit our website at: http://www.zedbooks.demon.co.uk

Contents

Preface

Many books have been written about transnational corporations (TNCs). None of them, as far as I am aware, has examined their impact on the world's poor. This is a serious omission. TNCs are now enormously powerful; in some respects they are more powerful than governments, not least because they are usually efficient at what they do – and what they do is make money for their shareholders. The cost in human terms of commercial success needs to be assessed. The impact of *government* policies on the poor is frequently analysed. In contrast, TNCs have escaped lightly.

When 'efficiency' is not accountable to people, it can become exploitation. When the impact of these unelected, and largely un-accountable, undemocratic corporations on materially resource-poor communities is analysed, a picture emerges of damaged livelihoods which brings no credit to the companies. Transnational corporations have used their money, size and power to influence international negotiations and taken full advantage of the move towards privatisation to influence the policies of governments. The most serious charge, however, is that the large corporations especially have used their power to effectively cause hardship for millions of the poor in developing countries. The story of how they do it is told in this book; it is a human story that needs to be revealed.

Most books on TNCs have been written by economists and teachers/lecturers in business management. This one is written by a former TNC employee, turned economic journalist, whose interest in trans-national corporations extends over almost half a century. On leaving school I worked for a TNC for ten years, including three years selling the company's products. This enabled me to 'see the inside' and provided a basic understanding of the rationale and thinking of the large firm with a global reach. More recently, as a journalist and writer for the last 20 years, I have travelled and worked in over 40 developing countries, to write about matters which affect the poor. TNCs are one of them.

Much of the research into TNCs has focused on their economic impact, in terms of efficiency, profit maximisation, capital flows, etc.; it has overlooked the economic, social and cultural effects on the world's poor. A learned journal, *Transnational Corporations*, examines TNC activities from almost every angle, but, like most literature on the corporations, rarely mentions the people affected by them. People are seen as links in a long chain who scarcely warrant a mention.

The academic community, in management and business schools, is largely failing to give students a perspective of how TNCs affect the poor. I make no apology for rushing in where academics fear to tread. In a book on the corporations, written in 1973, Louis Turner says: 'In researching the book, I found it chastening to discover how often journalists raised crucial issues years before academic authorities had begun their analysis.'[1] Academics urgently need to begin their analysis of TNCs and the poor. Too many years have already gone by.

As the academic literature is sparse about the effects of TNCs on people, let alone on the poor, I have supplemented my own direct research in developing countries by drawing on newspapers and special- ist journals which have given the matter more attention and also have the advantage of being more up to date. I have also drawn on the findings of non-governmental organisations which have done pioneering work in highlighting corporate activity. As I have researched this book, what has become clear is that the effects of TNCs on the poor are huge, but often hidden and rarely reported. A great deal more needs to be done to stop abuses of corporate power.

I have looked in this book at the main activities in which TNCs are engaged in developing countries and which touch the lives of the world's poor. These are chiefly agriculture, forestry, fishing, foodstuffs, mining, manufacturing, energy, tourism, and medicinal drugs. Some of the largest corporations are active in more than one of these sectors. As the corporate spread widens, so public concern over TNC activities is growing.

It is now hard to detect the absence of TNCs from any sizeable area of economic activity that could possibly yield a profit. David Korten describes TNCs as 'instruments of a market tyranny that is extending its reach across the planet like a cancer, colonising ever more of the planet's living spaces, destroying livelihoods, displacing people, render- ing democratic institutions impotent, and feeding on life in an insatiable quest for money'.[2] The worst aspect of this tyranny is that it hits hardest at the most vulnerable people, the poor.

'Market tyranny' effectively delivers developing countries into cor- porate hands. The outcome of the GATT Uruguay Round of trade talks, in 1994, strengthened the TNCs considerably because it means that governments are less able to regulate and control them. Words like globalisation and liberalisation bring joy to TNC directors. Although the corporations have become more powerful, the UN has abandoned its attempt to frame a code of conduct to regulate them. The TNCs may claim that self-regulation can control the industry, but this has not happened and is unlikely to happen.

Economic recession in developing countries has again, ironically, often strengthened the TNCs. In some ways it suits them to have an impoverished Third World. The corporations can then present themselves as a country's saviour. Often out of economic desperation, rather than conviction, do governments try to attract them. In some rural areas of Africa, government services, such as health, education and agricultural research, no longer exist. There is a vacuum that either TNCs or non-governmental organisations could fill. But there are huge dangers in TNCs filling such a role.

Countries are now competing to give foreign investors a 'favourable climate'. But this usually means that TNCs can do what they like. The corporations protest otherwise, but with little conviction. 'TNCs are implausible as social consciences, defenders of the poor, human value setters', says Reginald Green, 'their capacity and legitimacy for independent action in these areas is nil and such action contradicts their logic.'[3]

Running through this book is the impact that TNCs have on a country's physical environment. A company that damages the physical environment of an area, damages its natural resources to the detriment of local people. 'TNCs are the main economic agents responsible for the global environmental crisis', believes Martin Khor of the Malaysian-based Third World Network. When TNC activity damages a physical environment, it damages the ability of the people who live there to make a living. And it usually hits the poorest the most, for they have fewer options – they depend on natural resources rather than on purchased goods. They cannot very easily move and make a living elsewhere, although in desperation this may happen.

Effects

This book contains examples of the effects of large transnational corporations on the poor. Small transnational firms, employing less than 500 people, are not covered; these account for less than 10 per cent of foreign direct investment.[4] The examples are not necessarily the worst examples, they do not pretend to be comprehensive, but are rather an indication of what is going on. Some of the cases I have seen at first hand. While the book concentrates on the impact of TNCs on the poor in developing countries, this is not to say that these large corporations have no impact on the poor in Western countries. In the West, mainstream economic institutions, especially banks, often refuse to serve the poor, who are then forced:

> to turn to a shadow economy [which] is no longer made up of only sleazy hucksters. Ripping off the poor has become big business, with major companies, including Ford, American Express and Nationsbank among the major players.[5]

Worldwide, ripping off the poor has become big business. Control over human and natural resources is becoming inexorably ceded to TNCs at the expense of local communities. Although they are affected by the corporations, local people have little or no power to influence their decisions. Some TNCs are now talking of the need to consult people about their projects. This book shows the scale of what needs to be done.

Chapter 1 gives an overview of the role of the corporations; it examines how they have grown both in size and power since the late 1980s, especially in developing countries. In addition to direct investment, TNCs now have more non-ownership arrangements and non-equity links, such as sub-contracting. In this way, the corporations make profits without risking their money. But the risk is transferred to developing countries. The corporate attitude is 'let the poor take the risk'. TNCs are powerful enough to be able to do it. These types of arrangement are especially prevalent in the manufacturing and tourism sectors.

TNCs are not the only companies that make life difficult for the poor; many domestic companies also come into that category. TNCs, however, are fundamentally different from local Third World companies. Their size and internationalism give them a power over governments that national firms do not have. The sizeable amounts of money they have enables them to engage in activities that effectively harm the poor. More jobs is a carrot that TNCs often hold out for governments, yet the jobs created can be both fickle and few. TNC activity often makes only weak links with national economies.

Chapter 2 looks at why developing countries 'want' TNCs. Economic weakness is a major reason. In a world of structural adjustment programmes, globalisation, liberalisation and privatisation, governments of developing countries seem to have little choice but to attract the corporations. But these modern-day 'isations' are having a profound effect on the poor, playing straight into the hands of TNCs who could scarcely have imagined a more profitable scenario. Battered by economic recession, it is not always apparent to governments that the right of their country to develop its own economy and technologies is under threat.

Debt is a major reason why developing countries 'want' TNCs. They hope that they can earn more foreign exchange to help them repay debt. Both debt relief and development aid may be made conditional on countries liberalising their economies, which means making them open to the corporations. There is enormous pressure on developing countries to jump on board the globalisation bandwagon – the proposed Multilateral Agreement on Investment is part of this and is considered in Chapter 2.

The devil is in the detail, and most of this book examines, by sector, the details of TNC activities. Chapter 3 looks at the largest economic sector of all, agriculture. Transnational corporations are most visible and often most controversial when engaged in agriculture: they sell seeds, fertilisers and pesticides to farmers, patent new crop varieties, own plantations, and they are involved in biotechnology, genetic engineering and animal breeding, contracting out their activities, and giving advice. They also process, market and export a huge number of products, ranging from coffee to bananas, from tea to tomatoes.

Domination

Many food corporations have huge power, dominating world markets in internationally traded agricultural commodities, with a small number of companies accounting for a large percentage of the trade. The food giant, Cargill, for example, has a greater sales turnover in coffee than the GDP of most of Africa's coffee-producing countries. The expansion plans of such companies often threaten land which is at present farmed by smallholders. Chapter 3 also looks at pesticide sales in developing countries, and at how some leading chemical TNCs have shown disregard for the safety of people who handle their products.

Chapter 4 examines some of the major products in which TNCs are involved – in particular, tobacco and cigarettes, babyfoods, and non-traditional exports, such as fruit, vegetables and flowers. The production, trade and use of these commodities is again damaging the lives of millions in developing countries. With people in the North gradually giving up smoking, the TNCs that dominate the tobacco industry view the South as the market that will keep them in business. But the industry and its TNCs are having a damaging impact that far exceeds any benefits.

More than one million children are dying each year who might have lived if they had been breastfed in infancy. The promotion of breastmilk substitutes to mothers is done by some of the world's most prominent TNCs. The spirit, and even the letter, of the World Health Organization Code of Conduct on the marketing of breastmilk substitutes is not being observed by many of the companies. These activities can cost farmers their livelihoods, however, as the new crops replace traditional staple foods and give rise to unforeseen pest problems. The use of toxic chemicals in agri-business activities again appears to be causing huge damage to the health of workers.

Tropical rainforests are often of critical importance for the poor, and TNCs are again involved in the destruction of this precious resource. When they damage forests, they harm more than trees – they harm the livelihoods of the people who live there. Chapter 5 looks at the rampant logging which is now going on; at how, for example, in Papua New Guinea, some TNCs are roaming the countryside 'with the self-assurance of robber barons, bribing politicians and leaders, creating social disharmony and ignoring the laws'. For 'Papua New Guinea' can be read 'the world'.

Chapter 5 also looks at the role of TNCs in the overfishing which has caused stagnant world fish catches. Using 'modern technology', trawlers from Western countries, mostly owned by the corporations, are sweeping up fish from Third World waters in an unsustainable manner, threatening the catches and livelihoods of local fishers. Again, it is poorer communities who bear the brunt, not least because less fish is available for them.

By definition, mining is an environmentally destructive activity. It is also hugely profitable and in the wake of privatisation is expanding at an enormous pace, with TNCs again prominent. But, as Chapter 6 shows, much of their activity is not only damaging local environments, it is creating havoc with the economies and cultures of the poor. Across Asia, the Pacific, Africa and Latin America, mining is being done with little regard for the people who live in the immediate area. Mining often takes over land where people once lived and farmed, it produces huge waste dumps, which are often health hazards, contaminating water sources sometimes far beyond the immediate area. A UN report says of mining (and petroleum extraction) that TNCs 'often have adverse socio-economic impacts on rural populations, and these effects need to be addressed by Governments and the TNCs involved'.[6]

Toys, shoes and clothes are among the main manufactured goods that TNCs and their sub-contractors produce in developing countries. Many of these goods are top-quality brand names that fetch high prices in the shops, but the people who produce them see little benefit. As Chapter 7 shows, low wages, often lower than a country's minimum level, and long hours and poor working conditions are common in the factories in developing countries that have been sub-contracted to make toys, garments and footwear for TNCs. But now the people who buy them are getting restless and there is a clear need for independently monitored codes of conduct on different products. It is still not clear, however, whether TNCs really believe in such codes, or whether they are trying to get away with the minimum they think is necessary to keep consumers happy.

Every year between the mid-1980s and the mid-1990s around four million people were displaced from their homes by large hydro-electric dam schemes. Large corporations are a vital link in the big dam chain; their experience of such schemes gives them an expertise that national companies usually lack. Chapter 8 considers some of these schemes, including the planned, if now postponed, Bakun dam in Malaysia, which will still remove around 10,000 people from their traditional longhouses. This chapter looks at the energy TNCs, including the activities of some of world's largest corporations, for example Shell in Nigeria and BP in Colombia.

Tourism is the second largest foreign currency earner for the developing world, second only to oil in terms of revenue. Many countries see it as one of their few growth sectors and an attractive way of diversifying the economy, escaping from dependence on traditional exports. But most of the foreign exchange that developing countries earn from international tourism goes to TNCs rather than to the people of those countries. Through their ownership of hotels, airlines and tour operators, tourism's TNCs have woven a powerful corporate web which puts them in prime position to reap the benefits. Poorer people, especially, are often the victims rather than the beneficiaries of the tourist industry. As Chapter 9 shows, tourism also has a huge and often damaging impact on local environments.

Abuses

One of the most flagrant abuses of TNC power, and arguably the one with the most serious effects on millions of the poor, is highlighted in Chapter 10, which deals with drugs. Medicine for the poor is big business for the rich. In many developing countries, 20–30 per cent of the health budget is spent on drugs, most of them made by pharmaceutical TNCs. This chapter shows how the companies promote their products and how liberalisation hinders countries from pursuing a national drugs policy, which mean the poor are denied access to low-cost, locally made drugs. Susan George is right to point out that:

the drug scene [the *legal* drug scene, that is] is nothing short of scandalous. Decent people sometimes simply cannot grasp the lengths to which corporations and those who support them are prepared to go in the pursuit of power and profit.[7]

TNCs are the great persuaders. The money they spend on public relations can almost be seen as a measure of their abuse of power. They have to spend, because there is so much to explain away. In every single area of economic activity, TNC activity is controversial. Instead of acting more responsibly, they choose to spend large sums to put a good 'spin' on what they are doing. Chapter 11 examines how they operate. What is both startling and disturbing is the way that the United Nations and some of its agencies have been effectively nobbled by the TNCs – their influence on UN bodies is huge.

The concluding chapter looks at some practical ways of curbing the power of TNCs. Governments, producers, consumers and shareholders can make choices and decisions which influence the corporations. While TNCs may be powerful, they cannot force people to play their game. The corporations depend for their survival on the people who use their technologies and buy their products. They depend on the markets they promote, on the governments they try to influence, and on the people who own them, that is, their shareholders. They are international companies, mostly owned by a small section of the public, but they show few responsibilities to the wider public.

National governments can regulate the corporations, despite their power. Producers and farmers can use methods which cut out TNC inputs. Consumers can play a critical role by refusing to purchase goods and services made by TNCs that are acting irresponsibly. By purchasing fairly traded products, made by smaller producers, consumers can help to counter the power of the large corporations.

While codes of conduct on goods such as garments and toys seem to offer a way forward, they are by no means a panacea. In the late 1970s, on a visit to Nigeria, I talked to a British businessman who was the director of a transnational company. An international code of conduct for TNCs was then under negotiation in New York and I outlined what the code was aiming to do. He responded by telling me – point by point – of the ways TNCs would get round such codes and regulations. Two decades later, companies are now under more pressure to agree to codes of conduct and consumers must ensure that these codes are worth something. Chapter 12 considers the human-scale alternatives that offer a more people-centred and sustainable future, and whether there is any place for large-scale TNCs in communities where people matter.

As the world approaches the third millennium, we are seeing sovereignty shift into corporate hands. Power is passing from governments to TNCs and the poor are paying the highest price. All professions, wrote George Bernard Shaw, are a conspiracy against the laity. Yet transnational corporations have no need to conspire against the poor. Their power and practice, insensitivity and apathy towards the poor, have much the same effect. My hope is that this book will fill a hole in the debate and stimulate attention, research and action that will lessen the damaging impact of TNCs on the world's most vulnerable people.

Acknowledgements

In covering an activity as wide as the work of transnational corporations, I have been helped by many people and should like to thank, in particular, Barbara Dinham of the Pesticides Trust; Helena Paul, the Gaia Foundation; Brian O'Riordan, Intermediate Technology, who read the fisheries section of Chapter 4; Thea Sinclair, Tourism Research Centre, the University of Kent; Tricia Barnett, Tourism Concern; Peter Madden and Bethan Brookes, Christian Aid; Aditi Sharma, the World Development Movement, who read Chapters 6 and 7; Christopher Hall, Christian Concern for One World; Patti Rundall, Baby Milk Action; mining expert Roger Moody; David Ould, Anti-Slavery International; and Michelle Stratford, Oxfam, all based in the UK.

And, based abroad, Vandana Shiva of India, João Pedro Stedile and Jose Luiz of Brazil, Ogen Kevin Aliro of Uganda, Zafrullah Chowdhury of Bangladesh, Janneke van Eijk of Clean Clothes Campaign in the Netherlands; Francisco Morales of CIAT in Colombia; health expert Andrew Chetley, and participants from a number of developing countries at a consultation in 1996 on Mining and Indigenous Peoples. I should also like to thank the staff and writers of the excellent US-based *Multinational Monitor* magazine. This plays a leading role in highlighting abuses by TNCs, and is always a tremendous source of information. Also Martin Khor and Mohammed Idris of the Malaysia-based Third World Network for the insights I have gained from their work.

My thanks to the librarians at the Overseas Development Institute and the British Library in London, and at the University of the South Pacific in Suva, Fiji, for help with research into tourism. Also officials of the UN Food and Agriculture Organisation, the UN Conference on Trade and Development, the International Labour Organisation, and the World Tourism Organisation.

Ironically, I would like to acknowledge the role of Nestlé UK. In July 1994 Nestlé mounted an exhibition at a meeting of the Church of England General Synod in York. This claimed that the company was adhering to the international code on the marketing of breastmilk substitutes. But an agency report issued at about that time pointed to many hundreds of alleged violations of the code by Nestlé. It was health officials, doctors and nurses around the world who were making these allegations. To me, Nestlé's case simply did not add up. The idea of this book was born at that meeting, because it made me think about the claims of TNCs and to wonder what they are trying to hide. In researching this book, I found that the effects of TNCs on the poor are more severe than I had expected.

My thanks to Alison for her valued comments and skilled eye for textual errors, and to others, too numerous to record, who have inspired me with their insights. Any mistakes are entirely mine.

CHAPTER I

Introduction: The Corporate Spread

Government by organized money is just as dangerous as government by organized mobs (Franklin D. Roosevelt)

The problem of power is how to get men of power to live for the public rather than off the public (Robert F. Kennedy)

To the TNCs the poor are normally invisible (Reginald H. Green)

Transnational corporations are one of the most important actors in the global economy, occupying a more powerful position than ever before. Fifty years ago, only a handful existed. Now they number tens of thousands, and have a profound political, economic, social and cultural impact on countries, peoples and environments. Defined by the United Nations as 'an enterprise with activities in two or more countries with an ability to influence others', TNCs produce a vast range of goods and services for international trade, and often for the domestic markets where they operate. Sometimes called multinational corporations, they operate 'across national boundaries in a context of nation states'.[1] Their power is huge and often underestimated, as also is their impact on the poor.

Mostly based in Western countries, TNCs have become a significant adjunct of Western economies. When they operate in developing countries, their sheer size can give them a disproportionate effect and power. Third World governments nevertheless generally try to attract them, while non-governmental organisations (NGOs), especially those in the South which see corporations at work and the effects they have, are often fiercely critical. A huge gap in attitudes to TNCs has opened up between governments and most development and environmental NGOs.

In the late 1990s, TNCs are growing fast. According to the 1996 *World Investment Report* of the United Nations Conference on Trade and Development (UNCTAD):

The tempo of business globalization is accelerating at a dramatic pace. Companies from every developed country as well as from an increasing number of developing countries, are becoming more active globally.[2]

According to UNCTAD's 1998 *World Investment Report* there are now at least 53,000 TNCs compared to 7,000 in the early 1970s; two-thirds of them are based in 14 industrialised countries. These TNCs have over 450,000 foreign affiliates worldwide. The FDI (foreign direct investment) stock which the parent companies invested in their foreign affiliates reached $3.5 trillion in 1997, when these affiliates generated sales of $9.5 trillion – higher than the value of total world trade in goods and services. About 400 corporations account for more than half the total TNC sales. Owned by their shareholders, they have to make profits for shareholders. Their chief loyalty is to their shareholders.

The biggest TNCs have annual sales which exceed the output of most developing countries. In total, TNCs employ about 73 million people worldwide, some 60 per cent in their head offices, the remaining 40 per cent in their foreign affiliates. About 12 million people are employed by the corporations in developing countries – about 2 per cent of their workforce.[3] In their persistent battle to increase profits, they have increasingly turned to the developing world, a world which holds many attractions for them. Wages and operating costs are usually much lower than in developed countries, organized labour unions may not exist, environmental controls are often lax, there is scope for transfer pricing and governments may offer a 'tax-free holiday'. Under this arrangement, a firm pays no tax for the first five or even ten years of its operation. There are also geographical reasons; the Third World has land for agriculture, land with minerals and land for tourists to explore.

Foreign direct investment

Foreign direct investment (FDI) is dominated by transnational corporations. With TNCs boosting their investments, FDI in developing countries almost tripled between 1983–87 and 1992, from an annual average of $18.3 billion to $50.4 billion.[4] It then almost trebled between 1992 and 1997, rising to $149 billion out of a worldwide FDI total of $400 billion.[5] While FDI surged, development aid declined and commercial loans to many poorer countries almost dried up, largely because of foreign indebtedness.

The FDI is highly concentrated: 'about 80 per cent of FDI has gone to only ten developing countries'.[6] The smallest 100 recipient countries have received only 1 per cent. Almost two-thirds of the FDI to

Table 1.1 The top 20 TNCs, ranked by profits in 1998 (US$ million)

1. Royal Dutch/Shell	15,637
2. Exxon	8,460
3. HSBC Holdings	8,360
4. General Electric	8,203
5. Unilever	7,943
6. Intel Corporation	6,945
7. Ford Motor	6,920
8. General Motors	6,698
9. Philip Morris	6,310
10. Toyota	6,159
11. British Petroleum	6,132
12. IBM	6,093
13. ENI	5,735
14. British Telecom	5,414
15. Lloyds/TSB	5,318
16. Novartis	4,927
17. Merck	4,614
18. Glaxo Wellcome	4,517
19. Microsoft	4,490
20. AT&T Corporation	4,472

Source: Derived from 'FT 500', *Financial Times*, 28 January 1999.

developing countries went to Asia, only 5 per cent to Africa. About 100 TNCs accounted for one-third of all the FDI in the developing world. Linkages to other sectors of economies resulting from this investment have often been weak (see Employment section, p. 10).

The TNCs have concentrated their FDI in a small number of developing countries often because they had authoritarian governments and were judged to be reliable 'client' states. The corporations are more likely to invest in countries where the government appears stable. Instability is bad for business.

Nervousness among developing country governments about the activities of TNCs caused a brisk period of expropriation of their assets in the late 1960s and early 1970s. Governments believed that by nationalising TNCs they could expropriate for themselves the profits that were going to the companies. But the expropriation period was short-lived. TNCs are skilled at operating an economic activity at a profit – they would not stay in business otherwise. Governments quickly realised that they could not run the often quite complex, usually Western-style type of TNC operation with the same degree of profitability. The hoped-for gains from expropriation failed to materialise, and nationalisation of TNCs was dropped as the answer to the problem.

Royal Dutch/Shell, the world's most profitable TNC, had sales of $138,041 million in 1998 (four times the annual income of Nigeria's 100 million people) and profits almost twice as high as any other corporation.

The corporations control 'between a quarter and a third of all world production and are particularly active in processing and marketing', according to the Brandt Report in 1980: 'The marketing, processing or production of several commodities – including bauxite, copper, iron ore, nickel, lead, zinc, tin, tobacco, bananas and tea – is dominated in each case by a small number of transnational corporations.'[7] The extent of their activities has since become much higher. It is common for a small number of TNCs to account for over 80 per cent of the trade in agricultural products (see Chapter 2). 'Outside the primary sector, upwards of two-thirds of the world's exports of goods and services are accounted for by TNCs; and 30–40 per cent of these take place within these same institutions.'[8] One estimate suggests that the biggest 500 TNCs 'control about 70 per cent of world trade, 80 per cent of foreign investment and about 30 per cent of world GDP'.[9] About one-third of world trade is conducted by TNCs within their own organisations – a subsidiary in one country selling to and/or buying from a subsidiary in another, or with head office.

The case for TNCs rests on the theory of comparative advantage – that everyone gains when countries specialise and that TNCs help in that specialisation. According to John H. Dunning: 'One of the tasks of the international market place is to allocate resources and capabilities in such a way that each country engages in the kind of economic activities to which it is comparatively best suited.'[10] But the theory of comparative advantage, the very engine of the TNC motor, has lost credibility. Countries have specialised economically but millions have not gained. Nonetheless, the ability of TNCs to produce goods and services that can earn foreign exchange and create extra jobs puts them in a position of considerable power over economies, trade and people. But this position of power is open to abuse; it effectively gives TNCs a high degree of governance over a developing country, even over a democratically elected government.

The worldwide trend to greater privatisation, liberalisation and globalisation is putting TNCs in an even more dominant position (see Chapter 2). In the late 1980s and 1990s most developing countries liberalised their economies by removing tariff barriers, non-tariff barriers, price controls, subsidies, and other restraints on the free play of economic market forces. Privatisation of an economy usually makes a country more attractive for the TNCs. In the last decade there has been a big increase in the number of developing countries in which the corporations will consider investing. The outcome of the GATT Uruguay Round increases their influence in a number of ways – it means that governments cannot use the controls they once used, over trade-related aspects of intellectual property rights, for example.

Why TNCs are different

Investment by TNCs in developing countries is fundamentally different from investment by local companies. TNCs 'directly control the deployment of resources in two or more countries, and the distribution of the resulting output', says Dunning.[11] They can use international experience, knowledge and muscle in a way that is not usually open to domestic firms. They are more likely to be able to exert market power, says Sheila Page, 'they are more likely to have experience in trading in markets outside the host country ... more likely to be aware of and experienced in exploiting the advantages of moving between exporting and investing abroad, and therefore more likely to respond to new opportunities'.[12]

Transnational corporations can therefore exercise a far more powerful role than purely local Third World companies. The sheer size of the larger corporations gives them enormous power over the governments of most developing countries, especially smaller countries. With size, comes the promise of what they can offer. They can provide the capital that a country lacks – to invest, for example, in activities such as prospecting for mineral deposits – and national companies may not have. They may have superior management and organisational skills. These, combined with international marketing outlets and experience, make them a force that national enterprises are unlikely to match. When they negotiate with governments of developing countries, TNCs are in a position to get a deal which local companies could not usually expect.

Transnational corporations are also different because they tend to make decisions in their head office country and not in the countries where they operate. Decisions affecting the people of developing countries are made in TNC offices in Washington, London, Tokyo, etc. In the countries where they operate, TNCs are usually under no obligation to consult local people about their plans. Even the affiliate of a TNC that operates in a developing country may have little say over how its company is run. 'Most decisions, the outcome of which affects the behaviour of foreign affiliates, are taken by their parent companies on the basis of information and expectations known only to them.'[13] And they operate in a round-the-world 24-hour market 'that pays no homage to national economic planning'.[14]

The bigger the corporation, the bigger the problem. 'Decision taking rests outside the country which is affected by the decision', points out Dunning, 'the more global the investing force is in its activities, outlook and strategy, the more the pattern of output and growth of its affiliates will be determined by forces outside their control.'[15] TNCs intensify the effects of big business on the poor. Purely local firms are unlikely to have the same impact. The inherent conflict between profits and people's rights is sharper in the case of TNCs. Dunning also points out that 'foreign investment transmits a way of life from the investing countries to the host country'.[16]

The poor

In contrast to the world of the transnational corporations, the poor have little or no say in the way their country is run. Around 1.5 billion people in Africa, Asia and Latin America are materially poor, with incomes of less than a dollar a day; many are jobless, voiceless, rootless and apparently futureless. Millions of women and men are either landless or have tiny plots, often with poor soil. If they work in the informal economy, they are often under-employed. Women and girls make up 70 per cent of their number.

These 1.5 billion resource-poor people are hungry for much of the time, they are poorly educated and in poor health, their housing and shelter are meagre, they have few resources at their command. They may go hungry even when food in the area where they live is relatively plentiful. Their poverty means they do not have the land to grow the food they need, nor the money to buy food.

The life expectancy of the poor is short and their plight is hardly improving. According to the United Nations Development Programme's *Human Development Report 1996*, the poor are generally more worse off now than 15 years ago, and, in some cases, poorer than they were 30 years ago.[17] Globalisation has not helped them. Aid programmes designed for them frequently do more to help the better-off. In Africa, most people were worse off in the 1990s than in the 1980s.

The starkest contrast between the poor and the TNCs is that the poor have little or no power. And while the corporations gained in the 1990s from the changes in the global economy, the poor lost, often from those same changes. What millions of the poor do have is a sense of solidarity with each other. While frequently demoralised and disorganized, there are examples of the poor uniting in efforts to stand up to the power of the TNCs. In this way the power they have can be realised.

The poor aspire to a better way of life and this natural aspiration often brings them into contact with TNCs. With clever advertising the corporations present an image of the better life the poor can have if they only use their products. Throughout the developing world the poor have been persuaded to spend some of their scarce resources on luxury goods such as, for example, cigarettes and canned baby foods, and food and drink of low nutritional value. TNCs have successfully persuaded people in developing countries to adopt products such as Coca-Cola, Seven-Up, Pepsi, McDonald's beef-burgers and Kentucky fried chicken as part of their way of life. Such goods cost a sizeable proportion of the poor's earnings, with the result that traditional and usually more nutritious foods cannot be afforded, and health suffers. 'By consuming inappropriate products, the poor have less money available to buy basic necessities.'[18] (See Chapter 4, especially the section on tobacco, pp. 48–57). Also, by spreading the message 'West is best', TNCs can reduce the demand for locally produced goods, and therefore damage local industries.

The poor buy the products of TNCs, and work for the corporations on terms that the corporations decide; they live in areas where TNCs operate and are affected by changes in the environment brought about by the corporate presence. They exist alongside the TNC world of instant communications, mobile phones, the Internet, e-mail and web-sites. This provides perhaps the starkest contrast of all. Most of the world's poor have never made a telephone call.

Size

Size alone makes for an unequal relationship between TNCs and the poor, both governments and peoples. Government negotiations with a TNC that is thinking of investing are loaded in favour of the corpora-tion. Their size and character in relation to most national economies 'are a source of considerable uncertainty for developing countries in negotiations with them', pointed out a Commonwealth Experts Group, although it took the view that TNCs 'can have a positive role to play in their industrialisation process'.[19]

But once they are operating in a developing country, their size and power, the jobs they offer to create and the taxes they pay, put TNCs in a powerful position to influence government policy. This raises ques-tions about the democratic process itself. For example, what right does a TNC that is unaccountable to people in developing countries have over the way that a country is run? Does their power enable them to effectively subvert democracy? Are we getting close to the point when voters will say 'what is the point of voting in elections when our elected leaders are subservient to the corporations'?

Recent changes at the global level give governments even less control over the TNCs. Structural adjustment programmes and the emergence of the World Trade Organisation have weakened the sovereignty of government. 'There has been an erosion of the decision-making powers of government', in the view of Kenneth Dadzie, former UNCTAD Secretary-General, 'national governments cannot play the role they did in the past'.[20] Neither may the TNCs be too particular about standards. Marketing executive, Lewis Pringle, was quoted as telling a Nestlé-sponsored conference in November 1995: 'In many (if not all) emerging markets, it is simply impossible to make significant money without overt violation of normal Western ethical principles.'[21]

Transnational corporations have the money to make a big sales pitch to developing countries, financing millions of salesmen and women to go around selling drugs to doctors and pharmacies, and chemicals to farmers, for instance. With more funds usually available to them than government has at its disposal, the corporations can cover the ground more thoroughly than government services. This sales effort is reflected in the relatively high prices of TNC products. Therefore, ultimately, it is the consumers who pay the salesperson's wages.

When Western-based TNCs invest in the economies of other countries, they do so because they believe that a profitable operation is possible. TNCs are usually ruthlessly efficient. For small-scale companies in developing countries, such ruthless efficiency can, however, drive them out of business.

Gain or loss?

The money that TNCs invest in developing countries seems welcome, but the question is whether it results in a net gain for a country's economy. The money invested by a corporation is often not its own – it may have been borrowed from banks in developing countries, reducing the amount of money that the banks have available to lend to smaller businesses in their country.

Neither can TNCs be relied on to stay in a country, as they tend to be less interested in long-term *sustainable* operations in any one country. They are more concerned about their own profit than with the welfare of a host country. This sometimes results in the closing down of an entire operation, an action which can have a devastating impact. Again, what distinguishes a TNC from a domestic firm is that the corporation can more easily shift its operation to another country. The priorities of a TNC are unlikely to coincide with those of local people. 'They are not those of the majority of the population, even though they may coincide with those of a wealthy minority', say Dinham and Hines of TNCs in Kenya's food and agricultural sector.[22]

TNCs have been powerful enough to lead industrialisation in some countries. But there is evidence that such TNC-led industrialisation in several Asian countries has been achieved at a severe cost to agriculture and rural development. Governments have tended to keep farm-gate prices low, both to save money for industrialisation and to enable workers in new export-orientated factories to have cheap food and not demand high wages. Again, people had to be attracted to work in industry. In Taiwan, for example, 'the government has intentionally held down peasants' incomes so as to transfer these people into industry', admitted Taiwan president Lee Teng-Hui.[23]

Of particular significance is that the presence of TNCs in poorer countries has widened internal inequalities. Almost all the studies that have been done on the effects of FDI have concluded that it has led 'to an uneven income distribution in developing countries', according to Pan-Long Tsai. However, Tsai adds that 'only the East/Southeast Asian countries appear to be the ones really harmed (in terms of uneven income distribution) by the inflow of FDI'.[24]

TNCs produce goods and services for those who have purchasing power; they cannot meet the basic needs of people who do not have the money to express their needs in the market place. The corporations apply their knowledge to comparatively luxury goods and services. The nature of their products and knowledge 'create biases against the poor; very few [of the poor] are its direct customers, employees or sources of supply'.[25]

The impact of TNCs on a country's physical environment is often severe. Agri-corporations are more likely to be involved in the production of crops for export than domestic companies. The cultivation of export crops can mean the removal of the poor from their land, and involve monocropping, which damages soil more than food crops. The production of cotton and tobacco has severe environmental costs (see Chapter 4). TNCs import into developing countries goods such as chemical products which are banned in their home countries. They export hazardous waste to developing countries on a considerable scale, thus making disasters more likely to happen.

Employment

Low wages are one of the reasons why TNCs are attracted to developing countries. The hope that they can create jobs is one of the reasons why governments try to attract the corporations. The *World Investment Report 1994* says that 'for each job directly generated by a TNC, one or two may result indirectly from backward and forward linkages'.[26] But jobs in TNCs are vulnerable, and the linkages may be much weaker than expected. According to the Report:

> Greater mobility of capital and technology under TNCs may bring about dramatic shifts in production and employment at the local, national and regional levels, generating considerable albeit temporary strains on workers in certain industries and/or labour markets ... labour mobility does not match capital mobility.[27]

For workers who lose their jobs when a TNC moves to another country, the 'strain' may, however, be more than temporary. The workforce employed by TNCs 'generally enjoys superior wages, conditions of work and welfare services relative to conditions prevailing in domestic firms', the Report claims. Comparisons, however, can be misleading as TNCs tend to be concentrated in high-skill, capitally intensive industries.

But the majority of jobs in such enterprises are low-skilled, low-paid production and assembly jobs. They tend to be highly specialised, with a greater division of labour. 'Advanced' technology is used, on mass production lines. A worker will perform a small, specialised task of a large operation. This may be good for profits, but such tasks are likely to be monotonous and effectively turn workers into little more than the arm of a machine. Neither do they equip workers with skills they can use elsewhere, in domestic firms for example.

Employment by TNCs has also become more uncertain because of the outcome of the GATT Uruguay Round agreement on trade-related investment measures (Trims). This means that countries have to overturn laws that require foreign enterprises to purchase inputs from local sources. One of these inputs is labour. TNCs are therefore no longer under any obligation to use local labour or materials – they can shop around for the cheapest possible source. Because of the agreement, governments of developing countries cannot be sure that a TNC will employ its citizens (the 50 least developed countries are exempt from this requirement).

TNCs sometimes, but by no means always, pay higher wages than local firms. But for people who work for TNCs there is a serious downside. Their negotiating rights are likely to be more restricted.

TNCs, unlike trade unions, 'can operate on a global basis so that each union in one piece of a TNC ends up negotiating with the whole TNC', points out Reginald Green. 'TNCs are larger and better organized than other employers, and therefore more able to bear the costs of industrial action.'[28] For workers, the feeling of being a small cog in a large wheel is not unique to large corporations, but 'is shown in its extreme form by the large TNCs', says Dunning.[29]

According to an International Labour Organisation (ILO) report, the role of TNCs in job creation is 'at best marginal'. It points out that if TNC employment is growing at all, it is 'due to acquisitions and mergers rather than to new employment opportunities'.[30] A new TNC-owned factory may create jobs but at the cost of existing jobs in locally owned factories. A net gain of jobs may not result. While FDI has created 'some 12 million jobs in developing countries', says an UNCTAD report, 'many of the newly created jobs have displaced workers in competing domestic industries'.[31]

Dual economies

Attracting TNCs is costly. It demands that governments allocate resources for the purpose. This means there is less for other sectors of the economy, such as agriculture, education and health care. Exporting processing zones (EPZs) have been set up with the aim of creating jobs and increasing export earnings (see Chapter 7), but they have often led to 'dualism'. 'Dual' economies come into being, that is modern-style economies that are receiving abundant funds, and traditional, subsistence economies that have fewer funds as a result of the modern ones.

In theory the benefits of the modern sector might trickle down to the traditional sector or even pull it up out of poverty. But this has generally not happened. Rather, what happens is that dualism breeds inequality within countries, with two economies existing side by side, the stronger one feeding off the weaker, bringing no benefit to the vast majority of people.

As discussed above, a modern economy does not necessarily make links with the rest of the economy. Mexico, for example, has had an EPZ-type programme called *maquila* ('in-bond' assembly) since 1965. The promotion of employment in Mexico's border region is one of the programme's chief objectives. By 1993 it had given rise to more than 2,000 assembly plants, most of them foreign-owned. 'Mexican assembly operations are dominated by foreign ownership, with strong representation by the major multinational enterprises', says a survey of the programme in 1994.[32] Few linkages with the rest of the country's economy were created; less than 2 per cent of the materials used in the plants came from Mexican sources.

> The *maquila* industry in the northern border area has not gone beyond the stage of being, primarily, an enclave of foreign interests, that is, the location on the Mexican territory of an economic activity, which, although it employs workers and generates value added for export, is not integrated into the rest of the regional economy or the national economy.[33]

As a result of this lack of integration, a robust domestic supply sector has not developed in Mexico. The *maquila* programme has not helped sustainable development. Yet the country possesses 'the internal capacity for producing an array of intermediate products competitively'.[34] This capacity is not being realised. The enclave is hindering Mexico's ability to develop a balanced economy.

Transfer pricing

By having subsidiary companies, TNCs are able to make use of transfer pricing which operates to the detriment of developing countries. Under transfer pricing, the parent TNC sells materials to a subsidiary in another country at an artificially high price. Such materials are then used in a manufacturing process or service industry. Having to pay these high prices reduces the profits of the subsidiary company, and means that it pays less tax in the country where it operates, which is therefore cheated out of tax revenues. Transfer pricing is tax avoidance.

The difference between the declared profit of a TNC subsidiary and its real profit can be considerable. In Colombia, for example, the over-charging of drugs by foreign-owned drug companies meant that TNC subsidiaries reported a 6 per cent profit to the Colombian government, whereas the real profit was over ten times higher. While the extent of transfer pricing is unknown – TNCs are unlikely to give details in their balance sheets and observers find difficulty obtaining evidence – the practice appears to be widespread.

In addition to tax avoidance, a further reason why TNCs use transfer pricing is that profits are often difficult to take out of a developing country, which naturally hopes they will be reinvested there. However, with the liberalisation of trade there has been some relaxation of previous restrictions on financial flows, which could lessen the incidence of transfer pricing. The growing international mobility of capital allows the corporations to play one country off against another, in search of the cheapest production costs. Governments of developing countries are beginning to flex their muscle against this form of tax avoidance. Brazil, for example, drew up a corporate tax bill in October 1996 to clamp down on transfer pricing.

Services

An important growth sector for TNCs in developing countries is services, especially tourism, banking and finance, accounting, insurance, telecommunications, information, mail, radio and television, patenting and copyrighting, maintenance, advertising, transport and shipping. Liberalisation of economies is helping corporate growth and influence.

Post-liberalisation, developing countries are obliged to allow the giant TNC banks free access to their banking markets. This could be highly damaging to Third World banks, many of which are now struggling to find their feet, and have been accorded some protection from foreign banks. At the time of Malaysia's independence, for example, in the late 1950s, foreign banks controlled the overwhelming share of the country's banking business. In 1990, however, domestic banks had the dominant share, partly because of restrictions placed on the establishment or expansion of foreign banks. But in the current climate this situation may not last; the banks may again revert to foreign control.

In any country the banking sector can be a powerful instrument for controlling or influencing production and even the pace and character of economic development. Banks decide who has credit, how much and at what price. Micro-credit schemes for the poor – which have been a success in many developing countries – could suffer if TNC banks come to monopolise a developing country's banking sector and insist on borrowers offering collateral to guarantee repayment. Third World nationals may feel they have no way of redressing what they believe are injustices in the bank's lending policy. In this way, foreign-owned banking services are likely to be less democratic, accountable and useful.

The liberalisation of international trade in banking services has substantial dangers for developing countries, warned an UNCTAD report in 1990. A commitment to liberalise cross-border transactions in banking services would entail dismantling significant parts of national regimes of exchange control, it said.[35] In many developing countries these regimes are essential to micro-economic management. Liberalisation could also reduce the effectiveness of monetary policy in developing countries, which often rely heavily on direct methods of controlling credit and interest rates.

Mexico was the first major country to bear the brunt of liberalisation and increased TNC activity in the financial sector. In 1995, the banking sector went through a severe crisis of confidence – 'a long post-liberalisation spending spree had left the domestic banking sector in a fragile state'.[36] But it is East Asia, notably South Korea, Thailand and Indonesia, that have been severely affected since November 1997 by large currency movements, as international speculators lost confidence in these Asian economies and moved their funds elsewhere.

'A new political class has appeared on the world stage', say Hans-Peter Martin and Harald Schumann. 'It can no longer be shaken off by any government, any corporation, still less any ordinary taxpayer. Currency and security dealers acting on a world scale direct an ever-growing flow of footloose investment capital and can therefore decide on the weal and woe of entire nations, and do so largely free of state control.'[37] The dealers are difficult to name; while some work for large companies, others are relatively small-scale, but all are transnational in character.

For the poor, the results of these currency movements were tragic. Millions of livelihoods have been devastated. In April 1998, an International Labour Organisation report said that millions will lose their jobs in the worst-affected Asian countries as a result of retrenchments, especially in the construction, financial services and manufacturing sectors. Under-employment will become widespread and the real earnings of those who hang on to their jobs will fall substantially as a result of the decline in labour demand and the inflation induced by large currency devaluations. Most dramatically, the report predicted that the impressive trends in poverty reduction achieved in these countries over the past 20 years, will be reversed.[38]

Increased malnutrition seems all too likely. In 1998, the crisis led to increases in the prices of basic commodities, including some staple foods, which hit hardest at people with very limited incomes. Higher prices for farm inputs, and also sharply higher interest rates, forced some farmers into bankruptcy, with small farmers being especially vulnerable. When small farmers go under, it is farmers with larger landholdings and capital who gain by buying up more land, making the pattern of land ownership more concentrated.

A further effect of the crisis is that many thousands of displaced workers returned to the rural areas in a bid to survive. These workers previously sent some of their earnings back to their families in the villages, but this ceased. Rural families and services were put under greater pressure. The crisis also exposed the vulnerability of developing countries – even comparatively well-off countries – to violent capital swings; it showed that the poor need more protection from such forces and that means more protection from TNCs.

Apart from banking and finance (for tourism, see Chapter 9), many countries could find that an excessive dependence on imported services is detrimental to development efforts. When key service sector activities are not being run by local people, skills are not being developed. Furthermore, a heavy reliance on imported services means that value is added abroad rather than domestically. Services are more likely to make a contribution to development in poorer countries if they develop locally rather than being imported, via TNCs. Neither do service sector activities generally create many jobs. In many of these activities, the affiliates of TNCs are capital-intensive even compared to the corporate manufacturing sector.

Conclusion

Transnational corporations play an enormous role in both industrial and developing countries. As governments have retreated in recent years, so their role has become larger, with their economic and industrial power deepening and expanding. Northern governments have exploited the weak bargaining position of Southern countries to open up new opportunities for their TNCs.

TNCs are powerful, secretive and largely unaccountable, and their size often dwarfs the countries in which they operate. By their sheer power, the corporations appear to count a great deal more with government than do the views of the public who do not have such access to policy-makers. Acting with little or no government control, no effective responsibility to developing countries and peoples, and leaving few, if any, long-term benefits, TNCs can be highly detrimental to a poorer country's political, economic and social health. But the worst aspect is that resource-poor peoples and communities suffer the most.

CHAPTER 2

Why Poor Countries 'Want' the Corporations

Globalization is not a serious concept. We have invented it to disseminate our politics of economic entry into other countries (John Kenneth Galbraith)

If there is little or no net gain for developing countries from the presence of TNCs, the question is why do they continue to attract them. Economic weakness is largely responsible. Governments of developing countries are caught in a dilemma – apprehensive about TNCs they may be, but a wounded person needs help. TNCs offer help to countries that have economic wounds such as severe unemployment, chronic shortage of foreign exchange and sizeable foreign debts. The corporations appear to be the engineers of wealth, to have the money and skills to earn additional foreign exchange and create jobs. They seems to be an almost magical answer. The deeper problems they can bring may not be considered alongside more pressing economic needs.

The 'magic' is an illusion, but Third World governments will be persuaded by Western governments and international financial institutions that they have no option but to open their markets, embrace globalisation and attract the corporations.[1] It is made difficult for them *not* to 'want' to attract TNCs. Control of TNCs in developing countries is deliberately made lax, or even non-existent. And governments may even be unaware that their citizens are being exploited by the TNCs they have courted. The corporations are powerful, have considerable knowledge and experience of producing goods and services, and are often in a position to mislead ministers and officials who make policy. Governments may even end up defending the very corporations that are exploiting them.

In practice, the corporations are strong enough to write their own rules for their presence. According to Vandana Shiva: 'governments have been dismembered by TNCs'.[2] It is the corporations which run the show, with governments under their thumb, believes Shiva. The

Western government/corporate 'spin' has been skilful. The prescription of globalisation, liberalisation and privatisation is 'presented with an air of inevitably and overwhelming conviction. Not since the heyday of free trade in the 19th century has economic theory elicited such widespread certainty.'[3] When such 'widespread certainty' abounds, and when such 'spin' sounds so convincing, developing countries want to be part of it.

Globalisation and liberalisation

Globalisation – the world as a single market, without barriers, as opposed to a world divided up into separate markets – has become one of the most talked about concepts of the late 1990s. 'Globalization is not a policy choice – it is a fact', US President Bill Clinton told the World Trade Organisation ministerial meeting in May 1998, again putting a 'spin' on the concept which suggests that countries have no choice – all must have it.

Aided by structural adjustment programmes, liberalisation and privatisation, globalisation took off in the 1980s. According to World Bank economist Zia Qureshi, globalisation 'is driven by a widespread push toward the liberalization of trade and capital markets, increasing internationalization of corporate production and distribution strategies'.[4] Globalisation 'has profound implications for developing countries. It creates important new opportunities – wider markets for trade, an expanding array of tradeables, larger private capital inflows, improved access to technology', in Qureshi's view.[5] In this line of thought, the liberalisation reforms, which are being adopted by more and more developing countries, are seen as key to improvements in their economic prospects. And liberalisation – cutting import and export barriers to trade, and reduce the role of the state – has meant that more countries have policies the corporations like. So TNCs both benefit from and promote liberalisation and globalisation.

'Globalisation and liberalisation have decreased the role of the state as a social regulator of the market and increased the power of large corporations', said an NGO Declaration at the UNCTAD IX conference in May 1996. 'Globalization is the product of human decisions, not just inevitable forces', it added.[6] The corporations have become 'a major force leading towards closer integration of the world economy', claims the *World Investment Report 1993*. 'An estimated one-third of private productive assets are under the common governance of these firms, contributing to the emergence of an integrated international production system.'[7]

Globalisation locks developing countries into the global economy and makes it more difficult for them to pursue a genuinely independent economic course. It can affect the poor in fundamental ways, raising the prices of basic foodstuffs, and threatening to wipe out small-scale family farms in favour of TNCs. But globalisation *looks* both attractive and inevitable, and it may *look* to a Third World government as if it has no alternative. Third World governments may have no option but to go along with it if they want aid or help with foreign debt relief which is often made conditional on reforms that embrace the 'free' market.

Globalisation is widening the gap between the rich (including TNCs) and the poor, and is leading to a more divided, not united, world. The World Bank admits that between developing countries, globalisation is widening the rich–poor country gap.[8] UNCTAD's *Trade and Development Report 1997* says that evidence is mounting 'that rising inequalities are becoming more permanent features of the world economy'.[9] Far from helping to integrate, globalisation and TNC activity are widening the divisions between people.

Awareness of the negative aspects of globalisation is growing. According to John H. Dunning: 'There is a growing awareness, particularly among the citizens of smaller countries, of the need to preserve ... their distinctive cultures, institutional structures, life styles, working relationships and consumption preferences. Many TNCs ignore such country-specific difference ... at their peril.'[10] Some governments are heeding the message. At the May 1998 World Trade Organisation (WTO) ministerial meeting, 'many of the developing country statements echoed the apprehension expressed by people's organisations concerning the impact of liberalisation and globalisation'.[11] Citizens and government of developing countries are beginning to see 1990s-style economic globalisation for what it is – not a certainty, but a sham.

Privatisation

The third member of the liberalisation and globalisation trinity is the privatisation of state assets which is again part of the structural adjustment process. Worldwide, annual privatisation receipts were expected to reach $100 billion in 1996, a 50 per cent increase on 1995, according to a survey for the Organisation for Economic Cooperation and Development (OECD). Since the mid-1980s, most developing countries have sold off at least some state-owned companies to private companies, many of them TNCs. In Argentina, for example, 'some 60 per cent of the assets sold to date have been bought by foreign investors from 19 countries'.[12]

While privatisation may improve the efficiency of an enterprise that was formally run by the state, it means that state assets are sold off, sometimes cheaply, to private, often foreign interests. Privatisation effectively transfers some of the capital resources of a developing country to a TNC. For the corporations, privatisation is therefore bringing a boom, especially as they can often acquire state companies at knock-down prices. Under the government of Bahamas privatisation programme, for example, a local hotel that was sold to a hotel chain for $8 million was considered by opposition politicians to be worth $20 million.

Privatisation has come in for strong criticism from people affected by it. In Sri Lanka, disquiet among the labour force about the proposed privatisation of public utilities led to strikes that severely affected industrial output. The process can be very damaging for services of considerable importance to the poor – especially health care, education and agricultural research. Services the state used to provide free of charge are in private hands – at a cost. In health care, many state budgets and services have been drastically cut. People on very low incomes, who are more prone to ill-health, are particularly affected. In a number of countries, increased malnutrition and other diseases have appeared in the wake of health care privatisation. In Zimbabwe, for example, diseases such as cholera and TB, which had virtually been eradicated in the country, have begun to reappear.

Education is also affected, with people again having to pay for services that were previously free. One example of the effects of this can be seen in the North Western Province of Zambia. Under a project funded by the UN's International Fund for Agricultural Development, the province increased food output between 1985 and 1995 to become self-sufficient in maize. But the higher food output has not lowered malnutrition rates. A project official said that 'when people grow more food, they might sell it and use some of the money to send their children to school. They do not necessarily eat more.'[13]

Privatisation can effectively take away the capacity of the public sector to do agricultural research. Drought-tolerant varieties of staple crops such as beans, for example, rarely interest TNCs, which prefer to develop high-value crops. But the poor cannot afford such crops. If everything is left to the private sector, the market will fail to deliver the food that is needed by hungry people.

While governments have generally shown that they cannot run large-scale economic enterprises, many have jumped from one unsuitable vehicle 'running it themselves' into another, 'let foreigners run it'. This, however, could be even worse. TNCs can effectively turn developing countries into satellites of Western countries, seriously undermining national sovereignty and democracy. Widespread privatisation is a virtual abdication of government. TNCs are left to get on with their activities, with little control by the people's elected representatives who make up governments.

A way of developing the privatisation idea in Africa has been put forward by a right-wing think-tank, the London-based Institute of Economic Affairs. 'There is a radical free-market solution to Africa's problems', it says. The 'solution' is a revival of the charter company idea. These were companies such as the Imperial British East Africa Company that operated in colonial days. The way to do it today, it believes, would be:

> to auction leases to govern African countries, giving the successful applicant the right to levy taxes in return for the provision of specifically stated services ... because the sums involved would be large, bidders would be likely to be multi-national companies or a consortium of companies ... the various bids would have to be voted on the population.[14]

Such a proposal may seem bizarre, but the idea of the wholesale privatisation of African countries is only to develop what is now going on. Colonialism by companies, rather than countries, is already happening. TNCs would hardly be interested in the idea of taking over countries, however, because they now have power without ownership. Taking over a country would give them responsibilities.

Debt

The wish to earn more money from abroad, and lessen their foreign debt burden, is a major reason why poor countries 'want' TNCs. Debt became a new issue affecting development at the start of the 1980s, when international interest rates soared with the coming to power of governments in the USA, Britain and West Germany which were pledged to tighter monetary policies. Developing countries which may have borrowed money in the 1970s at around 10 per cent rate of interest – often for unwise, large-scale projects – found themselves in the 1980s having to repay at around 20 per cent. At the same time, commodity prices were falling sharply and Western countries were continuing to heavily protect their markets against Third World manufactured goods. With aid stagnating, developing countries were having to find more foreign exchange, while receiving less. Balance of payments problems resulted and the door was open for the World Bank and the International Monetary Fund (IMF) to come with structural adjustment programmes.

Developing countries were offered help, provided they liberalised and privatised their economics, slashed social services, cut subsidies, generally reduced bureaucracy, and made their economies more welcoming to foreign investment. While some reforms were needed, it was the poor who paid the price. And it was TNCs who gained as they came in on the coat-tails of the adjustment programmes.

Third World debt 'has grown from US$9 billion in 1955 to US$572 billion in 1980 and US$2,177 billion in 1996. Its debt service – including interest and the principal – is currently close to £245 billion a year'.[15] The money is owed to Western countries, international aid agencies, the IMF, and banks. By the mid-1990s, foreign debt had emerged as probably the biggest single factor keeping people in poverty.

Over 50 countries, mostly African, were carrying severe debt burdens and having to switch money away from essential services, such as health care and education, in order to make debt repayments. Sub-Saharan Africa's foreign debt (US$226 billion in 1995) is over three times more than its annual exports (US$73 billion in 1995). It costs Africa US$23 billion a year to service the debt, more than it receives in development aid.

Whereas servicing the debt costs developing countries US$245 billion a year, development aid (in 1997) was US$47.5 billion. Debt servicing is therefore five times higher than aid. The human cost of this burden is enormous, and so also would be the benefits of relief. The *Human Development Report 1997* estimates that if severely indebted countries were relieved of their annual debt repayments they could use funds for investments 'that in Africa alone would save the lives of about 21 million children by 2000 (seven million lives a year) and provide 90 million girls and women with access to basic education'.[16] With more of their own funds to invest, the indebted countries would have less need of TNC investment.

In 1996 the International Monetary Fund and the World Bank launched a Heavily-Indebted Poor Countries Debt Initiative. This is a modest scheme that will cancel US$7 billion of debt and initially covers only six countries – Uganda, Bolivia, Burkina Faso, Guyana, Ivory Coast and Mozambique. According to the Jubilee 2000 Coalition, a London-based network of NGOs campaigning for debt relief, over 50 countries need debt relief and have 'unpayable' debt of at least US$100 billion. The coalition is urging that this debt is cancelled to mark the millennium in the year 2000. But there is little sign that Western governments will agree.

Subtle pressure

There is enormous pressure on developing countries to jump on-board the globalisation bandwagon, pressure that leads to a fear of losing out if they don't. A stark example of this is the attempt of the 29 governments (mostly Western governments) belonging to the Organisation for Economic Cooperation and Development (OECD), to draw up a Multilateral Agreement on Investment (MAI). Business interests had persuaded them that such an agreement was a good idea.

The MAI would safeguard the rights of companies which invest in OECD countries. In particular it would remove government regulations on foreign investment, provide greater protection for investments, and establish a dispute settlement mechanism. According to NGOs such as the World Development Movement, the MAI would increase the power of transnational corporations to an enormous extent, giving them unprecedented power. A fast-food chain that wanted to open a restaurant in a country that had signed the MAI, for example, could sue the government of that country if it was denied entry or introduced environment or social legislation that might curb their investment.

'The agreement will erode the rights of citizens and the role of governments, while extending the rights of TNCs', said WDM director Barry Coates. The treaty could fuel a 'race to the bottom', he believes, in which governments 'will abandon their commitments to local communities and sustainable development in their scramble to attract foreign investment'.[17]

Although the treaty appears to affect only OECD governments and companies, non-OECD countries would be invited to join after the negotiations had ended. Argentina, Brazil, Chile and Slovakia have all indicated an interest to be among the first wave to join. Other developing countries may be pressurised to join, rather than risk isolation, because of their perceived need for foreign investment. Again the Third World 'wants' the corporations, even under the stringent conditions of the MAI, because of the subtle pressures of the international economic system.

However, a number of developing countries, including Malaysia and Pakistan, have been highly critical of the MAI, seeing it as a threat to their sovereignty. But the sovereignty of everyone, in both rich and poor countries alike, would be at risk from such an agreement. Unelected transnational corporations would be able to stop elected governments taking decisions they believe are right. By October 1998, negotiations (which began in 1995) on the agreement were stalled, partly because of the success of NGO campaigning on the issue. TNCs are likely to urge

Western governments to try again. But any multilateral agreement on investment should respect the rights of developing countries to determine their own development policy and to retain mechanisms that enable them to achieve national priorities.

The aid connection

Developing countries want aid to promote economic and social development and reduce poverty. But if they accept aid, they accept TNCs, for the corporations are major beneficiaries of aid spending. Donor governments 'tie' most of their bilateral aid to the purchase of goods from companies in the donor country. A developing country may receive aid for a dam project, for example, on condition that companies of the donor country receive the contract to build it (see Chapter 8). Power stations, agriculture and the tourism sector have all attracted aid which in turn has helped the corporations.

Over half the aid from the world's largest aid donor, Japan, goes through its financial aid agency, the Overseas Economic Cooperation Fund, to the electric power and gas, and transportation sectors – in practice to large-scale projects. The Japanese government makes no secret of the fact that the aid helps its own companies to win contracts abroad. In 1994/95, the Japanese government's technical assistance agency, the Japan International Cooperation Agency, loaned money to fund controversial golf course development in other Asian countries.

British aid helps to fund the Commonwealth Development Corporation (CDC), whose objective is to 'contribute to economic development by investing in and supporting the operations of financially viable and developmentally sound business enterprise'. In practice, this means that aid again helped TNCs. The CDC has encouraged tobacco-growing in Malawi where there is prominent TNC involvement and where farmers have been moved off their land to make way for large tobacco estates. Ivory Coast, West Africa, has the world's fastest deforestation rate, but CDC funds have resulted in natural forest being cleared to make way for timber plantations.[18]

The United Nations Development Programme (UNDP), a technical aid agency, has encouraged developing countries to open up their borders to, among others, mining and tourism TNCs (see Chapters 6 and 9). In the Philippines the UNDP helped to finance government's efforts to attract foreign mining investors, even though this could deprive many of the country's poorest people of their lands and livelihoods. Following public protests, the government imposed conditions on the corporations (see Chapter 6).

The World Bank, the world's largest multilateral aid agency, part-funded from donor government aid budgets, is using aid money to promote the interests of the TNCs. Many of the big dam projects that have boosted TNC profits but displaced millions of people, are funded in part by foreign aid from the Bank and other donors. The World Bank has also funded large-scale agricultural, mining and tourism projects. It has helped TNCs by providing loans to help finance the setting up of privatisation agencies in a number of African countries.

Through its structural adjustment policies, the Bank is at the forefront of efforts to persuade countries to deregulate and liberalise their economies, and remove controls, including controls on TNCs. The World Bank pressed for deregulation and liberalisation of the drugs industry in Bangladesh, so undermining one of the most important and successful national drugs initiatives ever taken by a developing country (see Chapter 10). It has promoted 'non-traditional' agricultural exports as part of trade liberalisation and structural adjustment policies in Latin America. The winners from such deregulation are TNCs, the losers are the poor.

The World Bank's 'direct financial links to the transnational corporate sector ... have received far too little attention', warns David Korten. Although the Bank lends to governments, its projects 'normally involve large procurement contracts with transnational construction firms, large consulting firms and procurement contractors', he points out.[19]

'Private sector investment is the most important source of growth in developing economies', claims the World Bank.[20] The Bank holds seminars, publishes material and holds exhibitions to do all it can to smooth the path for TNC investment in poor countries. Bernard Pasquier, who works for the Bank's Private Sector Development (PSD) group, says:

> we are creating a front gate so that we can help companies better. The idea is ... to, shall we say, put a little oil in the machine to help it go more smoothly. Our objective is to help multinational and home grown companies in the developing countries to build up a thriving private sector.[21]

The Bank's Multilateral Investment Guarantee Agency (MIGA), set up in 1985, is the fastest-growing institution in the World Bank group. It offers major benefits to the private sector – in many cases it provides guarantees against political risks, such as nationalisation, losses on currency transfers, wars and civil disturbances. The MIGA has guaranteed, for example, a new gold mine on Lihir Island, Papua New Guinea (PNG). The mine is to be operated in a joint venture led by Rio

Tinto. Bankers found it virtually impossible to raise money for schemes like this in PNG. The World Bank stepped in, providing the funds that the market failed to provide – the very market it preaches developing countries to adopt.

Aid agencies are supposed to help the world's poor. They are funded with aid money which is intended to combat poverty. Yet all too often the agencies' policies are helping not the poor but the rich – the world's big business corporations.

Conclusion

To the concepts of globalisation, liberalisation and privatisation, should be added a fourth, that the three together inevitably make possible, corporatisation. And it is corporatisation which poses the biggest threat to the poor. Developing countries do not necessarily 'want' the corporations. In an economic world order where Western countries control the purse strings, and where the purses of many developing countries are empty, the West and the international agencies they control have effectively cornered poor countries into submission – ever so diplomatically of course. Using its economic power, the West has used poverty in the developing world to force through its own ideological, free-market agenda. There is nothing inevitable about globalisation. It is a policy choice that has opened wide the gate for the TNCs to the detriment of the poor. It is a policy of the most dubious morality, a serious misuse of power.

CHAPTER 3

The Agri-corporations: From Production to Trade

Big agri-corporations create a curious capitalist mirror-image of former Soviet state farms (Christopher Jones, UK farmer)

Transnational corporations are at their most visible and often most controversial when engaged in the basic primary industry, agriculture. The agri-corporations sell seeds, fertilisers and pesticides to farmers, patent new crop varieties and are involved in plant genetic engineering, plant and animal breeding. They dominate production and trade in key agricultural inputs, such as chemicals and seeds, and process, market and export a vast number of products, ranging from coffee to bananas, tea to tomatoes. They also sell services, which might include advice on seeds, hybrid crop varieties and management practices. This chapter examines in particular the corporate role in seeds, trade and chemicals.

Such is TNC power that agricultural and food policy is in danger of being concentrated under the control of the corporations. Claiming to have the technology that will increase crop yields, destroy pests and disease and feed the world, the TNCs downplay traditional, organic agriculture, and local production systems, and say they have a key role to play in Third World agriculture. With governments of developing countries having little money for key areas of agricultural development activity, the TNCs are taking on an ever larger role – plant breeding, for example, has become a major corporate activity. But this growing TNC involvement threatens the livelihoods of millions of resource-poor farmers in developing countries.

The agrochemicals market was worth around US$32 billion in 1997; the largest agrochemical companies include Novartis (formed by a merger of Ciba and Sandoz), Zeneca (formerly part of ICI), AgrEvo (a merger of Hoechst and Schering crop chemical businesses), Du Pont, Bayer and Monsanto (see Table 3.1). Many agrochemical companies also have substantial interests in pharmaceuticals.

Table 3.1 Leading agrochemical TNCs and their 1998 profits (US$ million)

Novartis	4,927
BASF	3,134
Bayer	3,003
Du Pont	2,405
Hoechst	1,856
Zeneca	1,818
Dow Chemical	1,808
Monsanto	294

Note: Pharmaceuticals account for some of the profits.
Source: FT 500, *Financial Times*, 28 January 1999.

Seeds

Seeds are a US$13 billion a year business and one of the most concentrated areas of TNC activity in agriculture, with most chemical corporations having interests in seed companies. In the wake of seed and fertiliser developments in the 1960s – the so called 'green revolution' – the chemical TNCs began to buy up small family seed companies. But even as recently as the mid-1980s, the UN Food and Agriculture Organisation (FAO) 'was able to list more than 7,000 seed sources worldwide (public and private) and the seed industry was free to argue that its market was highly diversified and unconcentrated'.[1]

Takeovers were about to start, however, on a quite massive scale. Between 1985 and 1990, agri-corporations acquired 630 seed businesses, 'involving companies active in all sectors of the industry'.[2] The reason for their interest lay in the possibility of developing and establishing patents over, for example, higher-yielding seeds, which oblige farmers to pay for their use – even though the new products will have been developed from farmers' seeds. The late 1990s has witnessed another spate of takeovers of smaller companies as the TNCs geared up for exploiting the potential of biotechnology / genetic engineering.

In 1998, there were around 1,500 seed companies in the world, with 24 of them accounting for about half the commercial seed market. About 34 per cent of commercial maize seed sales in developing countries is now in the hands of TNCs. In 1997, the largest seed companies included Pioneer Hi-Bred, Novartis, Limagrain (French), Advanta (joint venture of Zeneca and Van der Haave of the Netherlands), Cargill, AgrEvo, Dekalb Plant Genetics (USA), which is 40 per cent owned by Monsanto, and Takii (Japan).

In 1996, Monsanto acquired Agracetus from W.R. Grace, giving it a dominant position in crop species patents. Under a slogan of 'Food – Health – Hope', Monsanto, a St Louis, US-based company, employs 21,900 people (1998) and produces and markets agricultural products, pharmaceuticals and food ingredients. In 1997, it took over Asgrow Seeds, the world's largest soybean breeder, Holden's Foundation Seeds, a maize genetics business 'that claims a third of the US market', and also acquired 40 per cent of Dekalb Plant Genetics 'arguably the second largest maize seed company in the world'.[3] Other companies too were on the acquisition trail. In August 1997, Du Pont acquired 20 per cent of Pioneer Hi-Bred; in December 1997, Zeneca paid US$500 million for a fungicide business owned by a Japanese chemical company. In September 1998, AgrEvo announced that it would acquire Cargill Hybrid Seeds North America for US$650 million (See also section on Genetic engineering, p. 32 below).

The corporations have become involved in the seed business because it offers good profits and fits in well with their other activities. TNC distribution channels for seeds are identical to those of crop chemicals, opening up the possibility of linking chemical and seed development and marketing. But for farmers, buying a company's seeds can lock them into buying its fertilisers and pesticides.

The agrochemical and seed TNCs have not been slow to develop new crop varieties that are responsive to their chemicals. Ciba, for example, marketed its own brand of sorghum seed which comes wrapped in three chemicals. The integration of these technologies into one marketing package allows the company to sell more seed and chemicals. A double market is therefore created – for both these products. But there are now serious doubts about the sustainability of the technology that made possible the seeds and fertiliser improvements of the 1960s, and helped to increase yields of rice and wheat. In tests that go back to the mid-1960s, the Manila-based International Rice Research Institute (IRRI) has found a steady decline in rice yields, from 10 tons to 7 tons per hectare. Furthermore, the technology promoted by the TNCs has led to the loss of thousands of traditional plant varieties. This loss of diversity could cause huge problems for food supplies in the future. It will make it harder for breeders and farmers to have the range of genetic material they need to develop improved crops that yield more food and resist pests and disease.

The Food and Agriculture Organisation says that around three-quarters of the world's plant species have been lost this century. It has warned that the large-scale loss of plant genetic resources, vital for agriculture and food security, is a matter of major concern. The warning is based on a survey of 154 countries, carried out in 1995. Over 80 countries reported that the spread of modern, commercial agriculture and the introduction of new varieties of crops was the main cause of the loss of plant genetic resources.[4]

TNCs not only dominate the commercial seed market, they are especially powerful in countries where laws give them patents or other rights over new varieties they develop. The effects on millions of resource-poor farmers of this TNC activity are profound. From the dawn of agriculture 10,000 years ago, farmers have produced and saved their seeds for sowing in the next season. This necessity has contributed to the development of genetic diversity and resulted in varieties that are well adapted to specific conditions. But the traditional practices of farmers are under threat, as companies take out patents on seeds that farmers have used for generations. The world of the poor farmer has thus become linked with the power of the transnational corporation. Farmers have something that TNCs believe they can turn into a profit. Seeds that have been developed and improved by farmers over centuries are now being used by the corporations to make further developments and profits. Whereas there was no question of farmers taking out patents on *their* improvements to seeds, the TNCs have sought to patent new seed varieties that they claim to have 'invented', but which farmers have helped to develop.

'The idea that farmers do not innovate or generate knowledge unless they can derive private profits is wrong', points out Indian environmentalist, Vandana Shiva. Patenting, believes Shiva, will mean farmers become dependent on TNCs for their seeds, and that the companies will decide what is grown by farmers. There is a danger, she warns, of 'a very slippery slope ending in multinational totalitarianism in agriculture', that leaves farmers with considerably less choice.[5] Farmers in India and elsewhere are particularly concerned that the TNCs, with their money and power, will jeopardise their independence and eventually push them off their land. Furthermore, the development of commercial varieties could work against the conservation and sustainable use of biodiversity.

Patents

Farmers face the possibility of having to pay the corporations high prices for patented varieties. Patents are the lifeblood of the agrochemical research industry, the means through which agri-business companies can exercise control. The companies argue that they can only afford to invest large sums of money in researching and breeding new crops if they have protection to safeguard that investment. Patents offer that protection. But protection for a corporation can mean the exclusion of the poor.

Patents were designed for industrial processes. Patents on plants, which TNCs are now taking out, are open to a number of objections. At an ethical level, they can be seen as a corporate attempt to patent a lifeform. For farmers, the concern is that patents could shift control of crop varieties from them to the corporations.

The USA was the first country to grant patents on plant varieties. Before 1997, other countries 'judged patent systems to be an unsuitable form of intellectual property rights for living things'.[6] Some patents create confusion. RiceTec, a Texas-based company, has taken out a patent, for example, on an aromatic rice grown in the USA which they label 'Basmati'. But about 250,000 farmers in India and Pakistan have traditionally grown basmati rice. Taking out a patent on it is like Australians taking out a patent on champagne. RiceTec is also marketing what it labels as 'Jasmine' rice. But jasmine rice comes from Thailand, where it is grown by over five million resource-poor farmers. US consumers could be confused into thinking they are products from developing countries. In reality they are buying patented domestic products.

In March 1995, the European Parliament rejected a directive that would have allowed the patenting of plants. While the decision initially influenced parliamentarians in other countries, especially in India and Brazil, pharmaceutical TNCs in Europe soon launched a major lobbying offensive to secure a new directive. In July 1997, the European Parliament changed its mind. It approved a revised Life Patents Directive which states that plant and animal varieties 'shall not be patentable', but the directive added that 'inventions which concern plants or animals may be patented if the invention is not technically confined to a particular plant or animal variety'. A Barcelona-based NGO, Genetic Resources Action International, pointed out that the directive means companies can patent plants and animals as long as they do not call their end product a variety.[7] The new directive could give industry patent control of the whole supply chain, from the basic genetic material, through the processes which make use of the genes and gene sequences, to the products which result. In November 1997, the European Council of Ministers approved the directive.

Important staple foods are therefore in danger of becoming the private property of a TNC. While it would be unthinkable for a car manufacturer to be granted a patent on the automobile, such a patent is in danger of happening on crops. A patent on an entire crop, such as soya for example, would mean that if a farmer did not pay royalties on the crop, it would be illegal for her or him to plant it. It would also mean that an activity such as baking biscuits from soya seed would be illegal. Broad patents on plants are therefore a threat to diversity, to men and women farmers, and to food output.

Patents invariably establish private, exclusive, monopolistic control over plant genetic resources, resulting in farmer dislocation which, in turn, is a threat to food security. Such 'rights' can deprive farmers of their rights – the right to develop and exchange their own seed, and, ultimately, the right of survival. Furthermore, the TNCs are often ceasing the sale of traditional varieties because no patent-like control can be obtained over varieties that predate patent laws. This could result in many traditional varieties falling out of use and becoming extinct.

Communities in developing countries are in danger of becoming dependent on outside sources of seeds and the chemicals needed to grow and protect them. Self-reliance in agriculture is therefore becoming harder. Saving agriculture's genetic diversity does not guarantee self-reliance or development, but losing this diversity reduces options and fosters dependency.

Protests in India

India is among the countries that have not allowed patents to be taken out on plant varieties. The Indian Patents Act of 1970 makes it clear that inventions relating to agricultural and horticultural processes are not patentable. In 1996, India's parliament rejected an amendment to the act on the grounds that apart from the unacceptable economic cost, it would end farmers' traditional ability to innovate and adapt their own varieties, wiping out centuries of biodiversity material and skill. Nonetheless, according to Devinder Sharma, TNCs have applied for 40 patents on Indian crops and species.[8]

The US-based company, W.R. Grace, for example, took out a US patent on neem-based bio-pesticides in 1995. The company estimates that the global market for this pesticide could reach US$50 million a year by 2000. But the pesticide is produced from seeds of neem trees in farmers' fields in India, and the patent is being challenged in the courts. Millions of Indian farmers have used neem-tree emulsions to protect crops from pests.[9] The farmers would be unlikely to see any benefit from a tree they have cultivated and improved for centuries.

Because of the way it strengthened the corporate hand, the clause on trade-related intellectual property rights (TRIPs) in the GATT Uruguay Round has generated considerable feeling. In July 1993, farmers in

Karnataka state burnt down an administrative building belonging to the seeds company, Cargill, because they were fearful that the TRIPs provision could make it illegal for them to replant seeds that their ancestors have used for centuries without paying royalties to patent holders. 'The installation of a patents regime in genes, plants and farm inputs, when none exists, is to gain control of a nation covertly', said M.D. Nanjundaswamy, president of the Karnataka Rajya Raitha Sangha, the farmers' association of Karnataka.[10] In October 1993, over three million Indian farmers came to the state capital, Bangalore, to demonstrate against the likely effects of the Uruguay Round on their livelihoods. Farmers were also angry at what they believed to be the misleading advertisements of the Cargill corporation for hybrid sunflower seed. Many claim that these seeds produce only a fraction of the advertised yield and that the hybrid crops are not fit to eat.

The US administration continues to try to marshall support for patents on agricultural products. US Secretary of Agriculture Dan Glickman told India's Institute of Agricultural Research in January 1996:

> I hope your new legislation will provide a responsible and reasonable protection to private seed companies, which will encourage them to provide the best seeds available for your farmers. There would be very few inventions of anything, particularly in agriculture, without patent protection because it is a fundamental fact of nature that people will not go through the expense of the development of new ideas just for the altruistic benefit of the human race.

There would, however, be little food today if farmers had not protected and developed plants over centuries, without any reward. The contribution that farmers make to the collective store of intellectual property is still not recognised.

Genetic engineering

The advent of biotechnology/genetic engineering holds out the promise of massive opportunities for TNCs but poses an additional threat to the poor. Biotechnology appears to offer large increases in crop yields – as high as 500 per cent for some crops like coconut, oil palm and cassava. In late 1996, Monsanto, which has taken the lead in applying biotechnology to agricultural products, released a genetically engineered soybean. It believes that genetically altered seed 'will become a US$6 billion annual market within five years'.[11]

Genetically modified food could, however, lead to lower rather than higher harvests. Once genetically modified organisms are released into the environment they are there to stay; they allow for no second chances. Their traits could spread to crops in neighbouring fields, seriously reducing food output. Genetically modified crops can be made to resist herbicides (weedkillers), but herbicide applications can kill other things, including beneficial insects, such as ladybirds, and also herbs and medicines on which the poor depend. Weeds in nearby fields could develop resistance to the applications, leading to 'superweeds' which will require higher doses of herbicide to keep them under control. The use of pesticides would undoubtedly increase should genetically modified crops spread and poorer farmers could be driven into bankruptcy by having to buy more of the poisons. Overall, the widespread adoption of these crops will mean the spread of monoculture and cause further loss of plant genetic diversity – the basis of food security.[12]

'Genetic engineering threatens to destroy millions of peasant livelihoods in the Third World', believes Shiva. 'Tropical crops like sugar cane, coconut, vanilla and cocoa can be grown anywhere with genetic engineering. Whole industries in developing countries would disappear.'[13] The technology would mean a further shift of power to the TNCs, concentrating power in corporate hands at the expense of local communities. The advance of genetic engineering would hand over the task of feeding the world to the TNCs. Already, research and development of maize, the world's third most important staple food, is being 'concentrated in the hands of smaller and smaller numbers of agribiotech giants'.[14]

A new genetic engineering issue opened up in March 1998 when a US firm, Delta & Pine Land, the world's largest cotton seed company, and the US Department of Agriculture (USDA) received a patent on a technique that means seeds can only be planted once. The technology genetically disables a seed's capacity to germinate if it is planted again – it switches a plant's reproductive processes on and off so that harvested seed will be sterile if farmers attempt to replant. This could bring about the most profound revolution ever to hit agriculture because it threatens the farmers' practice of saving seed from one season to use in the next.

'Crop geneticists who have studied the patent are telling us that it's likely that pollen from crops carrying the terminator trait will infect the fields of farmers who either reject or can't afford the technology', says Camila Montecinos of a Chile-based organisation, Centro de Educacion y Tecnologia (CET), which works with farming communities. 'When farmers reach into their bins to sow seed the following season they could discover – too late – that some of their seed is sterile.'[15]

While only cotton and tobacco seeds have been shown to respond so far to the new technique, it could be applied to 'potentially all cultivated crops', believes the Canada-based voluntary organisation, Rural Advancement Foundation International (RAFI). It has called the technique 'Terminator technology' because it could end the centuries of farming tradition of farmers saving and planting their own seed. RAFI's Research Director, Hope Shand, describes the technology as 'terribly dangerous; half the world's farmers are poor and can't afford to buy seed every growing season'. Around 1.5 billion people come into this category.

There could be pressure on national regulatory systems to marginalise saved-seed varieties and clear the way for Terminator technology. RAFI has joined with farmer-based organisations in developing countries to urge a global ban on the use of Terminator technology.[16] In May 1998, two months after the patent was granted, Monsanto began the process of acquiring Delta & Pine Land. The technology is again a threat to the food of the poor. In August 1998, India's Minister of Agriculture announced a national ban on the Terminator technology.

Also that month, Monsanto and Cargill (see Trade section, p. 36 below) announced that they had signed a letter of intent to form a worldwide joint venture to create and market new products enhanced through biotechnology for the grain processing and animal feed markets. The joint venture, said the companies, 'would draw from Monsanto's capabilities in genomics, biotechnology and seeds, and from Cargill's global agricultural input, processing and marketing infrastructure to develop and market new products with traits aimed at improving the processing efficiencies and animal nutrition qualities of major crops'.[17] This venture creates an entity that links biotechnology research and development with seeds, production and processing, right through to the customer. A month later Monsanto bought Cargill's international seed operations for US$1,400 million excepting its North American operations. Monsanto then announced that it would merge with American Home Products, a pharmaceutical group which also has interests in crop protection products. The merger would have created a huge company, with annual sales of around US$23 billion, that could apply genetic engineering to both agricultural and human health products. Although the deal was called off several months later, mergers and concentration of TNC power are likely to continue.

Bio-piracy

TNCs are making handsome profits out of genetic materials from developing countries, while local communities receive little or nothing.

RAFI has compiled a list of instances where genetic resources and/or local knowledge in the South have made, or are making, a contribution to agriculture, food processing, or pharmaceutical development in the North. The report lists more than 100 examples of developing country contributions to food and medicines in Western countries. They include Bayer's synthetic aspirin, the world's most widely used drug, which is derived from a traditional Arab medicinal plant. Wheat material from the Mexico-based International Maize and Wheat Improvement Centre is estimated to contribute US$3.1 billion annually to the total farmgate value of the US wheat crop – around 34 per cent. Pau D'Arc, a medicinal plant from Latin America, used to combat malaria and cancers, has a market value in the North of US$200 million a year.[18]

TNC activities have been equated with piracy. A RAFI report prepared for the United Nations Development Programme found that contributions of plant genetic resources and knowledge from farmers in the South is worth US$4.5 billion a year to the North. But the South received nothing for those contributions; it was effectively cheated out of that sum, alleged RAFI. This is just in agriculture; it is the value added to agricultural prices in the North.[19]

'Bio-piracy' can take the form of companies (sometimes via academic research departments, whom they sponsor) taking plant species from developing countries without permission and without offering any compensation. In 1995, RAFI documented 55 current instances of such piracy. 'Recent examples from Gabon, Thailand, Ecuador and Peru illustrate bio-piracy activities on a grand scale', according to RAFI's September/October 1995 newsletter. In one of these cases, the University of Wisconsin, USA, has received two US patents for a protein derived from the berry of a plant that growers in Gabon called *Pentadiplandrabrazzeana*. The berries were collected by a University of Wisconsin researcher, working in Gabon. The researcher found that a sweet protein could be derived from the berries. The University of Wisconsin call the protein 'brazzein', and estimate that it is 2,000 times sweeter than sugar. The university now has exclusive rights to brazzein, which it intends to license to corporations. 'Wisconsin believes it can make inroads into the $100 billion a year worldwide market for sweeteners', RAFI points out. Yet Gabon's contribution to the development of the new sweetener will go uncompensated. 'What is being pirated is not one invention of one individual or corporation, but the collective creativity and inventiveness of millions of people over millennia, a creativity … that is necessary for meeting the needs of our people in the future', insists Vandana Shiva.[20] Developing countries 'need to bring in tougher national legislation to prevent the unauthorised collection of germplasm especially by the transnational corporations', believes Sharma.[21] Many countries have already imposed such bans, he points out, including Ethiopia, Iran, Iraq and China.

Trade

TNCs dominate world markets in internationally traded agricultural commodities, with a small number of companies accounting for a large percentage of the trade. Six corporations handle about 85 per cent of world trade in grain; fifteen TNCs control between 85 to 90 per cent of world traded cotton; eight TNCs account for between 55 to 60 per cent of world coffee sales; seven account for 90 per cent of the tea consumed in Western countries; three account for 83 per cent of world trade in cocoa; three again account for 80 per cent of bananas; while five firms buy 70 per cent of tobacco leaf. Food products account for three-quarters of agricultural trade and raw materials the remaining one-quarter.

TNCs 'need a regular and reliable supply of good quality raw material to feed into the markets, preferably enough of an over-supply to keep prices of the raw materials low'.[22] By their demand for export crops, TNC effectively encourage farmers to grow them, but over-supply and low prices mean that farmers often get only a bare return. The best route for commodity producing countries would be to band together, reduce acreages or exports and win higher world prices. But such cooperation has been little tried and only rarely successful. Export taxes are another possibility. In 1984, a Commonwealth Secretariat report suggested that countries producing primary commodities could gain substantially by jointly agreeing to impose export taxes on their goods.[23] Although nothing has yet come from the idea, the possibilities remain (see later in this section). Higher commodity prices would not be welcomed by TNCs; low commodity prices mean lower production costs and make for higher profits.

Trade in agricultural products and foodstuffs grew from US$65 billion in 1972 to over US$500 billion in 1997. This increase – part of the globalisation process – has transformed little-known firms into major transnational corporations with significant political clout. But it has dire implications for the poor. Because of the need to earn more hard currency to repay foreign debt, developing countries have been en-couraged by the World Bank and other donors to pay their farmers more to grow and to trade agricultural commodities, such as coffee, cocoa and tea. But this has resulted in 'over-supply' of many com-modities, causing lower prices, often below the costs of production, leading to hardship and worsening poverty for growers. Some of the

Table 3.2 Major traders of some of the largest agricultural products

Grain	Sugar	Coffee	Cocoa
Cargill (USA)	E.D. & F. Man (UK)	Cargill	Cargill
Continental (USA)	Cargill	E.D. & F. Man	E.D. & F. Man
Mitsui/Cook (Japan)	Sucres et Denrées (France)	Neumann/Rothfoss (Germany)	Sucres et Denrées
Louis Dreyfus (France)	C.Czarnikow (UK)		
André/Garnac (Switzerland)			
Bunge and Born (Brazil)			

TNCs involved are well-known names, others are little-known family firms. The GATT Uruguay Round agreement ushered in an era which is favourable to their business. The Round reduced tariffs by an average of 40 per cent. As freer trade means more trade, this offers the possibility of higher profits for the traders.

In September 1994, a report by the Organisation for Economic Cooperation Development and the World Bank estimated that the reductions in tariffs and subsidies under the Uruguay Round would add US$213 billion a year to world income by the year 2002. Most of this gain – US$190 billion – is expected to come from reductions in tariffs and subsidies on agricultural products. Much of the extra income will go to those who trade the products and not the people who grow them in developing countries. Sub-Saharan African countries were expected to lose nearly US$3 billion a year from the changes.[24]

Cereals

World production and trade in cereals exceeds those of any other crop. Cargill, a private US company based in Minneapolis, is the world's largest international grain trader, accounting for over half the trade. Cargill is followed by another family firm, Continental, also of the USA, Mitsui/Cook of Japan, Louis Dreyfus of France, which is controlled by the French family of that name, the Swiss firm, André/Garnac, also named after its family owners, and Brazil's Bunge and Born, which again is a family firm. In November 1998, Continental announced that it would sell its grain trading operations. Cargill is the likely buyer, provided that the US anti-trust authorities approve. A small number of families and a Japanese conglomerate therefore run most of the international grain trade. These companies are estimated to hold about 60 per cent of all the world's grain stocks.

Cargill has many other interests besides grain. It describes itself as 'an international marketer, processor and distributor of agricultural, food, financial and industrial products with some 80,000 employees in more than 1,000 locations in 72 countries and with business activities in 100 more'. It is the world's largest oilseed trader, the second largest phosphate fertiliser producer, and a major trader in grain, coffee, cocoa, sugar, seeds, malt and poultry. The extent of Cargill's trade in coffee – the largest agricultural earner for developing countries – is seen in comparison to Africa. Cargill 'has a greater sales turnover in coffee than the GDP of any of the African countries in which it purchases coffee beans'.[25] In 1997 Cargill had an annual turnover of US$56 billion – roughly equivalent to the gross domestic products of the 16 poorest

Sub-Saharan African countries (including Nigeria) put together – making it one of the world's 12 largest companies. Descendants of Cargill's founder own 85 per cent of the company.

As a private firm, Cargill is not obliged to tell the public about its operations. Speaking of Cargill, US Senator Frank Church told a Senate Sub-committee on multinational corporations in 1975: 'No one knows how they operate, what their profits are, what they pay in taxes ... or much of anything else about them.' 'The ambience of secrecy has not altered appreciably', believe Clairmonte and Cavanagh. A Cargill subsidiary once claimed that both the firm and its employees would be open to criminal prosecution if it supplied information to the US government about some of its activities. 'It takes no great effort to imagine the response to an underdeveloped country which had the temerity to raise such awkward questions'.[26] According to Kevin Watkins, author of a study on the GATT, Cargill 'assumed responsibility for preparing the United States negotiating papers' for agriculture in the Uruguay Round.[27] This is denied by the company, which says only that it made its views known to the US States administration and European governments.

Land

Cargill's activities very directly affect the poor in developing countries. Brewster Kneen expresses this clearly: 'Cargill's corporate goal is to double every five to seven years, but the achievement of this goal requires the occupation of more and more territory, and the expulsion of whole societies from their settlements and their commons.'[28] The globalisation of the food industry means the major players – transnational corporations – require land that is at present in the hands of food crop smallholders. The transfer of land from food crops to export crops is growing fast; an extra million hectares a year is going under plantation crops.[29] Plantations are almost always geared to the export market. Such rapid conversion of land from smallholder agriculture to estates producing for export threatens the existence of resource-poor farming communities and indigenous peoples. It is bad for rural economies and peoples and is likely to increase the migration of people to urban areas. TNCs involved in agricultural trade are nonetheless likely to continue the globalisation process.

The issue of whether good land should be used for growing crops for export, rather than food for local people, has long been debated. While food is the most basic need, it is lack of money and purchasing power which is responsible for a great deal of hunger; the sale of export crops brings in money. The generally low prices of crops grown for export, however, might suggest that the food/export crop balance needs shifting in favour of more emphasis on food for local consumption.

Millions of smallholders who grow crops for export are benefiting little from the export trade. Faced with falling prices because of over-production, the leading coffee-producing countries agreed in October 1994 to withdraw supplies from the export market. World coffee prices rose, at least partly as a result. They reached their highest level for 20 years in May 1997, after producers had again made clear their intention to withhold supplies to keep up the price.

The widespread nationalisation of foreign companies by developing countries in the 1970s included many of the large-scale plantations growing export crops. In the late 1980s a number of developing country governments invited foreign investors back, often on a joint-venture basis. In some countries, the traditional plantations of colonial times have been replaced by out-grower schemes, in which large numbers of farmers grow and sometimes process a crop on contract. The farming-out of tobacco by British American Tobacco (BAT) is a classic example of this, but such arrangements have numerous pitfalls (see Chapter 4).

Pesticide effects

Eleven TNCs account for 81 per cent of worldwide agrochemical sales, which exceeded US$30 billion in 1997. Massive advertising campaigns by the chemical corporations have turned developing countries into a booming growth market for pesticides and also a dumping ground. While many pesticides are exported by Western-based TNCs, others are produced in factories in the Third World by subsidiaries of TNCs, set up through foreign investment. In developing countries, most pesticides are applied to crops that are grown for export. Insecticides to ward off pests, fungicides to tackle diseases, and herbicides to combat weeds, make up a profitable trio of products for the industry.

As subsidies to farmers in Western nations are being lowered, so sales of pesticides in the West are less buoyant. Pesticide manufacturers have increasingly looked to the Third World as an outlet for their products. Some companies 'predict over one-third of all pesticide sales will be to developing countries by the year 2000'.[30] The most dangerous pesticides (considered to be aldicarb, camphechlor, chlordane and heptachlor, chlordimeform, DBCP, DDT, aldrin, dieldrin, endrin, EDB, HCH and lindane, paraquat, parathion and methyl parathion, pentachlorophenol, and 2,4,5-T) are either banned or severely restricted in Western countries. But some are still exported to developing countries by agrochemical companies. 'A scandal of global proportions' is one description of such exports.[31] In developing countries, lack of information about restricted pesticides, together with the absence of regulation, can combine with illiteracy and repressive working conditions to turn them into deadly substances, poisoning people, land and water courses.

Under the Prior Informed Consent (PIC) clause of the Food and Agriculture Organisation (FAO) Code of Conduct on Distribution and Use of Pesticides, which came into effect in 1989, importing countries should be notified of intended exports of hazardous products, and they have the right to refuse them. The code is voluntary, although all the major agrochemical companies subscribe. The PIC procedure currently lists 12 pesticides and five industrial chemicals, among them aldrin, dieldrin, chlordane and DDT. Through the voluntary PIC procedure, importing countries can learn about dangerous and toxic chemicals that may be shipped to them. They can decide whether they want to permit or ban future imports. In March 1998, 95 countries agreed on a legally binding convention to curb international trade in the most dangerous chemicals and pesticides.

However, developing countries often lack the equipment to screen chemicals for their risks. Many pesticide formulations have not been screened by government research stations. In a study of Kenya, for example, a total of 96 formulations were recorded as being in circulation but not registered with the authorities. Unregistered products found on sale included DDT, aldrin, dieldrin, lindane. DDT has been banned for agricultural use in most countries for many years but is still authorised (with restrictions) for malaria control – application must usually be by trained Ministry of Health staff and only in mosquito breeding grounds.

DDT remains available in retail outlets throughout Kenya, where label instructions recommend its use on various agricultural crops. Both transnational companies (for example, Montedison and Murphy, part of Rhone-Poulenc) and local companies sell the chemical. Shell marketed the widely banned pesticide dieldrin as late as 1992, indicating use 'For Coffee'. Shell Kenya denied it was marketing dieldrin in Kenya, saying it must have been smuggled in from Tanzania where Shell's dieldrin is also not registered for use. The label, however, has an official registration number, implying intended use in Kenya, although the number is left blank. Shell stopped global production of dieldrin in 1989 but there are large obsolete stocks in Africa as a result of locust control strategies.[32]

The US-based TNC, Del Monte, has large plantations in Kenya, with both pineapple estates and canning factories; production is almost entirely geared to exporting tinned pineapples to markets in Europe and

North America. To grow its crops, Del Monte imports significant quantities of the highly persistent, bio-accumulative pesticide, heptachlor. This is one of the pesticides included in the PIC procedure and is banned in 21 countries and severely restricted in others. Kenya banned heptachlor in 1986 on the grounds of unacceptable health risks. Import records confirm that Del Monte has been regularly importing and using heptachlor.[33] In a 1997 report on Costa Rica, the World Development Movement accused the world's biggest banana companies, Chiquita, Del Monte and Dole, of the excessive use of toxic agrochemicals, saying that these had led to health problems for workers such as sterility, kidney failure, memory loss and even death.[34]

Bhopal

The worst single disaster for the poor involving pesticides happened on 2 December 1984 when a cloud of poisonous gas escaped from a tank at the pesticides plant of US chemicals group, Union Carbide, in Bhopal, central India. The tank spewed out a deadly cocktail of 24 chemicals. The effect on people who lived nearby was devastating. Sabra and Yacob Bee, for example, and their seven young children, who lived within a mile of the factory, were sentenced to a lifetime of illness. Said Sabra Bee:

> When the gas came, I thought I would die. I saw people dying on the streets. Old men were dead. Children were dead. Four hundred were dead in this street alone. Those who ran to the hospital lived. Those who stayed here died.

The Union Carbide plant lies in the north of the city. Fate took a hand. The wind was blowing from north to south, carrying the noxious gases into the heart of Bhopal. By daybreak, nearly 1,000 people were dead.

Sabra and Yacob Bee spent 20 days in hospital. Ten years later, in 1994, Yacob was once again in hospital, still suffering ill-health from the effects of the gas. The family was still waiting for compensation. Their agony has been compounded by administrative delays. India's judicial machinery has proved inadequate in dealing with the crisis. It took five years for the Indian government to extract US$470 million compensation – less than one-sixth of the US$3 billion they originally demanded – from the Union Carbide Corporation, the US parent company of Union Carbide India Ltd. Compensation claims did not start to be settled until 1992. By 1996 more than 800,000 claims for compensation had been received and more were pending. Those injured by the gas are indistinguishable from those who escaped and received few visible injuries, apart from eye problems like cataracts. But their lungs and immune systems have also suffered, and, in their case, they have received no compensation. Government officials say that around 6,600 died from the effects of gas, and 350,000 were injured, but local NGOs put the death toll at 16,000 and still rising, and estimate that as many as 600,000 could have been injured.[35]

Soon after the disaster, Union Carbide sold its interest in the Bhopal factory to Ever Ready Industries. In December 1996, a report by the International Medical Commission claimed that survivors' ailments were 'unrecognised, untreated and mistreated'. One of the commissioners, Dr Rosalie Bertell, said: 'at every point, Union Carbide has been as obstructive as possible', which had created 'an immoral international situation'.[36]

Questioning pesticides

The chemical TNCs have often persuaded farmers in developing countries to buy more of their products than they need. In Asia, in particular, the chemical industry has made deep inroads into the rice sector. Spraying large quantities of chemicals has, however, destroyed the natural enemies of pests, eaten into farm profits and lowered returns to farmers. Good business for chemical TNCs it may be, but Asian rice growers are beginning to question whether they really need these products. There is now considerable evidence, plus growing awareness among Asian rice growers, that yields can be maintained and even increased by using less pesticide. Like most other crops, rice attracts insects that cause damage. To control the pests, farmers have been persuaded to reach for the chemical can. 'For over 40 years, farmers in Asia have relied on chemical pesticides as though they're medicines', pointed out Dr Kong Luen Heong of the International Rice Research Institute (IRRI).[37] According to Dr Paul Teng of IRRI:

> Farmers are relatively uneducated, they are exposed to propaganda from companies about pesticides, and think of insecticide as insect killing medicine. It takes an effort to wean them away from that thinking. The companies are usually better organised and have more money than government services to get their message across.[38]

Handing out free T-shirts and company caps, the chemical companies have sought to encourage a brand loyalty among farmers who did not question the need for pesticide. Heavy radio advertising and large roadside billboards have played on emotions, chiefly fear of loss, to reinforce the message the companies want farmers to believe. 'A lot of the company advertising is very scary', according to Heong. But a dramatic change has started to occur. Despite the heavy advertising, farmers are showing a willingness to get off the pesticide treadmill, not least because it can give them higher earnings.

Integrated pest management practices are now becoming more common and rice farmers are using less pesticide. A project in the Philippines, carried out by IRRI in conjunction with the FAO, the Department of Agriculture of the Philippines and local organisations, has shown that farmers who apply much less pesticide than neigh-bouring farmers, harvest as much, if not more, rice from their land. A group of farmers in a village in central Luxon was asked not to apply pesticide on their rice for the first 40 days after planting. Beneficial insects were thus given a chance to survive and to keep down the damaging insects. Yields compared well with previous yields, even increasing for some farmers. Those who did not spray saved between 1,200–1,500 pesos over the season (about £30–£37), a significant amount for them. Many were persuaded beyond the confines of the project. 'Many of the farmers stopped spraying altogether, not just in the first 40 days but over the entire growing season', related Heong.

Peter Kenmore, an FAO official in the Asia region, pointed out that a nine-country FAO Inter-Country programme for Integrated Pest Management (IPM) has encouraged rice farmers in 8,000 villages to drastically cut insecticide use. In total, a 75 per cent reduction has been achieved in these villages, said Kenmore, and yields have increased by an average of 10 per cent.[39] In 1987, the Indonesian government banned 57 insecticide varieties and began training farmers in IPM techniques. The brown planthopper was then a serious threat to rice; 200,000 hectares were infested. Since 1987, pesticide use has dropped by over 50 per cent, rice output has increased by 12 per cent and only about 20,000 hectares are troubled with the brown planthopper.

In Bangladesh, training in IPM techniques is available in 64 sub-districts of the country. Again, with reductions in insecticide use of 75 per cent, farmers report increases in yields of 6 to 21 per cent. In Vietnam, the government launched a national campaign in 1994 to urge farmers not to spray insecticide in the first 40 days after planting. In trials in six states in India, the Indo-British Fertiliser Education Project, which trained rice farmers in IPM techniques, found that the profits of farmers who did not apply insecticide were 20 per cent higher than farmers who sprayed. Over half a million Asian rice farmers are now skilled in IPM techniques, estimates Kenmore. The rise in awareness about natural ways of pest control is providing small-scale farmers with higher returns at the expense of TNC sales. Rumbled by farmers, chemical companies are also facing action by a number of Asian governments that is likely to reduce their sales. In the Philippines, two insecticides made by Hoechst were declared environmental and health risks in January 1994 and banned by the government. One was endosulfan, sold under the name Thiodan, the most widely used by the country's farmers.

To save foreign exchange, other countries are restricting the imports of chemicals. To get around this, many of the chemical TNCs are building factories in developing countries and making the chemicals locally. In Asia, foreign corporations have cooperated with local companies to establish joint ventures. 'But the initial rush into South America has cooled, and some corporations are pulling out', said Barbara Dinham of a UK-based non-governmental organisation, The Pesticides Trust. Nonetheless, investment in chemical plants in the South is likely to grow. Over 30 developing countries have facilities for formulating pesticides and at least 11 produce their active ingredients.[39]

Obsolete pesticides

There are about 100,000 tonnes of obsolete pesticides in developing countries, 'posing a serious threat to the environment and public health', according to a 1996 FAO report.[40] The report says that most of these pesticides are left over from the donations of foreign aid programmes. The conditions under which these pesticides are stored rarely meet internationally accepted standards; many pesticide containers deteriorate and leak their contents into the soil, contaminating groundwater and the environment. In sub-Saharan Africa, thousands of tons of unused, obsolete and deteriorating pesticides – many of them made and sold by TNCs, some donated under aid programmes – are lying around, causing severe health risks. Over 6,500 tons of these have been identified in 20 African countries, with Morocco and Algeria having the largest stocks.

'There is not a single country [in Africa and the Near East] that is not affected by the serious environmental hazards associated with obsolete pesticides', the FAO report warns. There is now a serious disposal crisis over these products, which include the widely banned lindane, dieldrin and DDT. Only a handful of developing countries have the incineration facilities to dispose of them safely. The safest way to deal with obsolete pesticides is to bring them back to the countries which manufactured them. The FAO has started a programme for the disposal of existing stocks. During an FAO meeting on the Disposal of Obsolete Pesticides, in March 1998, representatives of the agrochemical industry indicated a commitment to paying part of the disposal costs for obsolete chemicals in developing countries.

Health problems

Pesticides are poisons made chiefly by TNCs. In the developing world they are applied mainly by poor people, often causing health problems, and even death. They are difficult to use safely. Labels on cans may not be understood, soap and water may not be available to wash chemical off the skin after an accidental spillage, and protective clothing may be too expensive to buy or too warm to wear. Pesticides also cause damage to the environment, by running off into rivers and reservoirs, contaminating drinking water and fish stocks.

A growing awareness of the dangers to health posed by these chemicals has led to sufferers taking action. Workers on banana plantations, for example, are bringing lawsuits against the manufacturers of DBCP, a chemical used in the plantations, for the damage they allege has been done to their health by these chemicals. In 1995, Dow Chemical, Shell and Occidental Chemical faced lawsuits from 16,000 workers in 11 countries. The workers allege that the companies went on selling DBCP even after its harmful effects had become known. In 1979, the USA banned the use of DBCP. Dow Chemical invited Standard Fruit, one of its biggest customers, 'to sign a waiver absolving Dow from all legal responsibility arising from the use of Fumazone, the trade name of DBCP. As late as 1984, "Fumazone" was being applied to plantations in Cote d'Ivoire and in Ecuador, the world's leading banana-exporting country.'[41] The workers allege that the companies acted with negligence in a number of countries between 1965 and 1990.

The most recent threat to health is coming from the large amounts of pesticides that are being applied to non-traditional crops, such as fruit, vegetables and flowers (see Chapter 4). Persistent exposure to highly toxic chemicals is now causing serious health problems in a number of Latin American countries, especially for women engaged in flower production, who suffer high miscarriage rates, and recurrent headaches and dizzy spells. Economic problems arise too. Producers can lose the entire value of a crop, and also face stiff penalties, if pesticide residues in foodstuffs violate an importing country's standards. Between 1984 and 1994, the US Food and Drug Administration detained more than 14,000 shipments of fruit and vegetables from ten Latin American and Caribbean countries because the produce failed to meet US pesticide residue standards. The TNCs had encouraged the use of these products, the growers had paid with their purse and maybe their health, only to find that their crop was worthless.

In the power game that is being played out across the fields of the developing world, it is the poor who lose when anything goes wrong, not the corporations. The challenge facing resource-poor growers is to mobilise the power they do have to fight back against corporate might (see Chapter 12).

CHAPTER 4

Agri-commodities Take Their Toll

Transnational corporations have major investments in the production, trade and distribution of foodstuffs and processed agricultural commodities. This chapter examines, in particular, their involvement in tobacco and cigarettes, babyfoods, and non-traditional exports, such as fruit, vegetables and flowers. The production and use of such commodities touch the lives of millions in developing countries. A growing share of the business of leading food TNCs in processed agricultural commodities is coming from developing countries. Some (Unilever and BAT, for example) also have substantial interests in sectors other than agri-commodities.

Tobacco

In May 1998, the small Latin American country of Guatemala sent shock waves through the tobacco industry. Guatemala's gross national product of US$14.2 billion (1996) is tiny compared with, for example, Philip Morris's US$54.53 billion profits. But the government of Guatemala announced that it was filing a lawsuit against the US tobacco industry 'in an attempt to recover the costs of treating tobacco-related illnesses'.[1] It was the first developing country – or indeed any country – to file such a lawsuit. A sum of around US$500 million was being sought. If successful, the lawsuit, which came on top of other lawsuits from US states, would almost certainly be followed by other developing countries, for the cost of treating tobacco-related illnesses is heavy and mounting.

Tobacco is not only one of the world's largest traded crops, it is also the most concentrated in TNC hands. Five corporations, Philip Morris, BAT Industries, RJR Nabisco (formerly R.J. Reynolds), Rothmans and Japan Tobacco are responsible for around 70 per cent of global tobacco production (excepting China which is a state monopoly). The corpora-

Table 4.1 Largest food transnationals, by turnover, 1998

	Sales	Profits	Chief products	Employees
	\multicolumn{2}{c}{(US$ billion)}			
Philip Morris	56.11	6.31	Tobacco, cereals, beverages	152,000
Cargill	51.00	4.68	Cereals, seeds, oils, beverages	80,600
Unilever	50.06	7.94	Oils, dairy, beverages, meals	287,000
Nestlé	49.96	4.11	Beverages, cereals, infant food	225,808
Pepsico	20.92	1.49	Beverages, snacks	142,000
Sara Lee	20.01	-0.53	Meat and bakery	139,000
Coca-Cola	18.87	4.13	Beverages, foods	29,500
McDonald's	11.41	1.64	Restaurants	267,000

Source: FT 500, *Financial Times*, 28 January 1999, excepting Cargill, website: www.cargill.com.

tions often contract-out production to small farmers, giving advice, selling them the necessary seeds, fertilisers and other inputs, and then buying the dried tobacco leaf from them. American Brands was, until recently, among the major tobacco TNCs, owning the US-based American Tobacco and the UK-based Gallagher, but it sold American Tobacco to BAT Industries, and, in October 1996, announced that it would sell Gallagher and change its name to Fortune Brands, 'to expunge any memories of the tobacco connection. Its shares jumped ... after the announcement'.[2] The move led to pressure on BAT to hive off its US tobacco interests.

Millions of people in developing countries might wish that they could expunge the tobacco connection. Tobacco has worsened the lives of millions of the poor, with the damaging impact of the industry far exceeding the benefits. With smoking in the North on the decline, the industry has increasingly targeted the South, seeing it as the market that will help maintain profits. In *Tobacco: Supply, Demand and Trade Projections, 1995–2000*, the Food and Agriculture Organisation (FAO) points to a rapid expansion of potential smokers – people above the age of 15 – throughout developing countries and Eastern Europe.[3]

In the North, less than three out of ten adults now smoke, compared with around six out of ten 40 years ago, and smoking is no longer socially acceptable in most homes, public places and workplaces. Smoking-related disease kills around two million people a year in the North, where most people now recognise that smoking is a killer. Tobacco TNCs are on the defensive as chronically ill smokers begin to sue them for the damage they allege has been caused to their health. Some doctors believe that within 30 years, smoking in industrialised countries could very largely be a habit of the past.

In the South, however, smoking is on the increase. With some subtle persuasion from the tobacco companies, 50 per cent of men and 8 per cent of women now smoke. Forty years ago, virtually no women and only about 20 per cent of men in the South smoked. A million people in the South are dying each year from smoking-caused disease. According to the World Health Organisation, 'on current smoking patterns' this will grow to around seven million within 30 years.[4]

To Ministries of Agriculture, there is money in tobacco. Developing countries produce over four-fifths of the crop – 5.18 million tonnes in 1996, out of a global total of 6.41 million tonnes. China is the biggest producer (2.32 million tonnes in 1996). About 4.3 million hectares of arable land are under the crop in the South. Most of the tobacco produced is used domestically; 43 developing countries export tobacco, with nine countries (Argentina, Brazil, Turkey, Thailand, India, China, Indonesia, Malawi and Zimbabwe) earning over 90 per cent of the South's foreign earnings. Most developing countries, however, are net importers of tobacco, spending scarce foreign exchange on a product with a proven record of damaging health. If the rise in smoking in their countries continues, more foreign exchange will need to be devoted to importing tobacco products.

Tobacco TNCs claim that cultivation of the crop is a major source of rural employment and that it constitutes an important source of foreign exchange for many developing countries. It claims that the global market for tobacco is continuing to expand, with smokers in developing countries increasing in number by around 2 per cent a year. Much tobacco farming is only for limited periods of the year, claims the industry, and uses land which is often unsuitable for other crops. It also claims that tobacco is more profitable for farmers than other crops. What is certain is that tobacco generates good profits for the companies. Like the other tobacco giants, BAT, for example, has made excellent profits in poor countries, even in the world's poorest continent, Africa. In 1996 it reported 'strong sales growth' in its Asia-Pacific and African, Middle Eastern, Southern and Central Asian regions. According to tobacco control expert Simon Chapman, between 1985 and 1992, 'BAT made £299 million in profits from African operations – an average of £43 million a year'.[5]

Impact on the poor

Under contract with BAT (Uganda) Ltd, John Angiepado, a resource-poor farmer in Arua, in the West Nile region of Uganda, sold 200 kilogrammes of tobacco in 1990 for 100,000 Ugandan Shillings (about US$100) from three acres of land. For this, he and his family worked hard over the nine-month tobacco preparation and growing season. The earnings he regarded as a pittance: 'I don't know what to tell my children and wife who worked so hard to produce the tobacco.'[6] Yet this level of earnings seems about average in Uganda.

Some four-fifths of Uganda's tobacco is grown in the West Nile region, in the northwest of the country. Around 10,000 small-scale farmers grow the crop under contract for BAT, which has a monopoly on tobacco in the country. The company supplies farmers with a package deal (usually on credit) that includes inputs such as fertilisers, seeds, pesticides and technical advice, and buys the cured tobacco from them. In Uganda, as in most countries in the South, tobacco is grown by small farmers on plots of around half a hectare, and sold to the company at a price the company determines. Contractual arrangements with tobacco companies are normal practice.

In Sierra Leone, a subsidiary of BAT has over 15,000 farmers under contract to the company. BAT in Kenya has a contractual arrangement with around 20,000 small farmers; it offers them a package deal of advice, and buys tobacco leaf from them after it has been dried (cured). Farmers have to build their own curing barn – a thatched hut with horizontal poles to hang the leaf, and with a furnace for burning the wood. Curing can take from seven to ten days, during which time the barn has to be kept at a constant temperature, around 35°C. It is not uncommon for families to sleep around their barns at curing time. The price that farmers receive for their tobacco leaf is dependent on the company's evaluation of its quality. There are usually no independent assessors. The farmers are powerless to do anything about the price the company offers; they have no option but to take it or leave it.

In the Philippines, the National Tobacco Authority set a floor price for tobacco leaf of 20 pesos a kilo (about 50p), says Simon Chapman. But Philip Morris and R. J. Reynolds, which jointly control over 60 per cent of the country's cigarette market, pay farmers only 7 pesos a kilo (about 17p).[7] According to Chris Palabay, spokesman for Solidarity of Tobacco Planters Against Exploitation, interest rates for tobacco growers in the Philippines for a four-to-five-year loan 'range from 75 to 100 per cent'.[8] Debt could explain why many farmers continue to grow tobacco, because they owe money to companies. Malawi is often cited by tobacco

TNCs as a country where the crop plays a major economic role, but ordinary Malawian farmers – mainly women – 'do not benefit from the tobacco economy', points out a former employee of the Commonwealth Development Corporation in Malawi: 'Thousands of Malawian farmers have been moved off their land to make way for large tobacco estates.'[9]

Health

For the poor who smoke, tobacco worsens poverty by worsening their health. For health services in developing countries, the need to treat smoking-related disease puts an additional strain on often already over-stretched budgets. Smoking undermines a nation's health service. When a country has to spend money treating smokers, it inevitably has less money for treating other diseases.

The attraction of tobacco, for governments, is that it brings in tax revenues. Smokers in China, for example, earn the Exchequer more than US$5,000 million a year. But, as in many countries, there are no published figures about how much it costs the health service to treat the diseases which are caused by smoking. Ministries of Health in developing countries try to counter the apparent 'benefits' by pointing to the cost of treating smoking-related diseases and to the working days that are lost. They want legislation to control smoking before the diseases and the deaths it causes reach epidemic proportions. But often with limited budgets, these Ministries find it hard to tackle the powerful tobacco industry with its multi-million marketing budgets.

Hospitals in developing countries are now taking the strain of smoking-caused illnesses. In Zimbabwe, for example, lung cancer resulting from heavy smoking has become one of the commonest complaints at the Mpilo Hospital in Bulawayo. In Sudan, coronary heart disease has become one of the most common causes of death.[10] Other smoking-caused health problems include respiratory diseases, peptic ulcers and pregnancy complications, including low birth weight. Among malnourished mothers, low birth weight threatens children's lives. Children born to smoking mothers also risk impaired physical and intellectual development. Struggling, with some success, to overcome long-standing diseases such as leprosy and yellow fever, the health services of developing countries are hit by new diseases that are industry-made.

Tobacco production and use also means less food production. According to the FAO, Malawi has 4.3 per cent of its land under tobacco, and Zimbabwe 2 per cent. While these percentages are small on the national scale, they can rise dramatically in specific areas where peasant farmers have been persuaded to put a sizable part of their land under tobacco.

Dr Judith MacKay, Director of the Asian Consultancy on Tobacco Control in Hong Kong, claims that tobacco's 'minor' use of land denies 10 to 20 million people of food. 'Where food has to be imported because rich farmland is being diverted to tobacco production, the government will have to bear the cost of food imports', she points out.[11]

Heavy advertising of tobacco by the TNCs can convince the poor to smoke more, and to use money they might have spent on food or health care, to buy cigarettes instead. According to Dr D. Fami-Pearse of the University of Lagos, people in Bangladesh on low incomes, who had been persuaded to smoke five cigarettes a day, had to cut food purchases by 15 per cent, which reduced their daily calorific intake by 300 from an already low 2,000.[12]

Transnational corporations are especially keen to expand in Africa because it has the lowest tobacco consumption rate. Awareness of the health risks of smoking is generally low in Africa, as it is in most of the South where people have often not been informed about the risks – health warnings on cigarette packets are in their infancy. Bans or restrictions on tobacco advertising are only imposed in about 40 developing countries, which means there are no restrictions in three-quarters of the countries of the South.

Non-smoking women are one of the industry's chief targets. The World Health Organisation (WHO) warns that it is highly probable that the aggressive marketing of cigarettes to women 'will be intensified'.[14] The First International Conference on Women and Smoking, held in Northern Ireland in 1992, heard of the marked proliferation of 'women's brands' in recent years. The conference noted that TNC advertisements for women's brands tend to portray smoking as a glamorous, fun-loving activity enjoyed by independent women. But health workers take the view that smoking is worse for women because of gender-related diseases such as cervical cancer, osteoporosis and reduced fertility. It is urgent, says the WHO, to counteract the 'deceitful advertising' that links smoking 'to images of seduction, slimness, elegance, physical fitness and emancipation'.[15]

Young people are also a prime target of the tobacco industry's bid to maintain profits. 'The industry concentrates almost exclusively on children and young people to recruit new smokers', warns the WHO.[16] The advertising pays off. Every day, at least another 4,000 young people start smoking. An article in the December 1991 issue of the *Journal of the American Medical Association* points out that very young children see, understand and remember advertising. It says that some cartoon-style advertisements were far more successful in marketing cigarettes to children than to adults. Another pernicious form of advertising is that

of depicting cigarettes or their logos on toys. The industry also pro-
motes itself through sponsorship of sporting events that are popular
with children; it has an ongoing and pressing need to recruit people as
smokers to replace the ones who are dying, and the earlier in their life
the industry recruits them, the sooner they can contribute to company
profits.

A family burden

Tobacco production imposes economic as well as health burdens on
families. Women carry the heaviest burden of smallholder tobacco
growing; in addition to carrying out farming-related tasks, they have to
collect wood for the barns as well as for domestic use. Meals become
irregular and sparse during the busiest months. Vegetable gardens and
markets are often neglected. Tobacco growing often makes use of child
labour and this has serious consequences for education. Attendance by
children at school becomes more erratic. 'Tobacco growing in West
Nile (Uganda) is a family undertaking', says Aliro. 'Children are needed
at all stages of cultivation and curing, particularly for tasks such as
weeding, watering, stringing and sewing sheaths of tobacco leaves
together for hanging along flue-pipes in a barn.'[13] Fewer children of
tobacco growers attend school, Aliro points out, compared with children
from non-tobacco growing families, and they start primary school at an
older age. Even when school fees have been paid, children are kept at
home in periods of peak activity in the tobacco fields. While child
labour is not unique to tobacco, the crop's longer growing season and
the curing process cause particular strains.

Land degradation

Most tobacco in developing countries is grown in semi-arid areas
where trees are sparse. The industry claims that this is one of the
benefits of the crop, but the disappearance of yet more trees can remove
the land's natural protection and turn food-growing land into a barren
waste. In Uganda, for example, 'the most striking effect of tobacco-
growing is the near depletion of both natural and planted forests'.[17] In
Uganda's West Nile region, the area most affected by deforestation is
Maracha, which is in danger of becoming a desert. Wells and streams
in the area are drying up, forcing people to walk further in their search
for fuel. Women, already working long hours, have shouldered most of
this extra burden. As trees have been axed, so soil has less cover and is
more likely to be washed away in heavy rains. Farmers complain of

falling soil fertility and reduced crop yields. BAT claims that trees are being replanted in Uganda and that it is improving the efficiency of barn furnaces to reduce wood consumption.

About half the South's output of tobacco leaves is cured with wood. This curing causes a serious loss of trees, putting an additional strain on tropical forests. An Economist Intelligence Unit report points out:

> one of the major consequences of tobacco production in the Third World results from the considerable energy requirements of the flue-curing and fire-curing processes … as such, tobacco is a contributory factor in some countries to the problems of deforestation now being encountered. The clearing of forest land opens the way to erosion of the soil and other environmental repercussions which ultimately reduce the productivity of adjacent agricultural land.[18]

Tobacco therefore causes trees to be axed, affecting food production in some of the world's hungriest countries. In Kenya, BAT says that farmers can only become tobacco farmers if they agree to plant 1,000 eucalyptus trees a year on their land. But enforcement of this policy is another matter. A former senior employee of BAT Kenya has alleged:

> the company is shouting about massive tree planting but this, I'm afraid, is nothing less than an outrageous attempt to veil the whole problem. There can be no argument that trees in the tobacco-producing areas are being felled willy-nilly and that in the not too distant [future], there won't be any left at all. The trouble is that BAT, as well as the farmer, can get away with it and they do.[19]

The average smallholder in Kenya has less than four hectares of land. If she or he plants tobacco, that might take up half a hectare and the trees a further hectare. Land for food and other purposes is squeezed. Even fast-growing trees can take five years to grow and many farmers are not interested in planting trees today that will be ready to cut in about five years time. They have rather more pressing problems, such as growing enough food to make sure that their families survive today. Furthermore, many farmers prefer to use trees like eucalyptus for building purposes and they continue to cut native forest for tobacco curing. Also, the newly planted trees do not always survive. BAT Kenya claim, however, that their contracted farmers do have enough wood and that 40 million trees, planted by these farmers, are surviving.[20]

Deforestation in Malawi, the African country most dependent on tobacco for export earnings, is not well documented but could be reaching a critical level. In Sierra Leone, one of the world's six poorest countries, 'in Bombali district in the north of the country, the adverse effects of tobacco cultivation are clearly seen', warns an Action Aid report: 'The area was once forested ... but now it is bare and rocky and incapable of supporting crops.'[21] Tobacco deforestation is serious in parts of Brazil, one of the world's biggest producers. BBC Panorama presenter, Peter Taylor, said of a visit to a farm in Santa Cruz, Brazil: 'There were once forests around the farm, but they have been cut down for fuel, mainly to cure tobacco.' The country's 100,000 tobacco farmers, he estimates, need the wood of 60 million trees a year.[22] The industry claims that 24.7 million trees were used for tobacco curing in Brazil but that 217.5 million new trees were planted. But it does not say how many survived.

Tobacco growing also affects the environment by depleting soil nutrients 'at a much faster rate than many other crops, thus rapidly decreasing the life of the soil', warn Goodland, Watson and Ledec.[23] In some countries (Malawi, Sri Lanka, Zambia and Zimbabwe, for example), tobacco often grows on hilly land and this speeds up soil erosion. Tobacco needs heavy applications of pesticides. An instruction leaflet given to tobacco farmers in Kenya lists BAT's recommended seedbed programme for the crop (preparing seeds for planting). From making the seedbed to transplanting the seed in the field takes about three months. During that time, 16 applications of pesticide are recommended. Some of the world's most dangerous chemicals are available to the tobacco sector in Kenya, and hence to the farmers, including aldrin and dieldrin, (which Britain phased out in 1969), DDT, ambush and drinox. Besides being hazardous to users, these chemicals can contaminate water supplies. But figures are rarely published on poisonings that occur because pesticide has run off fields into water courses and local supplies.

Eucalyptus, the tobacco industry's favourite tree, is highly controversial. It grows quickly, even in dry areas, by drawing on underground water. But its fast growth can be at the expense of the water table. If a lower water table results, then the ability of land to grow food can be damaged.

Medical associations and the World Health Organisation have recommended that cigarette advertisements be withdrawn completely from the mass media. China has banned television advertising of tobacco. In Kenya, the industry agreed to withdraw radio and television advertisements, although a BAT weekly programme continued. Some of the cigarettes exported from the North to the South by tobacco TNCs have been found to have a higher content of tar and nicotine (the substance which makes them addictive) than brands sold in the

North. James Wilkinson says, for example, that in Pakistan, 'two of the most popular brands, Capstan and Morven, each have a yield of 29 mg tar per cigarette. Tar concentrations for a range of popular cigarettes sold in the United Kingdom and in Australia in 1981 never exceeded 19 mg per cigarette.'[24]

Alternatives

There are alternatives to tobacco. Many crops can grow on land that is now under tobacco cultivation They include the majority of grain crops and vegetables, such as paprika and chillies, fruits such as citrus, kiwi, avocados and mangoes, and nuts, including macadamia, pecan and cashew.[25] The best alternative crops for small-scale growers are those which can be sun dried, stored and sold for export at the end of the season. Dr Bernard Chidzero, Zimbabwe's Senior Minister for Finance, has told farmers that 'more mixed farming and less land under tobacco is needed'.[26] Horticulture could be a more sustainable crop in the long term and is a large employer of labour and foreign currency earner, said a Zimbabwe Minister of Agriculture (but see also below).[27]

The bottom line for governments of developing countries is that the net economic costs of tobacco are profoundly negative – the cost of treatment, disability and death exceeds the economic benefits to producers by at least US$200 billion annually, 'with one-third of this loss being incurred by developing countries'.[28] Facing coordinated international action against smoking, the tobacco industry can be expected to step up its promotional activities in developing countries. The tobacco TNCs have more money at their disposal to fight against control than the health lobby has to fight for control. But unless governments take action, they will be faced with an increasingly unhealthy population and huge epidemics of smoking-related diseases.

Babyfoods

'Welcome to Nigeria where babies are healthy and happy', read a billboard near Lagos airport. Not surprisingly, it was the advertisement of a babymilk manufacturer. However, according to the UNICEF 1995 report, *The State of the World's Children*: 'In 1990, more than one million infants died who would not have died if they had been exclusively breastfed for the first six months of their lives.' An earlier UNICEF report had pointed out that bottle-fed babies are '25 times more likely to die in childhood than infants who are exclusively breastfed for the first six months of life'.[29] The promotion of breastmilk substitutes to mothers therefore affects the lives of some of the world's most vulnerable people. Milk company TNCs do most of the promoting.

Feeding a baby with breastmilk is universally recognised to be superior to bottle-feeding; it gives the right blend of nutrients, antibodies and white blood cells which protect against disease. Recent research also suggests that breastfed babies have higher intelligence.[30] Yet breastfeeding in many industrialised and developing countries is losing out to the bottle. In China, home to more than one in five of the world's population, it is dropping quite dramatically. In Muslim Bangladesh, it more than halved in ten years – from 96 per cent in 1983 to 46 per cent in 1993, although the Koran instructs that babies are to be weaned only when they are two years old. Probably, the chief reasons for the fall is the powerful promotion and advertising by TNCs of breastmilk substitutes, competing for a share in an US$8 billion a year market. The TNCs have persuaded millions of mothers to foresake breastfeeding and to use powder instead. Free supplies to hospitals have been particularly persuasive but is the most detrimental practice, inducing mothers away from breastfeeding, believes UNICEF.

In 1973, the *New Internationalist* magazine published an article by two paediatricians on the effects of breastmilk substitutes.[31] The following year, War on Want published a booklet *The Baby Killer*, with a telling cover showing a sick baby inside a feeding bottle.[32] The booklet was a best-seller and led to television films and translations which gave the matter wide publicity. When translated into German by the Third World Action Group in Berne, Switzerland, it was given the title *Nestlé Totet Babys* which means *Nestlé Kills Babies*. Nestlé filed a successful libel suit against the group, but the Judge, imposing only a modest fine, said in his summing up that Nestlé's advertising in developing countries went considerably further than in industrialised countries. There was a need, he said, for Nestlé to 'fundamentally rethink its advertising practices in developing countries' if it wanted to be spared the accusation of immoral and unethical conduct.[33]

The Swiss-based Nestlé is the world's second largest food company. Its chief products are coffee, confectionery, mineral water, milk, ice cream and pet foods. In 1988 Nestlé paid almost US$4,000 million for the British company Rowntree, and owns numerous smaller businesses including Gales honey, Sun Pat peanut butter and Sarsons vinegar. Worldwide, it has around 40 per cent of the world market in breastmilk substitutes – or 'infant formulae' as the company prefers to call it. Other prominent babymilk manufacturers are Cow and Gate, Wyeth, Carnation, Boots, Ross-Abbott and Mead Johnson.

In 1975 a group of Catholic nuns, the Sisters of the Precious Blood, filed a suit against the American company, Bristol Myers, charging them with 'making mis-statements in its proxy statements'. 'In other words, lying', according to Gabrielle Palmer:

> When the nuns as shareholders, had challenged the company to provide detailed information about its promotional practices abroad, they were informed there was no promotion where chronic poverty or ignorance could lead to product misuse.[34]

Yet Bristol Myers marketed their product in countries such as Guatemala where only about half the population had access to drinking water. The nuns collected evidence from 18 countries and the company settled out of court. But the industry was not moved. 'In spite of all the publicity and the lawsuits, the companies, including Nestlé, continued their widespread promotion', says Palmer. Churches and concerned groups in the USA began a consumer boycott of Nestlé products which soon spread to Canada, Europe and New Zealand. As the boycott grew under the coordination of the newly formed worldwide NGO coalition, the International Baby Food Action Network (IBFAN), Nestlé stepped up its spending on public relations in an attempt to counter the threat to business. Palmer notes that the company paid a US$1 million fee to the public relations firm Hill & Knowlton which sent 300,000 glossy booklets to clergy and religious bodies.

The Code

The World Health Organisation and UNICEF became convinced that a Code of Conduct was needed for the marketing of breastmilk substitutes. This was approved by governments at the World Health Assembly in May 1981 by 118 votes to one. The vote against was cast by the USA. The Code's first four provisions call for 'no advertising of breastmilk substitutes, no free samples to mothers, no promotion of products through health care facilities, no company mothercraft nurses to advise mothers'. The idea behind the Code was that each country should put its provisions into effect in either a legally binding or voluntary way. It says that NGOs have 'the responsibility of drawing the attention of manufacturers to activities which are incompatible with the principles and aims of the Code' (article 11.4).

After the Code was adopted each company wrote its own version, 'none of which came near to the WHO basics', claims Palmer.[35] By 1984, Nestlé said it would keep to the WHO Code in developing countries, even in the absence of national laws. In response, the consumer boycott was lifted. Much of Nestlé's large-scale advertising of breastmilk substitutes stopped. But other marketing practices continued. In 1986 an investigation in the Philippines revealed that 37 per cent of babies were fed in hospital on free supplies from Nestlé. The provision of such supplies is in direct contravention of the Code. In Pakistan, Malaysia and Singapore there was also evidence of the milk companies breaking the WHO Code. The consumer boycott of the market leader, Nestlé, was reimposed.

As public pressure for change intensified, UNICEF's Executive Board called (in 1991) on 'manufacturers and distributors of breastmilk substitutes to end free and low-cost supplies of infant formulae to maternity wards and hospitals by December 1992'.[36] In effect, it asked the companies to stick to a Code that had been agreed ten years earlier.

An IBFAN report, published in September 1991, investigated the practices of babymilk companies. It found that 'no company demonstrates full compliance with the International Code. Nestlé ... is found to violate the Code more often than any of its competitors, but scant regard for the Code is shown by most other companies, including Hipp, Mead-Johnson, Meji, Milupa, Nutricia/Cow & Gate, Snow Brand and Wyeth.'[37] Nestlé said it would stop supplies to health facilities by the end of 1992.

In May 1994, in an attempt to tighten up any loopholes in the Code, the World Health Assembly adopted *unanimously* a resolution to strengthen breastfeeding worldwide. This resolution removed any possible ambiguities which the companies claim existed with the 1981 Code. But little seemed to change. A follow-up IBFAN report, published in August 1994, based on a survey carried out in 62 countries from September 1993 to July 1994, said there was:

> little improvement on the part of most baby feeding companies. Many of the marketing practices reported in 1991 continue to be used today. However, some successes can be reported, and the current climate among governments and international bodies is increasingly one of desire for change.[38]

The publication alleged that the TNCs were giving free supplies of their products in 41 countries, 'at least 28 of which have government bans in place. ... The industry's promise to end free or low-cost supplies to hospitals has been exposed as a sham.' And it alleged that Nestlé violated the Code 'as least twice as much as its nearest competitor'. The report said that 588 complaints about Nestlé were received from 22 countries; the majority referred to samples, free supplies, gifts etc. which it is alleged were distributed.

Nestlé responded by investigating 455 of the allegations. In late 1994, it reported that 'just three required corrective action ... a large number were simply untrue ... many were so vague as to be unverifiable'. It claimed that there were 'fundamental flaws' in IBFAN's monitoring and that the company had not promoted infant formulae in the developing world for ten years. But Nestlé's response had little credibility. The report quoted the 'National Director of Maternal and Child Health, Gabon', as saying 'you may use this note to deny the allegation made without foundation against your company which is in complete contradiction of what is happening in the field'. The director was unnamed. When the UK group Baby Milk Action asked Madam Marcelle Epouolou, head of the Nutrition Division at Gabon's Ministry of Health to comment, she replied:

> I am categorical about this: Nestlé, represented by SoGapral in Gabon, does donate free supplies ... as for the famous Director of Maternal and Child Health, he's a fictional character ... let Nestlé give us his name. We have visited several private clinics and the staff admit that they receive supplies of milk from all the companies.[39]

The company felt able to dismiss the allegations, said Baby Milk Action, because its interpretation of the Code 'is much weaker than WHO or UNICEF intended'. The company claims, for example, that the Code applies only to infant formulae and not to 'follow-on milks'. Such milks were virtually unknown when the Code was adopted in 1991 and 'are not safe for babies under 6 months because they contain too much salt and protein', in Baby Milk Action's view. Nestlé seems to believe that free supplies of babyfood can be given in some cases; it appears to interpret free gifts to health workers differently and thinks that pictures of its products are allowed on leaflets given to mothers. Such interpretations are, however, inconsistent with both the spirit and letter of the WHO code. According to Leah Marguiles, former legal advisor at UNICEF:

> the fact that Nestlé says that only three of the charges made against it by the International Baby Food Action Network were accurate, doesn't make it so. For example, the IBFAN report included violations that I found in a hospital in Bangkok which I monitored while I was legal adviser to the UNICEF Baby Friendly Hospital Initiative. Nestlé's response was that these free supplies were donated for the purposes of a scientific study and of course Nestlé didn't consider this among its three violations. The reality is that I went to the ward, interviewed nurses, and was told of the regular donations of Nestlé infant formula. When I asked for proof, I was given copies of invoices marked 'complimentary'. The invoice didn't indicate that the donations were for a study, and neither did the nurses – they just told me about the regular visits and showed me where the donations were kept – in the wards, alongside of the donations given by other companies.[40]

In 1996 Nestlé was under attack from another voluntary agency for allegedly violating a ban on free and low-cost supplies of baby milk to hospitals in China. Nestlé claimed that it voluntarily stopped free supplies to China in April 1994. The government of China banned this practice in 1992, but in February 1996 a report from the aid charity Save the Children Fund (SCF) alleged that Nestlé was undermining breastfeeding practices in Kunming City, Yunnan Province, by providing free supplies to seven hospitals. The SCF report said there had been a drop in breastfeeding and a large increase in the use of Nestlé's baby milk because of its free provision to mothers leaving hospital. Nestlé said that the government of China did not notify manufacturers of its change of policy in 1992. It also claimed to have stopped free supplies to hospitals in China in April 1994. But an SCF spokesman alleged that Nestlé was still providing free supplies in June that year. In a letter to Nestlé's chief executive, the SCF director-general Mike Aaronsen wrote: 'in view of the position that Nestlé takes publicly ... we would like you to investigate the practices in China and ensure they do not continue'.[41]

While it is for governments to develop codes of conduct for the companies, and to monitor those codes, Nestlé and other babyfoods companies have put pressure on governments not to introduce strong codes. Gabon, Pakistan, South Africa, Sri Lanka, Swaziland, Uganda, Uruguay and Zimbabwe came under pressure in 1997 and 1998. 'In Zimbabwe, Nestlé reportedly threatened to disinvest from the country if strong measures were introduced', alleged Baby Milk Action.[42]

Monitoring

Monitoring a code can be expensive and difficult, especially in a country that has many remote areas. The companies have more money to get their promotional staff and material into those areas than governments have to monitor their work. In May 1996 the World Health Assembly passed a resolution calling on governments to ensure that monitoring the Code is carried out in a 'transparent and independent manner, free from commercial influence', and that 'complementary foods are not marketed or used in ways that undermine exclusive and sustained breastfeeding'.

Violations of the Code of Conduct appear to be continuing. In 1996, the Interagency Group on Breastfeeding Monitoring – consisting of 27 voluntary organisations, including UNICEF (UK) and Save the Children – monitored the experiences of 3,200 women who were either pregnant or had babies under six months old, and 480 health workers in Bangladesh, Poland, South Africa and Thailand 'to obtain objective evidence of violations of the Code'. Their report found that some of the women interviewed in all four countries 'reported receiving information associated with a company name, which either promoted bottle feeding and/ or discouraged breastfeeding'. Across the four countries, 'Nestlé, Gerber, Milco, Nutricia and Wyeth were the main companies identified with these messages'. In all the countries surveyed, 'health facilities ... had received information from companies which violated the Code', alleges the report: 'Company personnel were found to have visited health facilities with the stated aim of giving product information to mothers.' Posters and displays of products were found, it claims, in violation of the Code. The Interagency Group believes that its research 'proves that many companies are taking action which violates the Code and in a systematic rather than one-off manner. ... Breastfeeding continues to be threatened by the marketing activities of companies.'[43]

Transnational corporations appear to be interpreting the Code in a way that does not interfere too much with their promotion of the products. In April 1998, IBFAN, which by then comprised more than 150 groups in over 90 countries, published a new report, *Breaking the Rules, Stretching the Rules 1998*. Based on the monitoring of company practices in 39 countries, this alleged that manufacturers are still giving samples to mothers and breaking and stretching the rules.

The allegation was nothing new, but also in early 1998 there was an additional factor – that of possible legal action against the milk companies. Lawyers from the USA, the UK, India, Bangladesh, the Philippines, Norway and Sweden formed a research group 'to tackle the continued problem of abuses of the international conduct of marketing of breast-milk substitutes by major manufacturers'. The lawyers specialise in personal injuries and human rights. The group plans to help authorities in developing countries to coordinate 'potential litigation initiatives, said one of the lawyer firms, Ross & Co. of the UK. In appropriate cases, this may involve 'damage claims for families losing babies', it said. Families who were persuaded to use a company's products and whose babies died may in future take a manufacturer of breastmilk substitutes to court, in much the same way that smokers have taken the tobacco companies to court. 'It is the ultimate consumer battle', believes Ross & Co., 'pitching the wares of the largest transnational corporations against the best product nature can supply'.[44]

The long-term commercial wisdom of the milk companies' marketing practices is hugely doubtful. As long as the controversy continues, and as long as it is even suspected that Nestlé products, for example, could be harming the poor, then many who examine the company's record may decide they do not wish to buy its goods and contribute to its profits. Hanging on grimly to promotional practices that minutely increase sales in the short term will never improve company images. In December 1998, IBFAN was awarded the prestigious Right Livelihood Award. In the words of the citation, the award was 'for its committed and effective campaigning ... for the rights of mothers to breastfeed their babies ... free from the commercial pressure and misinformation with which the companies promote breastmilk substitutes'.

Non-traditional export crops

Farmers in developing countries have long grown fruit and vegetables for their families and local markets; producing them for export markets has recently become more common. TNCs are increasingly involved in the production of crops that have traditionally not been exported. But export crops are replacing staple foods in some areas, resulting in food scarcities and rising food prices that hit hard at the poorest. And they are also causing pesticide problems which are spreading to food crops. Latin America provides a stark example.

The last ten years have seen a huge growth in the export of vegetables from Latin America, especially to the USA, with countries courting TNCs to earn foreign exchange and repay debts which have mounted partly because of low prices for traditional export crops. Much of Latin America's best farmland has for years grown export crops such as coffee, banana, sugar and cotton, again generating substantial export earnings and profits for TNCs. But when prices of such crops plummeted in the 1980s, it seemed to governments that expanding exports of high-priced crops – from mangos to snowpeas to roses – was a way to compensate. International aid agencies, particularly the World Bank, promoted these non-traditional exports as part of trade liberalisation and structural adjustment policies, and the trade is now booming. It brings North American shoppers an all-the-year-round supply of fruits, vegetables and flowers, but causes severe problems for Latin America's poor.

The economic gains appear impressive:

- The value of non-traditional exports increased by 48 per cent in South America (excluding Brazil) between 1985 and 1992, and by 17.2 per cent in Central America. During the same period, Ecuadoran flower exports grew 15-fold in volume and 30-fold in value.
- Although non-traditional crops represent a small fraction of total exports, they can fetch high prices. While world grain prices range from US$75 to US$175 a tonne, a tonne of fresh fruit and vegetables can fetch US$500. For those who succeed, the business is profitable.

- Because many of these crops are labour-intensive, expanding production has generated hundreds of thousands of jobs, especially for women.
- The trade boom has spurred growth in the transport, packaging, and marketing industries, as well as in intermediary firms that broker sales.[45]

Yet this market success 'has frequently come at a cost in workers' health, inequitable distribution of economic benefits, and environmental degradation in many of the exporting countries'.[46] In most Latin American countries, the main beneficiaries of the growth in non-traditional exports are large companies, including both TNCs and the large national investors.

Chile was the first Latin American country to embrace non-traditional export crops. In 1980, Chile exported about the same amount of beans, an important staple, as it grew for local consumption. But by the early 1990s the quantity of beans exported was almost three times higher – 55,000 tonnes a year, compared with 20,000 tonnes grown for local consumption. Between 1989 and 1993 the area in Chile under basic food crops fell by nearly 30 per cent, from 1.2 million hectares to 0.86 million hectatres. Fruit, flowers and other crops destined for the export market, have replaced beans, wheat and other staple foods. TNCs are heavily involved in this trade; three of the top four companies in Chile's non-traditional export crop sector are owned by foreign corporations. This involvement 'has changed the face of the country's agriculture and embittered many small farmers'.[47] Large-scale fruit producers bought out small farmers who could not afford to invest in the new crops.

Brazil's big new export earner was soybean. In 1970, soybean grew on 1.4 million hectares of land; by 1988, it was growing on 10.5 million hectares. Argentina followed Brazil's example. The area under soybean has risen, since the early 1970s, from 10,000 hectares to 5 million hectares. Mexico and other Central American countries have greatly increased their export of vegetables, notably tomatoes, to the USA. Tomatoes now account for nearly half Mexico's vegetable exports.

In every South and Central American country, TNCs are major players in the new business. In Central America, the corporations control about 25 per cent of total production of non-traditional export crops, and they handle the distribution and transport of a large percentage of the exports. Often they are the same corporations who produce and sell the traditional exports. In Bolivia, where there has also been a big expansion of soybean, Cargill has a joint venture with a local company. Fruit companies, Del Monte and Dole, have 'created strong networks in bananas and food access to information and technology which allowed them to rapidly expand into newer export products'.[48]

Consequences

The benefits of these 'new' crops are concentrated in the hands of wealthy investors, foreign companies and distributors. Although many of them can be grown on small plots of land, most are grown by wealthy entrepreneurs. 'Larger businesses have accumulated land in agro-export crops while poorer farmers have been squeezed out of this market and pushed onto marginal land.'[49]

Government support for farmers to help them sustain the production of food staples has fallen dramatically in many Latin American countries. Governments are now more interested in how they can use land for export crops. Scientists have been switched to work on these crops. This is reflected in research spending. In the 1980s, around 90 per cent of the money that Latin American countries spent on agricultural research went on food crops, especially beans. There has now been an almost total change. Only about 20 per cent of agricultural research spending is devoted to food crops, while 80 per cent is going to export crops. These are now the priorities of Latin American countries. Land is not seen, primarily, as the place on which to grow food for local people, but as something from which a country can earn more foreign exchange. In some countries on the continent, research into small farming problems has been completely abandoned. 'In the absence of adequate technical assistance to sustain the production of food staples, small farmers have been forced into growing export crops', points out Francisco Morales, of the Colombia-based International Centre for Tropical Agriculture (CIAT).[50]

Small-scale farmers and consumers in Latin American are paying the price of this drastic shift to export agriculture. In towns and cities across the continent, beans are now frequently scarce as land which once grew beans now grows vegetables for export. Beans contribute around 30 per cent of the protein consumed by the continent's 200 million low-income families. Most bean farmers are now trying to grow vegetables for export and devoting less of their land (often already small) to beans for their own use.

Further constraints

The switch to non-traditional export crops has brought other costs. The international market demands fruit and vegetables with no blemishes and farmers feel they have to use large amounts of pesticide – far more than is used on most traditional crops, say Thrupp, Bergeron and Waters, authors of a study into non-traditional crops.[51] Encouraged to grow vegetables and fruit for export, farmers regard pesticides as the way to guarantee that their produce arrives in top-notch condition.

Many farmers over-use pesticides and apply them at the wrong times, including right up to harvest. In Colombia, farmers who are going to apply pesticides say *Voy a banar el cultivo* (I'm going to bathe the crop). 'If you ask them why', says César Cardona, a CIAT entomologist, 'they're likely to answer, *parque es martes* – because it's Tuesday.'[52] A serious 'side-effect' is that the heavy applications of pesticide applied to these crops is leading to new pests and viruses, causing huge damage to food crops. Dependence on chemical pesticides 'has become almost total', says Morales:

> The expansion of vegetable crops has resulted in the appearance of new virus problems; more than one million hectares previously planted to beans in South America are now abandoned due the incidence of whitefly-transmitted viruses. The boom in soybean cultivation coincided with one of the worst virus epidemics that Latin American agriculture has ever suffered – golden mosaic disease – caused by a virus transmitted by the whitefly.[53]

This has seriously affected traditional bean-growing areas and crops for local people. In Argentina the whitefly has caused virus epidemics. Consumption of beans by Brazilians has almost halved since 1981. Bean production in Chile is increasingly affected by epidemics of viruses. There are also direct side-effects to health. 'The growth [in fruit and vegetable exports] has frequently come at a cost in workers' health, inequitable distribution of economic benefits, and environmental degradation in many of the exporting countries.'[54] There are economic uncertainties as well; while export prices are normally high for fruit and vegetables, they are nonetheless highly volatile. Inputs are costly, market requirements are demanding and competition is fierce. Producers can lose the entire value of a crop and face stiff penalties if pesticide residues on fruits or vegetables violate an importing country's standards. As mentioned in Chapter 3, the US Food and Drug Administration has detained thousands of shipments from Latin America because the produce failed to meet US pesticide-residue standards.

Floriculture

With a buoyant market for cut flowers in Western countries, floriculture is now earning a small number of developing countries large amounts of foreign currency. In European Union countries the cut-flower market is worth around US$14 billion a year, with imports making up more than one-fifth of the figure. The growth of this trade has been made possible by improvements in air cargo transport. Flowers from Africa can be on sale in Europe within 48 hours of being picked.

Colombia is one of the largest exporters of cut flowers; it began exporting them 30 years ago but only in the last five years has the trade taken off. The US administration encouraged the Colombian government to expand this activity because it might provide an alternative to the cultivation of coca and the processing of coca into cocaine, and so help to keep drugs off American streets. Cut-flower exports now earn Colombia over US$350 million a year, but the country's 80,000 flower industry workers appear to be paying the price. 'Poverty wages, child labour, pesticide poisoning and severe health problems' are endured by many of these workers, alleged a Christian Aid report.[55] Women engaged in flower production suffer high miscarriage rates. Some of the pesticides in use are banned in Western countries. TNCs are again heavily involved. Colombia's cut-flower industry was started by a US-based company, Floramerica. In neighbouring Ecuador, two-thirds of the flower plantations involve foreign investment, mainly from Colombia, the Netherlands and the USA.

In Africa, Kenya and Zimbabwe are enjoying a boom in exports of horticulture produce. In the case of Kenya, Unilever and Lonrho are involved, but also a number of local companies. Flowers and vegetables are supplied to supermarkets, including Marks and Spencer. In one area – around Lake Naivasha – there are conflicts over land 'between the rapidly expanding horticultural schemes ... and Maasai cattle owners who claim the surrounding land is theirs. ... Unless drastic action is taken in time, people, their livestock ... in the region could perish.'[56] While jobs have been created, most employees are women workers on short-term contracts. In February 1997, a documentary programme on BBC television showed the huge power that the supermarket Tesco has to decide how a farm in Zimbabwe that was growing 'mange-tout' peas for Tesco ran its business. The company's demands meant a very high wastage rate – around half of the peas were considered unfit and had to be fed to animals or thrown away. Returns to the farm's workers were small and declining. It was Tesco that effectively set the wages and the standards.[57]

The drawbacks of the trade in non-traditional export products call into question its sustainability and the strategies behind it, say Thrupp, Bergeron and Waters.[58] They suggest that policies must be changed if adverse impacts are to be avoided. Policies need to change also in the tobacco and babyfood sectors. Products with the potential to kill people, even when used as the manufacturers direct, will eventually be rumbled by a public that will demand action.

Del Monte in the Philippines

The operations of Del Monte in the Philippines show something of the complexity of TNC activities and their impact on employees. The company began business in the Philippines in 1926 with the establishment of the Philippine Packing Corporation. In 1988 the name was changed to Del Monte Philippines Inc. (DMPI). This reflected the changes that occurred in the corporate affiliations of its US-based parent company, Del Monte Corporation. At the time of the joint delegation's visit in 1987, Del Monte Corporation was a subsidiary of R.J.R. Nabisco (itself a merger of the tobacco company, R.J. Reynolds Industries. and the food company, Nabisco Brands). In 1988, R.J.R. Nabisco was taken over by Kohlberg Kravis Roberts (KKR) for US$25 billion (one of the biggest buy-outs in corporate history). KKR then sold off slices of the R.J.R. Nabisco empire to pay for debts incurred in the buy-out. Among the parts disposed of in this manner was Del Monte. In 1989, while retaining the Del Monte processed foods operations in Canada and Venezuela, R.J.R. Nabisco sold off the rest of the Del Monte processed foods business to a partnership composed of Merrill Lynch & Co., Citicorp Capital Investors Ltd., Kikkoman Corporation and members of Del Monte Corporation's senior management. The fresh food business was sold to the ill-fated Polly Peck International.

The Philippines-based DMPI became a wholly owned subsidiary of a Panamanian-registered corporation, Central American Resources, Inc., which in turn was an affiliate of the US-based Del Monte Corporation. DMPI's corporate lineage therefore traces its roots to the USA, Japan and Europe. The composition of DMPI's board of directors is multinational and reflects this complex mix of business interests: two Americans representing Del Monte Foods, one Japanese from Kikkoman, an Englishman from Del Monte International, and executives from DMPI (four Filipinos and two Americans). In 1982, following protests in Switzerland about its activities, Del Monte agreed to improve working conditions in the Philippines with a social clause. At first glance, Del Monte workers seem better off than most workers in the country considering that they are paid above the legal minimum wage. However, the minimum wage has not kept pace with the poverty line. In 1990, the government estimated that a family of six had to earn at least 130.50

pesos a day to cross the poverty threshold. The daily cost of living for the same family in the countryside was estimated at 184.22 pesos a day in 1991.[59]

The company has continued to use the services of short-term and contract workers who do not seem to be enjoying the legal minimum wage or additional company benefits, such as housing and rice allowances. 'In 1994, concerned that the [social] clause was not being properly monitored, NGOs urged Migros (the leading food retailer in Switzerland) and Del Monte to agree to the creation of a more permanent monitoring body.'[60] This was agreed and Migros undertook to continue importing pineapples from the Philippines even if they became more expensive because of the social clause.

CHAPTER 5

Extracting Logs and Fish

If they continue to extract logs and timber from our forest, our lives will wither like leaves on the trees, like fish without water (Tribal leader)

Forests

Forests are of critical importance for the poor in developing countries; they maintain climates and prevent soil erosion, acting like a sponge to absorb moisture and releasing it slowly to adjacent land. When forests go, the land loses that natural water supply and protection. Droughts and flash floods become more likely. Rivers and fisheries can be badly affected by sediment which has run-off from cut forest areas. It is the poorest, who have less protection from such calamities, who suffer most from deforestation. Indigenous peoples who reside in forests are among those who are badly affected.

Transnational corporations are leading actors in the axing and burning of the forests. Some of the forests they clear through burning will make only short-term range-land for cattle, and some of the timber they axe will be used to make temporary products such as chopsticks and toothpicks. Other areas of forest are being cleared by TNCs to grow plantations such as eucalyptus trees and oil-palm.

Around 154 million hectares of tropical forest were lost in the 1980s, according to the United Nations Food and Agriculture Organisation (FAO), that is 15.4 million hectares a year. While the rate is slowing down, losses are still heavy. According to a 1997 FAO report, a further 65.1 million hectares of tropical forest were lost between 1990 and 1995, about 13 million hectares a year.[1] Enormous human suffering is being caused by this destruction. The devastating floods in the Philippines in October 1991, for example, which killed 7,000 local people, were widely attributed to forest destruction. Scientists have linked the loss of forest cover to the warming of the global climate, which again hits hardest at the poor.

The causes of deforestation are many. The FAO has argued that logging is responsible for only 6 to 7 per cent of degradation and that just over a quarter of the damage occurs when people move into and settle in the forest after the logging has removed the biggest trees, and made forest areas more accessible for settlement and cultivation. A further 10 per cent is destroyed due to infrastructure, such as road-building and dams, it says, while around 55 per cent is damaged because of human encroachment in forest areas, shifting cultivation, 'slash and burn' techniques, the demands of agriculture – cattle ranching, for example – and because of fuelwood gatherers.

But the FAO argument has been discredited. The evidence suggests that logging is the chief cause of deforestation. Ordinary people do not have the equipment or the machinery to axe huge trees. The most recent and detailed study of deforestation in Asia (by researchers at Rutgers University in the USA, published in May 1996) found that it is loggers who have done most of the damage. The axing of forests by logging companies, usually TNCs, in order to sell timber to the West, emerges as the major cause.[2]

Asia and the Pacific

Japan is responsible for much of the deforestation that has occurred in Asian developing countries. In order to protect its own forests, Japan has purchased the forest products of poorer countries and its companies have reaped the reward. Since 1945, Japanese TNCs have logged and brought back to Japan a large slice of Filipino forest. Whereas the Philippines then had 17 million hectares of tropical forest, only one million hectares remained by 1989. The Philippines has one of the most severe deforestation problems of any developing country. The Japanese firms involved in the deforestation include Mitsubishi, Mitsui, C. Itoh and Sumitomo.

Mitsubishi figures among the world's top 100 TNCs. In addition to the Philippines, it has logging companies in Malaysia, Indonesia, Papua New Guinea, Thailand and Burma. It is also one of the world's largest importers of timber. According to the California-based Rainforest Action Network (consisting of 150 groups in 45 countries), Mitsubishi 'contributed to the fastest liquidation of a primary rainforest ever in human history by logging Sarawak, Malaysia, over opposition from native communities'.[3] In 1990, in protest about its alleged logging practices, Rainforest Action Network called for a boycott of Mitsubishi goods (see Chapter 12). The network claims that the company is selling paper, plywood and veneer made from rainforest wood. A Mitsubishi spokesperson said that the network's charges were groundless because the company practised sound logging.[4]

Malaysian companies are prominent in logging operations in other Asian countries. They appear, for example, to be winning substantial logging concessions in Cambodia. According to one report, a Cambodian Ministry of Agriculture document lists 30 contracts for 6.4 million hectares of precious forest in Cambodia, which have either been recently approved or are in the pipeline and scheduled to be signed soon. Patrick Alley, a spokesman for the British NGO, Global Witness, concluded: 'I cannot cite another example in the world where such a vast proportion of a country's forests have been sold in such a short time, in such great secrecy to foreign companies.'[5]

According to Tom Fawthrop, writing in the Thai paper, *The Nation*, the decimation of Cambodia's forests has already been appalling. Before 1970, the country had 17 million hectares of forest, covering 70 per cent of total land area. Ministry of Agriculture figures revealed that forest cover in 1992–93 had fallen to around 10 million hectares, with logging companies getting the benefit. According to Fawthrop, 'the Cambodia government has signed all the remaining rainforest to foreign logging companies – even perhaps down to the last tree outside of national parks'.[6] Behind logging often lurks mining. In Malaysia, 'many timber concessions are being translated into mining concessions'. Twenty-five mining licences have been granted, for example, to 17 companies 'to mine for gold in the Bau area'.[7]

Malaysian timber TNCs are also active in Indonesia, often in joint projects with local firms. The effects of the scramble for land at Indonesia's forest frontier were vividly demonstrated in 1997 by forest fires. These burned continually for over three months, causing smoke to cover a huge area and disrupting agriculture and the lives of millions of people. Large areas of forest were burnt so that companies could use the land to grow crops such as oil-palm, the oil of which is used in cooking (invariably just once before being discarded). According to the Bogor, the Indonesia-based Centre for International Forestry Research, the government (of Indonesia) 'has licensed and stimulated many companies to develop new industrial plantations of rubber, oil-palm and pulpwood, as well as transmigration sites. These activities require the clearing of hundreds of thousands of hectares of land, and fires are their cheapest option.'[8]

Malaysian companies also have interests in South Pacific states, including Vietnam, the Solomon Islands and Vanuatu, while the Samling conglomerate controls two-thirds of the timber exports of Papua New Guinea. The forests of the Solomon Islands are now being eagerly logged by the companies. The government ignored the findings of an expert report which recommended that no more than 325,000 cubic metres of rainforest should be cut each year. Instead, it issued licences to loggers that allow a cut of up to 4 million cubic metres a year. 'This is a resource [tropical forests] that is growing more precious by the minute, and they are selling it off as if it were firewood', pointed out Gordon Bilney, an Australian government minister, of the Solomon Islands' government decision. 'The logging will condemn thousands of rural fishermen and their families to a life of struggle.'[9] Coral lagoons, suffocated with the run-off from the eroded slopes, and rivers thick with sediment are just two of the problems that local people will have to cope with.

Foreign companies, mostly from Asian countries, have tried to bribe villagers in Papua New Guinea to let them log their forests. An unpublished report of an official inquiry into logging in PNG found: 'Some of these companies ... are roaming the countryside with the self-assurance of robber barons, bribing politicians and leaders, creating social disharmony and ignoring the laws in order to rip out and export the last remnants of timber.'[10] Local pressure sometimes pays off. In 1989, Survival International mounted a successful campaign to stop the TNC paper producer, Scott Paper, building a eucalyptus woodchip and pulping plant on southeast Irian Jaya. The scheme would have involved the felling of tropical forests in the Digul valley of Irian Jaya which is home to 15,000 tribal people. Many of these peoples are hunter-gatherers and rubber tappers, and it would have been impossible for them to continue their way of life. Scott Paper withdrew its funding.

Latin America

Asia's timber TNCs are now moving into South America. According to Brazil's environment minister, the Malaysian timber companies WT and Samling:

> have acquired 15,000 square kilometres in the Brazilian state of Amazonas and 50,000 square kilometres in neighbouring French Guiana. ... Timber production in the state of Amazonas totalled 600,000 cubic metres in 1995. The [Brazilian Environment] Institute believes that a three-fold increase would be required to meet the demand of Asian logging firms in the Amazon.[11]

Samling is also reported to have taken an 80 per cent stake in a huge timber operation in the Latin American state of Guyana, one of the few countries on the continent where most of the forest is intact. 'Indonesian and Korean companies are buying up large tracts of Amazon rainforest and trucking mahogany all the way to the Atlantic coast for export.'[12]

The Barama Company (80 per cent owned by Samling and 20 per cent by the South Korean trading TNC, Sung Kyong) has a 25-year licence to cut 1.69 million hectares of forest in Guyana's Northwest region. 'The company will enjoy a ten-year exemption from income tax, corporation tax ... consumption tax, property tax, most timber export taxes and most import duties.'[13] The Amerindian Peoples' Association expressed strong criticism that the concession did not respect the land rights of Amerindian people and that there was no consultation with them.

The Japanese-based, Mitsubishi, has logging interests in Brazil, Ecuador, Chile and Bolivia. In Brazil it owns Eidai do Brazil Madieras, the largest logging and milling operation in the Amazon. The Rainforest Action Network alleges that Mitsubishi is processing mahogany 'illegally obtained from native lands'.[14] In July 1996, the Brazilian National Congress placed a two-year moratorium on new mahogany logging, but logging of mahogany in indigenous peoples' areas was already illegal, and the question is whether the new law will be enforced. In Chile, Mitsubishi is converting forests into eucalyptus plantations.

Another TNC that has converted forest land into eucalyptus plantations, this time in the Brazilian state of Espirito Santo, is Aracruz Celulose, a member of the World Business Council for Sustainable Development.[15] The company is 28 per cent owned by the Brazilian cigarette company, Souza Cruz, a subsidiary of BAT, and 28 per cent owned by a Norwegian company, Lorentzen. Brazilian interests own the remainder. Aracruz Celulose is the world's largest exporter of hardwood bleached pulp (which is turned into paper products). The pulp is made from eucalyptus trees. But according to local NGOs, who represent workers and Indian peoples, tropical forest was removed to make space for the eucalyptus. They claim that the company's activities have meant the eviction of thousands of Indians and forest-dwellers from their forest homes, and that land, water courses and fisheries have been damaged.

In 1967, Aracruz acquired large areas of tropical forest that was inhabited by local smallholders and by Indian Tupiniquim people, claim groups including the Workers' Union for Extractive Wood Industries, the Workers' Federation of Agriculture in Espirito Santo and the Indian Counsel Missionary. Aracruz now owns 203,000 hectares of cultivated land in the area, including 132,000 hectares on which eucalyptus is growing. According to these groups, 70 per cent of the land 'appropriated by Aracruz used to be rainforest' and a total of 80,000 hectares of natural forest was cleared to make way for the eucalyptus. Aracruz denies this, claiming that it planted the trees on land that had been 'exploited, degraded and ultimately abandoned'. The Indian people claim that their rainforest homes were destroyed to make way for eucalyptus trees. According to José Luiz, one of the Indians affected:

> We had no idea what was going on. I was only seven at the time but I remember that heavy equipment suddenly appeared and my parents were told that the company had bought the forest from landowners.[16]

The groups claim that about 7,000 families had to leave their homes, including several thousand Tupiniquims, who received no compensation. While some stayed in the area, it seems that many had no choice but to drift into nearby towns to try to make a living. 'We were too disorganised to fight the company', admits Luiz. Only a few of the Indians found employment with Aracruz.

Eucalyptus grows quickly in the area; the trees are cut down near the base and regrow to a height of almost 40 feet within seven years, giving the company a regular supply of raw material for its factory. However, the trees achieve this rapid growth by tapping large quantities of groundwater, impoverishing surrounding vegetation and threatening to dry up local water courses. In the area around the Aracruz factory, the eucalyptus appear to be having devastating consequences. The groups allege that 176 lakes and numerous rivers in the area have dried up as a result of the plantations. Said João Pedro Stedile of Brazil's Landless Workers Movement:

> this used to be one of the best fishing areas in the country but local fisheries have been devastated. 50,000 people in the area used to eat fish every day. Now they eat fish no more; some fishermen have stopped fishing because there are so few fish to catch.[17]

Eucalyptus trees are turned into woodpulp by a five-stage bleaching process which uses chlorine dioxide. The groups allege that 200,000 tons of chemicals, including highly toxic dioxins, have been dumped in the Atlantic, killing and poisoning fish and vegetation. 'Fish that could feed 30 million Brazilians are poisoned by dioxin', estimates Luiz. Local farmers say that their land is now dry and yielding less food. Eucalyptus has a worldwide reputation for lowering water tables and causing problems for farmers. It appears to be causing problems for Aracruz itself; the area is now so short of water that its plant has come within weeks of closing. Water has, at times, had to be brought from 60 kilometres away.

After years of pleading their cause with the state government of

Espirito Santo, some of the Indians won the right, in the early 1990s, to return to 1,900 hectares of their former land. But those who returned say that the eucalyptus has destroyed the forest foods which were a central part of their diet, dried up their water courses, destroyed fisheries and made land cultivation extremely difficult. One of the returnees expressed his feeling:

> If I could eradicate the eucalyptus tree, I would because it has eradicated us. A hell has been created in our region, even the birds don't go where eucalyptus grows. And the worst ecological backlash is yet to come.[18]

The poor continue to pay the price. Aracruz is the world's largest woodpulp exporter, shipping 70 per cent of its output to paper-making factories in North America, Europe and Japan. Annual exports are running at around US$330 million. The company claims to be running a sustainable forestry operation. Mr Carlos Alberto Roxo, the company's general manager for environment and public affairs, said that Aracruz does not accept that its activities have damaged fisheries. He believed that damage to water courses in the area has been caused by general deforestation and not by the eucalyptus plantations, and that the eucalyptus trees are not lowering the water table. He agreed that fewer Indians live in the area but points to a general decline in the Indian population.[19] Responding to the company's claims to be running a sustainable forestry operation, Manuel Carol Gomes, a workers' group official, said: 'What does Aracruz sustain? It sustains misery, it sustains the degradation of people.'[20]

In 1997, the Indians launched a claim with the Brazilian government to have a further 1,300 hectares of their land restored to help them regain their original lifestyle. The official government agency for indigenous affairs concluded that their claim was justified. Aracruz opposed the claim and put considerable pressure on the government to rule against the Indians.[21] In March 1998, the government ruled against the Indians and furthermore decreed that NGOs that had supported their struggle were forbidden entry into the indigenous lands.

The need to earn more foreign exchange is encouraging other Latin American governments to consider schemes to log forests for papermaking in a manner that seems unsustainable. In late 1991, for example, the government of Honduras considered entering into a contract with a US pulp and paper manufacturer, the Stone Container Corporation, which would have given the company control of up to 1.6 million hectares of tropical forest – one-seventh of the country's land area. It was apparently intended that timber should be chipped and exported for conversion into paper products all over the world. 'Absent from the agreement are any requirements for Stone to produce environmental impact studies or reforest logged-over areas', said Oliver Tickell.[22] The agreement could have brought an extra US$20 million a year in foreign exchange to Honduras, but the environmental cost, in terms of a huge degraded land area, could have been much higher. Such costs were publicised by environmentalists and, after sustained domestic protests, the government pulled out of the deal, fearing that its popularity was at stake – elections were beginning to loom. The case is an example of how, in a democratic society, local protest can thwart the power of transnational corporations.

Africa

Africa has lost over half its tree cover in the last 100 years. The continent's forest has been seen by logging companies as a rich resource. European logging TNCs, chiefly French, are active in Cameroon, Central Africa Republic, Congo, Gabon, Ivory Coast, Liberia and Zaire. Cameroon is losing around 200,000 hectares a year to deforestation, and Gabon some 250,000 hectares. French timber companies, especially Isoroy and Rougier, are dominant; some are involved in logging and plywood manufacture.

Gabon, one of Africa's biggest oil producers and a wealthy country by African standards, did not, until recently, need to exploit its forests. This, combined with its low population of just over one million people, means that Gabon's forests have remained largely intact. But a slump in oil prices reduced the country's revenues so sharply that it was left with the second largest debt in Africa. Allowing more logging, the government has now parcelled out most of its forests to foreign companies. While Isoroy is the biggest logger, over 50 timber companies are known to be operating in Gabon, logging 2,500 square kilometres of forest every year, very little of which is sustainable.

Isoroy has been granted a concession to log in Gabon's biologically rich Lope Reserve, a 5,000 square kilometre area of tropical forest and Savannah. The company claims to be operating under environmental guidelines laid down by the Forest Stewardship Council (FSC) which was set up in 1993 by the World Wildlife Fund. These guidelines require that a company conforms with national laws. The FSC plans to give Isoroy timber products a 'green' label, but this has aroused some consternation among wildlife NGOs, which say that Gabonese law states that all plants and animals should be protected in the Reserve.

In neighbouring Congo, an alarming picture comes from a World Bank report. It claims that a lack of government controls mean that

TNCs thrive while the Congo forest suffers. The report stresses that 'forestry administration is non-existent. The forest is left to the mercy of the loggers who do what they like without being accountable to anyone.'[23]

In Nigeria's Cross River State, a Hong Kong-based TNC, Western Metal Products Company Limited (WEMPCO), is logging a 541 square kilometre area of tropical forest 'for plywood, toothpicks, veneer and chopsticks', alleges Lori Pottinger.[24] Conservationists have warned that the scheme could threaten the whole Cross River forest (about 6,400 square kilometres), around 40 per cent of Nigeria's remaining rainforest. The company is building a large wood processing factory on the banks of the Cross River which could threaten the water supply of some 200 million people in at least 300 communities. 'Our entire lives are dependent on the forest. Harming it has many implications for our people', said the coordinator of an NGO Coalition for the Environment.[25] The coalition is trying to stop the logging and has put forward proposals for sustainable forest management of the area.

It is the government rather than the company that is chiefly culpable in this case. 'Neither WEMPCO's logging operations nor the building of its factory were subject to an environmental impact statement in the planning stages, in clear violation of Nigerian law', believes Pottinger. 'Preserving the forest is like preserving our identity, our soul, our life', an NGO worker, Oliver Enuor, points out. 'It is our life-line.'[26]

Like the Philippines, over 90 per cent of forest in Ghana, one of Africa's poorest countries, has been logged since the 1940s. Corruption and fraud on the part of timber TNCs have been alleged in a Friends of the Earth report, which claimed that British, German and Dutch companies tricked Ghana out of £30 million revenue from its forests. Some 'corrupt agents' were used, alleged the report, to make fake declarations about the value of the timber being shipped. The agents would submit prices to a government bureau that were lower than the prices the timber would fetch on world markets. The timber that was exported was sometimes of a higher grade than that declared to the Ghanaian authorities, it alleges. In both cases, the exporting firms would then get the higher price, the government the lower price. The report also alleged that companies inflated prices of imported machinery and professional services and invoiced the government for more than the goods and services had cost them. It believes that by these and other methods, Ghana was cheated out of the real value of its timber exports, losing around £30 million. Investigating the alleged plunder, the Ghanaian authorities found that the TNCs did use a number of methods intended to defraud. In the late 1980s the government granted an amnesty for companies to return money; by the end of 1990, 106 firms and individuals had voluntarily paid back a total of £6.6 million, just over one-fifth of the money lost.[27] The damage to Ghana's forest had, however, been done. All this happened at a time when Ghana was under pressure from the International Monetary Fund and the World Bank to step up exports of timber so that it could pay off its foreign debts.

Fisheries

The technology used by transnational corporations is killing the world's marine fishing grounds and causing huge problems for millions of people in developing countries. TNCs are involved in fishing in order to secure supplies of a valuable raw material for selling to fish markets and also for processing. But the corporations are causing one of the world's most critical food problems – overfishing and plundering seas for short-term gain without any thought of sustainability.

Global fish catches increased five-fold between 1950 and 1989, rising from around 20 million tons to just over 100 million tons. But in the 1990s, catches virtually stagnated, staying at only just above the 100 million ton mark, with quality declining and with a lower proportion coming from the seas. Some 40 per cent of the fish catch enters international trade; fish is therefore often eaten and processed far away from where it is caught.

According to the Food and Agriculture Organisation (FAO), virtually every commercial species of fish has been depleted, fully exploited or over-exploited. Nine of the world's 17 fisheries are in serious decline with four depleted commercially. The most heavily over-fished seas are the Gulf of Thailand, seas in Southeast Asia, the southern part of the North Sea and the northern Mediterranean. Much of the damage is being done by trawlers owned by Western and Asian-based TNCs.

For millions of people in the Third World, fish is a vital source of low-cost protein: it provides 29 per cent of the total animal protein of Asians; 18.6 per cent of Africans; and 7.6 per cent of Latin Americans, according to FAO estimates. Around a billion people in Asia rely on fish as their primary source of animal protein. But over-fishing by trawlers from the North is damaging the near-shore fishing grounds of developing countries and reducing fish catches. This is having especially severe effects on the economies of coastal communities, as it means less fish for local people.

At least 10 million people are full-time artisanal fishermen and women in developing countries, and a further 10 million are part-time.

These fishers provide most of the seafood consumed by local populations, yet they number among the poorest of the world's poor. An estimated 98 per cent of the traditional fishers of India, for example, live below the poverty line. Third World fishers, their families and dependents, number around 100 million; in India alone almost 8 million people depend directly on fishing for a livelihood. Women play a key role in fishing communities, chiefly by processing, marketing and distributing the fish.

Fishers in developing countries haul in about one-fifth of the global fish catch but face an unprecedented challenge to their way of life. Tens of thousands of jobs in the small-scale fishing sectors are being lost each year because of declining catches and competition from large vessels. According to fisheries experts: 'Traditional ways of life, which for centuries have been sustained by fisheries, are collapsing. Fishing communities managed to sustain themselves well enough until the arrival of modern technology.'[28] The modern technology is owned mostly by TNCs. Trawlers from Spain, Germany, Norway, Korea, Japan and the USA fish the world's oceans using vessels with huge nets, often several times bigger than a football field, sweeping up virtually everything for miles. The fish do not stand a chance. Although there are regulations over net size, many of the young fish that should stay in the water and grow, are inevitably scooped up.

TNCs control 'significant proportions of the global fish stocks, dominate global trade, and wield huge influence with governments'.[29] The Spanish-based company, Pescanova, owns one of the world's largest fishing fleets, with around 140 trawlers fishing in foreign waters. The African coast is one of its chief destinations. A fishing and frozen food transnational, Pescanova has an annual turnover of PTA 60,000 million (about £300 million) and a network of around 30 companies in 18 developing countries. Pescanova controls 50 per cent of the market for frozen fish in Spain and, through its worldwide factories, processes about one-fifth of world hake production. It also has 25,000 retail outlets.

The seafood TNC, the Seattle-based Tyson Enterprises Seafoods (part of the world's largest chicken company, Tyson Foods) has a joint venture with an Indonesian seafood company, the Jakarta-based Ika Muda, which is part of another Seattle-based company, a fish processor called Ocean Beauty Seafoods. Tyson Foods was named by *Multinational Monitor* magazine as one of the ten worst corporations of 1997. Kjell Inge Rokke of Norway accounts for about 10 per cent of the world's white fish production. Starkist, a large US-based fishing company, controls a significant part of global tuna production.[30] Unilever, Kraft Foods and Nestlé all have major stakes in the fishing industry.

Through fishing agreements, TNC trawlers can fish in the 200-mile Exclusive Economic Zones (EEZs) of coastal developing countries. These zones were agreed in 1982 under the United Nations Convention on Law of the Sea. Countries have the exclusive right to exploit marine resources within these EEZs – it means that some 80 per cent of world fish stocks are under their control. While trawler fleets from the North usually fish in the South under agreement or licence, international piracy, that is fishing without a licence, is common.

The high seas beyond the EEZ have, until recently, been a free-for-all, and have given rise to serious disputes between trawlers and countries. Coastal countries have a considerable interest in such fishing, as fish often migrate and straddle between their EEZs and the high seas. Fish caught on the high seas in the area immediately beyond a country's EEZ can mean there is less fish in its zone. But these seas are now subject to international regulation (see below).

European Union and Africa

The European Union is the world's largest market for fish, but its waters can meet only a fraction of consumer demand. Overfishing by European boats in European waters has caused stagnation in some fish catches and a decline in others – cod from the North Sea, for example. To help keep up the supply of fish for European consumers, the EU has had to look abroad; some 60 per cent of the fish sold in EU countries now comes from the fishing zones of other countries.

In particular, the EU has made access agreements with 16 African countries that enable its trawlers to fish in their EEZs. These agreements help TNCs, such as Pescanova, and also fish consumers in Western countries, by increasing the supply of fish and therefore keeping down prices. (Spanish boats own about 60 per cent of the EU's fishing fleet.) But the agreements usually fail to take into account the interests of local fishing communities. In the African countries they promote the establishment of an export-orientated fishing industry that threatens the local traditional fishing sector. The foreign vessels can damage fish habitats and contribute to the process of stock depletion in African waters, thus undermining the economic base of thousands of fishers.

According to the Coalition for Fair Fisheries Agreements (CFFA), a Brussels-based group of EU non-governmental organisations, the agreements between the EU and Africa have led to 'the depletion of fish stocks, the impoverishment of coastal fishing communities and the destruction of opportunities for sustainable development in ACP [African, Caribbean and Pacific] countries; they are also inconsistent with EU development policies'.[31] The CFFA claims that the EU's approach to these fisheries agreements directly contradicts the terms of the Masstricht Treaty. Fostering the campaign against poverty and the sustainable economic and social development of developing countries are among the aims of this treaty.

Senegal is one of Africa's largest fishing nations and by far the continent's largest exporter to the EU, with fish being the country's biggest earner of foreign exchange. Senegal effectively earmarks almost its entire earnings from fish exports for interest payments on its foreign debt. Under an EU–Senegal agreement, fish are caught in the country's 200-mile EEZ, mostly by Spanish trawlers.

However, representatives of Senegal's 35,000 artisanal fishers say that the trawlers are catching fish that would otherwise swim into near-shore areas. This undermines local livelihoods and threatens food security. They point to dwindling catches in the country's 10-kilometre near-shore area reserved for small-scale fishers. While the trawlers cannot fish within 10 kilometres of the shore, their dragnets haul up such huge catches of sole and hake that fewer fish swim into this area. Local fishers are forced to venture further out to sea in boats not designed for deeper waters, and some have been killed in accidents involving trawlers. The large EU vessels 'often run through nets and fragile boats, mainly at night, killing many Senegalese fishermen and causing great economic loss', according to one of the fishermen's leaders.[32] Their dwindling catches mean 'there is less affordable fish on the [local] market', according to Aliou Sall of CREDETIP, a support group for small-scale fishers.[33] A decline in the supply of fish for Senegalese people is set to lead to additional malnutrition. The situation in Senegal is now dire, according to Brian O'Riordan. 'The EU, having fished out first shrimp, then tuna, then demersal (sea bottom) stocks, is currently fishing down the food chain', he says, a 'characteristic of so many industrial distant-water fishing fleets'.[34]

Lower fish catches are affecting the social structure of coastal villages in Senegal. Young people are declining their parents' offer to take up fishing. They want other jobs because they see their parents' problems. Local fishers want the government to extend the zone reserved for them from 10 to 20 kilometres and for more investment in surveillance equipment to detect the foreign trawlers.

India

In 1994, the government of India decided to open up its 200-mile EEZ to foreign fishing vessels through 'deep sea joint ventures'. Some

170 licences were issued, covering 800 vessels. 'The licences were 100 per cent export orientated', says Brian O'Riordan. 'All the fish caught would be exported, contributing nothing to either the local economy or to local food supplies.'[35] India's fishermen and women were incensed, making strong protests to government. Nationwide protests resulted in the formation of the National Fisheries Action Committee Against Joint Ventures.

The government claimed that India's fishing grounds were not fully exploited and that poaching had resulted. It said it hoped to earn another US$500 million a year in foreign exchange from the move. Trawlers from Denmark, Japan, South Korea and the USA are among the foreign fleet. The fish caught by some of these vessels is enormous compared with the catches of local boats, say the fishers – sometimes up to 2,000 tons, which is equivalent to the catch from 1,500 artisanal boats.

Fishers claim that the government has given subsidies to encourage deep-sea trawler fishing since the 1980s and that this has led to a big depletion of marine stocks. Artisanal fishworkers, on the other hand, 'have received no incentives from the government, except for minimal subsidies for kerosene in some states', stresses the National Fisheries Action Committee Against Joint Ventures. They pressed for all licences for joint ventures to be withdrawn, for fish to be 'ensured for local consumption', and for local fishers to be equipped to fish further from the shore.[36] Their action was a success. In January 1995 the government decided to freeze the issue of new licences and to review its joint venture policy. Only 30 or so (rather than over 200) foreign vessels are still fishing in Indian waters.

Fishers near Bombay who belong to the Warlis, one of India's remaining tribes, launched a strong protest in 1998 about plans by the P&O company to build a port that would be eight times the size of the port of Liverpool. While the state government is encouraged the port, fishing in the area would have been disrupted, affecting the livelihoods of over 30,000 Warli families who rely on fishing. A report, commissioned by P&O, concluded that the port would destroy the Warli way of life.[37] Around 20,000 Warlis attended a meeting in early 1998 to make their views known; in November 1998 the company called a halt to its plans.

Regulation

A voluntary FAO Code of Conduct for Responsible Fisheries was approved by governments in October 1995. The Code covers the capture, processing and trade of fish and fish products, fishing operations, aquaculture, fisheries research and the integration of fisheries into coastal area management. It provides:

> principles and standards applicable to the conservation, management and development of all fisheries. ... The right to fish carries with it the obligation to do so in a responsible manner so to ensure effective conservation and management of the living aquatic resources. ... States should prevent over-fishing and excess fishing capacity and implement management measures ... to ensure the fishing effort is commensurate with the productive capacity of the resources and their sustainable utilisation. ... Selective fish gear and practices should be further developed and applied.[38]

Also in 1995, governments adopted the UN Agreement on Straddling Stocks and Highly Migratory Stocks to manage and conserve the fish that swim in the high seas – about 10 per cent of the marine fish stocks. When ratified, this will become an internationally binding convention. Under the agreement, countries will either have to cooperate to regulate fishing on the high seas, or their vessels will not be allowed to fish. If a country has reasonable grounds for believing that a fishing vessel on the high seas is violating conservation rules, it can board and inspect the vessel and, if need be, notify the flag state, that is the country where the vessel is registered. If the flag state does not respond within three working days, then the inspecting state may detain the vessel in port for further action.

These international agreements are general in character. The best route for controlling foreign trawlers seems to lie in regulation at national level. Namibia provides an example. In order to keep foreign trawlers out of its rich fishing grounds, Namibia refused a fisheries agreement with the EU on the terms it was offered and is successfully developing its own sector. At independence in 1990, Namibia's fish stocks were down to a dangerously low level because of unregulated overfishing by foreign fleets, chiefly Spanish fleets. Some 30 Spanish vessels were then estimated to be fishing illegally in Namibia's 200-mile exclusive economic zone. Namibia's new government asked all foreign fleets to stop fishing in the zone. But Spanish fleets failed to respond to requests.

In November 1990, Namibia's Ministry of Sea Fisheries mounted a helicopter raid and seized five Spanish boats, but the illegal fishing continued. In March 1992, the Spanish boats the *Egunsentia* and *Hermanos Garrido* were spotted fishing in Namibian waters, and on one occasion the Namibian authorities opened fire. Although relations between Namibia and Spain slowly improved, the Namibian government showed its determination by drawing up regulations which severely limited the right of foreign trawlers to fish in the country's EEZ. They can now only do so on a joint venture basis. The aim is to change the nature of European involvement. Instead of Europe's boats freezing and processing catches on board, Namibia insists that boats land the fish fresh so that it can be processed on land.

Giving the seas a chance to recover has proved a sound policy. Catches are again high, more fish are available locally and fish exports are growing at over 20 per cent a year, giving a boost to foreign exchange earnings. Jobs, as well as fish catches, have been boosted. Namibia's Ministry of Fisheries believes that the policy encourages the right kind of investment, and estimates that 1,500 new jobs a year are being created in the fisheries sector. Taking action to control the activities of the TNCs has paid off. The hope for the beleaguered seas, and for the people in developing countries who depend on them, is that governments will take action to discourage TNC technology and give more encouragement to small-scale community fisheries.

CHAPTER 6

Mining the Poor

We [at RTZ] see problems virtually everywhere (Robert Wilson, Chief Executive, RTZ)

Mining is the world's fifth largest industry. It has helped to give humanity electricity, television, vehicles, planes, fridges and whiter toothpaste. It has also provided guns, bullets and huge problems for the poor. For in the course of digging out minerals to make products of enduring and not so enduring value, mining has caused huge social and environmental damage, much of it done by transnational corporations in developing countries.

By definition, mining is an environmentally destructive activity. It is also a thriving industry, measured in terms of company profits – in the mid- to late 1990s it was probably more buoyant than at any time in history. In recent years, the TNCs have increasingly moved to the Southern hemisphere where the opportunities are larger and the mining industries are less regulated; the environmental standards that are expected of the companies in the North do not apply in most of the South.

Most mining is high-tech, and much is open-cast, spreading over vast areas. A mine planned for West Papua will explore an area 300 times larger than Wales, for example. Yet a great deal of mining is short-lived and is dependent on volatile markets and changing fortunes. Of greater human significance is that much of it creates havoc with the cultures and lives of the poor, and with the environments where they live.

During the last hundred years, mining has meant that probably 100 million people, most of them in developing countries, have been removed from the land where they lived and farmed. In many cases the land had been forest, which again had to be removed. Mines produce huge waste dumps, which are often health and safety hazards, threatening, for example, to slip down hillsides. These waste dumps can contaminate water sources, both near the mine and far away, and sometimes very far away from the immediate area of a mining activity.

Table 6.1 World's largest mining companies in 1996 (outside the former Eastern bloc)

Company	Base country	Percentage of production (by market value)
Anglo American	South Africa	8.04
Rio Tinto	UK	6.12
Broken Hill Pty (BHP)	Australia	4.17
Cia Vale do Rio Doce	Brazil	3.46
State of Chile (Colelco & Enami)	Chile	2.38
Gencor	South Africa	1.87
Noranda	Canada	1.65
Freeport McMoran	USA	1.54
Phelps Dodge	USA	1.46
Asarco	USA	1.44

Source: *Who Owns Who in Mining, 1998*, The Minerals, Metals and Mining Society, Roskill Information Services. Website: http://www.roskill.co.uk.

In the wake of liberalisation and privatisation, mining is expanding at an enormous pace. Governments of developing countries, which were once suspicious of mining TNCs, are now changing their laws, easing their regulations and offering tax concessions to attract them. Since the beginning of the 1990s, 70 countries, including 31 in Africa, have opened their doors to international mining companies, and governments are selling state-owned mines at a rapid pace. Throughout the world, TNC mining companies are 'again reestablishing their control over local companies, creating a global industry which is more similar to the regime that existed in the old days'.[1] Table 6.1 lists the world's largest mining companies in 1996.

In October 1996, a study by a Canadian company, Metals Economics Group, found that mining companies are spending record sums on exploration as countries open up to foreign companies and compete to attract them.[2] The TNCs have the money to exploit these opportunities. Fuelled by the good profits it has made in recent years, the mining industry is in 'an intensive phase of transformation' according to the Raw Materials Group (RMG) of Sweden.[3]

Some countries see the privatisation of mines as a central plank in their economic strategies. In West Africa, for example, Guinea has announced plans to deregulate the country's mining laws to make mining 'the standard bearer for foreign investment'.[4] In 1998, Zambia was pinning hopes of economic recovery on privatising its state-owned copper mines. In the Philippines, a new mining law, which was 'drafted by transnational mining companies', says mining specialist Roger Moody, was introduced in March 1995. It gives foreign companies 100 per cent ownership of mines whereas previously only 40 per cent foreign ownership had been allowed.[5] The law effectively opened up Filipino mines to TNCs but aroused fierce local opposition.

For some developing countries, minerals rather than agricultural produce are the chief export earner. This is the case for Ghana where the minerals that are extracted include gold, diamonds, manganese and bauxite. Since the liberalisation of Ghana's economy in the mid-1980s, all the former state-owned mines have been privatised and almost 200 mining companies from abroad have moved in. The development of the gold sector has been an important factor in Ghana's economic growth since 1985.

The companies

The biggest mining company, the South African-based Anglo American, is the world's leading producer of gold, diamonds (De Beers), platinum and chromite, the third largest producer of cobalt and manganese, and the fourth largest producer of nickel. Until the mid-1990s its mining activity was mostly in South Africa. The company also has a vast range of other interests, extending into financial services, such as banking and insurance, heavy industries, publishing, agriculture and processed foods; in 1992 it acquired Del Monte's fruit business.

In the mid-1980s it was estimated that Anglo American controlled more than 60 per cent of the companies that were quoted on the Johannesburg stock exchange. While its grip has since loosened, the company still controls around a quarter of the quoted companies. Anglo American has benefited from cheap and accessible labour, from both South Africa and neighbouring countries, and 'from low expectations about health and welfare and the ability to fire militant employees'.[6] In 1996 the company sacked the entire 28,000 strong workforce of a platinum mine, following an official strike.

The accident rate in the company's mines is high by international standards – South Africa has suffered more mining accidents than any other country – and is causing considerable concern. The country's National Union of Mineworkers has pointed out that in 1994, 424 people were killed and 5,727 were injured in 5,851 accidents. In May 1995, 106 miners were killed when an underground train cable snapped at an Anglo American mine. 'We blame management for the negligence which caused the disaster', said the mineworker's president. 'Safety shortcuts had become routine working practices in order to save time and to save money.'[7] The company denies the charge of negligence.

In the apartheid years, Anglo American could only make acquisitions of other companies within South Africa. But in the post-apartheid era, it has moved quickly to expand its international activities. In 1995, the company announced plans to invest in two of Africa's poorest countries, Mali and Zaire, and bought 10 per cent of Lonrho's business.[8] It was also interested in investing in mines owned by the state-owned, but up-for-sale, Zambia Consolidated Copper Mines.[9] The world's largest mining company therefore seems likely to become a significant new force in exploiting mining opportunities in developing countries. This could have a major impact on some of the poorest communities.

Rio Tinto (known as RTZ–CRA until February 1997), the world's second largest mining company, is the most widely spread, with more than 200 subsidiaries in over 40 countries. RTZ–CRA had come into existence in 1995 when RTZ merged with its 49 per cent-owned associate Conzinc Riotinto of Australia (CRA). RTZ had been formed in 1962 through a merger between the companies, Rio Tinto and Consolidated Zinc Corporation. The new name therefore reverts to an old one. Rio Tinto mines and processes a wide range of minerals and metals. It is the world's largest private producer of aluminium and one of the global top ten miners of bauxite, iron ore and copper. Coal is among its interests, and it also delivers 'more than a third of the world's gems and industrial diamonds from just one Australian mine'.[10] Most of its operations are open-pit; relatively few mines are underground.

Like Anglo American, Rio Tinto is highly profitable. In 1995, for example, its turnover was £5,637 million, and profits £1,560 million – 57.7 per cent higher than the year before and a phenomenal 28 per cent of turnover. (In 1997, turnover was about the same but profits were below £1,000 million; profits were again lower in the first six months of 1998, in the wake of the East Asia crisis.) The company's corporate philosophy 'is driven by its belief that success in a commodity business such as metals depends almost entirely on an ability to produce goods more cheaply than anyone else'.[11] Its aim, the company says in its 1995 Annual Report, is 'to act responsibly as the steward of the resources in its charge ... to work with local communities, sensitive to their cultures and way of life – particularly when indigenous people are involved'.

Rio Tinto Zinc has enormous power over countries and over the lives of millions who live near its mining operations. Its subsidiary companies are usually managed by nationals of the country where it operates. Often the name of Rio Tinto, or RTZ, does not figure in a national company name. And yet the mining giant has sometimes acted,

Moody points out, 'as if it were a national government. In the early 1980s, RTZ's lawyer in Panama declared that if the country's pro-Union labour law got in the way of exploiting the huge Cerro Colorado copper deposit, situated on the territory of the Guyami Indians, "We'll get rid of the law!"'[12] Fifteen years later and this threat has become an effective reality in Papua New Guinea and Argentina, where Rio Tinto lawyers are helping to draw up new mining legislation to entice foreign direct investment. Neither has the corporation always stayed clear of intimidating those who dared to oppose it. In 1981, one RTZ director said he would 'crush Survival International like a fly', says Moody, if the organisation did not call off its campaign against the Cerro Colorado mine. Things have changed, Moody believes: 'today the company invites its detractors to lunch'.[13]

Another controversial proposal was to mine titanium from the coastal dunes in South Africa's north Zululand in the area around Lake St Lucia. A company called Richards Bay Minerals, jointly owned by Rio Tinto and Gencor, planned to mine the titanium, which is used to make products such as white paint and toothpaste. St Lucia has been called 'one of the most beautiful places on earth' and in 1996 the government banned the scheme on environmental grounds, not least because it was incompatible with tourist development.[14] But the effects of Rio Tinto's mining operations on the poor reveal a gap between words and performance. 'Problems everywhere' seems appropriate.

Effects

While an influx of mining workers and sub-contracting personnel into a mining area can give a boost to local economies, the boost soon passes, often leaving detrimental long-term effects. Despite their protestations, TNCs frequently ignore or at best overlook environmental and cultural aspects. The impact of mining can go beyond the immediate area of a mine in a number of ways. Roads, railways and townships for workers have to be built, hydro-electric dam schemes may come in the wake of mines, and water courses and sacred sites can be affected.

In Ghana, the rationalisation of mines has meant that over half the industry's miners have been sacked. For those who still have jobs, discriminatory waging is practised. Local people earn about a tenth of the wages of white workers 'for comparable jobs or the same jobs', alleges Thomas Akabzaa of the African-based secretariat of Third World Network. He maintains that many of Ghana's large mines:

are now operating surface pits with devastating consequences for the environment. Apart from the destruction of forests and farm lands, cyanide, mercury, sulphide and other heavy metals, resulting from mineral processing, contaminate the rivers, soil and air.[15]

The Melanesian Environment Foundation points out that huge copper and gold mining development in the Pacific has brought with it Western lifestyles which have been damaging for local communities. Mining projects have disrupted traditional social systems by the introduction of money, imported foods and alcohol. The employment of men at the mine sites, while bringing the opportunity to participate in the cash economy, increases the burden on agriculture and on women who remain in the villages. The extra workloads, domestic violence and alcohol abuse mean that the quality of women's lives often seriously deteriorates as a result of mining activity. 'Good relationships between individuals have now been replaced and pervaded by the concept of competition.'[16] A meeting in London in May 1996 of indigenous peoples affected by mining, concluded:

> We are alarmed at how our inherent and fundamental rights as indigenous peoples are systematically trampled on, disregarded and violated by the dominant world neo-liberal economy through their transnational corporations in the name of greed and profit. ... Nothing justifies the destruction of our air, forests, waters, lands and territories, or the destruction of our lives.[17]

Grasberg

In 1973, a US-based TNC, Freeport McMoran, began the opencast mining of copper, gold and silver in rainforest at Grasberg in the forested hills of West Papua (Indonesian Irian Jaya). Rio Tinto has a 12 per cent stake in Freeport McMoran and has provided £500 million to fund the expansion at Grasberg. The forest has since been transformed into a vast complex of mines, towns, roads, and the world's longest tramway, and is now the world's largest gold mine and third largest copper mine. It is also probably the most controversial.

Local peoples, the Amungme and the Koromo, say that the Grasberg mine has had devastating consequences for them. Hundreds of people have been displaced from their forest homes by the mining activity and now live in an unhealthy and crowded township. While the mine employs 7,500 people, less than 150 of them are local indigenous West Papuan people. Local people claim they were not consulted about the mine, nor did they receive adequate compensation – only a few, they say, have received any compensation at all. They claim also that their hunting grounds have been taken over, that they have lost some of their sources of food and that their rivers have been severely polluted. On an average day, around 110,000 tonnes of waste and 20,000 tonnes of sediment are dumped into the local rivers. Siltation is causing flooding and damaging fishing and also crops of sago, the staple food. The Koromo maintain that the traditional fish they used to catch – yuaro, lifao, mufao, irao and ufarao – are now hard to find.

The Amungme say that a sacred mountain, the Puncuk Jaya Mountain, has been ravaged by the mining, with a huge crater gouged out of the top. 'Freeport McMoran has shaved off more than 120 metres ... to extract copper and gold.' The Amungme believe the mountain is home to the spirits of their ancestors. 'Freeport is digging out our mother's brain. That is why we are resisting', said a tribal elder.[18] Although the company presents itself as a steward of the environment, it took it ten years to do an environmental assessment, claims the World Development Movement. The WDM also alleges that only after Freeport McMoran was questioned about its environmental record in the USA, its home ground, did it set up an environment unit to monitor activities at the Grasberg mine.

Shareholders have done well from Freeport McMoran; in 1995, US$11 million of RTZ–CRA's profits came from the mine. A US government agency, the Overseas Private Investment Corporation, withdrew its political risk insurance cover for the company in 1995 because of the mine's impact on the rainforest. The agency said that the planned increase in the mines' production would overwhelm the rivers with waste. In a letter to Freeport McMoran, it said: 'These and other effects of the project have posed an unreasonable or major environmental health or safety hazard.'[19] In April 1996 the policy was re-instated, on condition that Freeport McMoran implemented certain environmental measures. But in October 1996 Freeport McMoran itself cancelled the political risk insurance cover. This appeared to suggest that the company was unable to take the necessary environmental steps.

In March 1996, violence erupted at the mine when 3,000 local people, armed with bows, arrows, sticks and stones attacked Grasberg's security office. The protest was triggered by the death and ill-treatment of local workers which 'ignited long-smouldering embers of resentment'. An Amungme leader stressed:

> We want development but at our own pace; we want the right to decide our future. Corporate rights seem more important than human rights. Land is our life but there is no guarantee that the TNCs will respect that.[20]

Bougainville and Lihir

The Papua New Guinea island of Bougainville has been seriously affected by years of civil war, provoked by operations at the Panguna copper–gold mine. As many as 10 per cent of the island's population may have died in the war, most of them innocent civilians. The mine, which is 53.6 per cent owned by Rio Tinto, has 'devastated the rainforest, wiped out all life from the Jaba river and silted the Empress Augusta bay to a depth of 30 metres', alleges Roger Moody.[21] The strength of their feeling was summed up by Perpetua Serero, one of the leading women campaigners: 'We don't grow healthy crops any more, our traditional customs and values have been disrupted and we have become mere spectators as our earth is being dug up, taken away and sold for millions.'[22] After their demands for compensation were rejected, local people, angry at the way they had been affected, began attacking the mine in 1988, forcing it to close down. The government sent in troops and lives were lost in the conflict. The mine which sparked the controversy stays closed.

The tiny PNG island of Lihir contains one of the world's largest unexploited gold deposits. However, the ore is located deep in the ground in a semi-dormant volcano, and millions of tonnes of earth will have to be moved to extract it. RTZ–CRA admitted that the mine would destroy the most revered religious site on the island, culturally significant hot springs and graveyards. 'Some 64 per cent of the ore will be stockpiled for future use', says Moody. 'This will cause run-off of heavy metals straight into the ocean.'[23] The diversity of coral species and fish is expected to decline. Again, it is the poorest who will suffer most as they see their ocean polluted, their fish stocks reduced and their food supply put at risk.

The impact of mining around the world

Other countries are also affected. In Namibia, between 1976 and 1982, RTZ's Rossing uranium mine was rushing to fulfil nuclear contracts. Twenty years later it was apparent that Rossing miners had paid a grim price. The Mineworkers Union of Namibia claims that hundreds of (Rossing) workers now suffer from lung diseases and cancers caused by appalling conditions between 1976 and 1982.

In Madagascar a Rio Tinto-owned company, QIT, is considering a joint operation with the country's state mining company to mine titanium dioxide (used for whitening). The project, still in its pre-feasibility stages, could involve the destruction of two-thirds of Madagascar's coastal forests, 'as the proposed mining areas lie directly below the last three remaining areas of forests', say Friends of the Earth. The forests are rich in biodiversity, and FOE believe it would be 'a crime against future generations to destroy them'.[24] Fishing communities in 27 coastal villages would be threatened by increased salinity which is likely to result from the construction of a weir.

While the activities of Rio Tinto seem to have had the biggest and the most adverse impact on the peoples of developing countries, other mining companies have also aroused fierce opposition because of fears that their operations threaten people's lives. In Papua New Guinea, the largest stakeholders (with a 60 per cent stake) of the Ok Tedi copper mine, BHP of Australia, were sued by local villagers because of the environmental damage they alleged the huge mine had caused to their area. The mine produces around 200,000 tonnes of copper a year. Under the agreement which set up the mine, in 1976, the operation was made exempt from most of the country's environmental laws. Over 40,000 people live in the area of the mine; they claim that *every day* about 80,000 tons of 'tailings' (waste residues) and 90,000 tons of waste rock flow into the waters of the Ok Tedi river, and also that a massive landslide from mine has caused severe damage. A 700-kilometre stretch of the river is reported to be 'biologically dead'.[25] BHP was named by *Multinational Monitor* as one of 1995's '10 Worst Corporations'.

The community of Nieuw Koffiekamp in Surinam is concerned at the possible efforts of a gold mine to be operated by Canadian companies, Golden Star and Cambior. Indigenous groups in Venezuela allege that 24,000 people are threatened with extinction because of TNC open-cast mining operations in Zuila and Guajira provinces. The government of Brazil has changed its regulations to encourage mining companies, especially TNCs, alleges Elaine Potiguara of an indigenous organisation called GRUMIN (The Women's Group for Indigenous Education). Over 30,000 requests have been made by the companies to explore for minerals on indigenous lands, Potiguara points out:

> Now is the worst time for the indigenous people of Brazil. The lands are used by the mining companies without any consultation with local people. The environmental consequences are incalculable. I want to send a message to those companies – stop entering our land, stop violating our rights.[26]

Gold

Unlike any other metal, gold exemplifies a huge gulf between those who dig it from the ground and those who wear and use it. Gold has long been associated with wealth; pagan societies, for example, built goddesses made of solid gold. Around 85 per cent of gold is beaten into jewellery, and the wearing of gold is a symbol of individual wealth. Gold is also the most lucrative sector of the mining industry. Yet the conditions under which gold is often produced, and its effects on communities in gold mining areas, are a world away from the glamorous glitter. The oppression of gold miners is grim history, with miners being paid poor wages for working in unsafe conditions and often living in disease-prone metal shacks.

Gold mining is still a risky activity that can have huge health and environmental costs. Extracting gold involves evacuating billions of tons of ore, removing trees, topsoil and vegetation, and 'usually involves the use of either cyanide or mercury. Almost three out of four miners in the Philippines who were exposed to mercury for some time, showed symptoms of poisoning.'[27] In mid-1995, South America's second largest gold mine, the Omai in Guyana, cracked open and 3 million cubic metres of cyanide-tainted water and other residues, including heavy metals, flowed out. The mine is owned largely by Canadian companies Cambior Inc. and Golden Star Resources. The government declared the area a disaster zone, and a report said that life in two rivers was seriously affected. Some people were hospitalised with suspected cyanide poisoning, while others complained of blistering of the mouth after drinking water. There is a danger that toxic metals may build up in the food chain as fish ingest polluted micro-organisms. Six months after the spill, the mine reopened.

Despite the accident, the Carib people of the Baramita region of Guyana are now seeing their land parcelled out to companies prospecting for gold and diamonds. Chief among them is the Canadian-based Canarc which has a prospecting agreement with Golden Star Resources and another company. Many of the Carib people 'regard the rapid spread of mining as a very serious threat to their future. Already it is leading to forcible evictions and the spread of disease', according to Survival International.[28]

Earnings from gold have benefited a number of developing countries but a high price is often paid. The small island country of Fiji seems typical. The gold mining industry in Fiji 'remains responsible for a wide variety of health and ecological disasters – leaking ponds of hazardous mineral remnants, fouled air and water, and a laundry list of health problems affecting miners and their families'.[29] Global demand for gold is higher than ever and gold mining is set for a huge expansion. At the annual Mining Industry Forum, held in Denver during October 1996, many companies promised 'to double reserves and output within a few years'. The increase in output will be 'accompanied by a wave of mergers as managements attempt to build their companies to a size large enough to attract institutional investors, who prefer big companies'.[30] Barrick Gold, for example, the largest gold producer outside South Africa, said it was sure of doubling output in the next ten years.

While giant-sized TNCs such as Rio Tinto and Anglo American dominate the gold mining industry, a new breed of what has been called 'aggressive junior companies' is now active. For example, in 1995, Canadian mining companies were opening up fields of exploration in countries such as Peru, Ecuador, Ethiopia, Laos, Vietnam, Surinam and Guyana. On locating a deposit, a 'junior' will often enter into a partnership with a giant TNC. Some juniors, however, are little more than prospectors, and their claims do not always add up. The Canadian-based firm Bre-X Minerals claimed in March 1997, for example, to have made the biggest gold discovery of the twentieth century at Busang in Indonesia. Its shares soared on the news. The company's senior partner, Freeport McMoran, later reported that Busang's gold was insignificant. Bre-X Minerals shares fell to almost nothing, amid speculation that Busang's ore samples had been tampered with.[31]

Sub-Saharan Africa is expected to be an expanding and lucrative region for gold mining and the TNCs. A conference in London, in November 1996, heard that more than 200 mining companies are actively exploring in Sub-Saharan Africa 'and at least 15 of them had established world class gold deposits in Ghana, Ivory Coast, Senegal, Burkina Faso and Mali'.[32] Prospects for further discoveries are said to be excellent.

While this 'glittering gold–poor region' connection may bring joy to TNC balance sheets, the question is whether ordinary people in these countries, who include some of the world's poorest, see any benefit. The new wave of gold mining threatens to leave a legacy of pollution and destruction that will damage the livelihoods of vulnerable people.

Culture

Cultural factors are usually of the highest importance to indigenous communities. A mine that threatens their culture can be regarded as the most serious threat of all. The Waanyi Aborigines of Australia, for example, claim that a proposed Rio Tinto mine – Century Mine at Lawn Hill in Queensland – could seriously damage their culture. This is potentially the world's biggest zinc mine, with a capability of producing 450,000 tons a year.

The Century Mine was given the go-ahead in December 1995, subject to agreement with the Waanyi Aborigines. About 150 Aborigine families would be affected by the mine. In February 1996, the Waanyi Aborigines staked their claim to 247 hectares of land in the area, including the mine site. They claim that Lawn Hill is a deeply spiritual site, 'where many rivers meet [which] symbolises the heart. To dig there would be to drain the blood from our system.'[33] They also claim that the mine's effluent would be held in an area prone to cyclones.

Rio Tinto offered to pay the Aborigines A$60 million (about £30 million) over a 20-year period. This caused a split, and they voted very narrowly to accept the offer. But knowing that it had the support of little over half the Aborigines, the company decided to suspend its plans. Damage, however, already seems to have been done, with huge amounts of water being pumped out of rivers *before* approval was granted. 'Our elders are seeing rivers drying up that were never dry before', says Aborigine, Greg Phillips. 'We have been treated with contempt.'[34]

Women: the impact

The impact on women of mining activity can be especially acute, but is rarely taken into account when mines are planned. According to Kerima Mohideen, coordinator of an international conference on women and mining, women:

> often bear the brunt of the projects' human costs. Mining-related environmental damage has cost women their health and traditional livelihoods, and increased their burden of work. In some cases, mining companies have undermined women's status in a community.[35]

Women's objections to a mine may be ignored even if they have the land rights. On Bougainville, for example, the island's matrilineal society gives women the final say over all land-use decisions. But when Bougainville Copper Ltd. was negotiating in the 1960s to develop the Panguna copper mine, they went over the heads of the women landowners and signed agreements with men. As soon as the company made its first move on the land, women were at the forefront of the opposition. Perpetua Sorero, chairwoman of the landowners association, pressed the case for compensation and finally led the aggrieved landowners into a guerrilla war.

In the Philippines, women in Itogon battled to stop open-cast gold mining by the Benguet Corporation on land their communities have mined sustainably on a small scale for centuries. According to Kerima Mohideen: 'As childbearers, the women have experienced devastating side-effects of pollution caused by opencast mines and smelters. Filipino health researchers in the Cordillera region have documented sharp increases in miscarriage rates in communities near gold and copper mines.'[36]

If mining replaces them from their land, women who have worked as farmers or animal herders may be forced to seek other means of survival, including prostitution. In the gold-rush areas in Brazil, the illegal trade in women and children for sexual purposes is particularly widespread. In Bolivia, thousands of women work the tailings of old mines, picking out minerals from the discarded muck. They work in low temperatures at 4,000 metres above sea level, their bare feet immersed in chemical-laden water. Many are widows who were forced to become directly involved in mining after their husbands died in mine accidents or from mining-related illnesses such as silicosis. Elsewhere in the Andes, large projects, such as Peru's enormous mining complex at Cerro de Pasco and nearby smelter at La Oroya, have created environmental disaster areas that have disrupted women's lives, according to Mohideen.

Women have also been at the forefront of protests against mining at the international level. In a declaration issued at the 1995 Women's Conference in Beijing, indigenous women called for a ban on uranium mining on their lands.

Philippines: government action

The Philippines is estimated to have the seventh largest gold reserves and the tenth largest copper reserves in the world. The country's 1995 mining law (see above, p. 89) lowered environmental standards by permitting increased open-pit mining and gave companies the right to evict villagers from houses, farms or other 'obstacles' to their operations. Following the law, TNC mining companies registered claims 'which cover a land area equivalent to at least a quarter of the Philippines'.[37] Many of the mining areas are the ancestral lands of the country's 8.5 million indigenous and Moro (Muslim) population. It is claimed that the United Nations Development Programme and others 'have financed the government's efforts to attract foreign mining investors, even though their operations could deprive many of the country's poorest people for their lands and livelihoods'.[38] But in 1996 the Filipino government came under pressure from the public to change the law after Marcopper, a local company part owned by Canadian mining TNC, Placer Dome, leaked toxic 'tailings into the Boac river south of Manila'.[39] Two foreign mining executives working for Marcopper at the time face criminal charges of violating five separate environmental laws. The case prompted widespread domestic debate about whether majority foreign ownership of mining companies should be permitted.

Transnational corporations seeking exploration licences protested that 'the positive momentum generated [by the mining liberalisation] has been stalled. ... The significant progress and investment that has occurred over the last 18 months is in danger of being derailed.' Twenty of the world's top mining TNCs said the environmental provisions in the 1995 Mining Act were 'comparable with best practices worldwide' and urged the Philippines government to resist pressure from domestic environmental groups to rewrite the country's Mining Code. The government's commitment to develop a vast gold and copper mining industry in the Philippines would be in jeopardy if it gave in to 'green' pressures, suggested the TNCs.[40]

Environmental and indigenous groups countered by appealing for international help to stop such expansion. They pointed out that in one region, the Cordillera, the 1995 law could threaten the livelihoods of 100,000 small-scale miners who are now barred by the companies from mining on land they have used for decades. In October 1996, the Filipino government announced a revision of the new law, requiring foreign companies to set aside 10 per cent of mining costs to environmental improvements, a move that will help to protect the livelihoods of small-scale miners. The foreign mining community was reported to be 'outraged' at the revision, but Mr Victor Ramos, Secretary of State for the Environment, said that companies with good environmental track records had nothing to fear.[41]

Responsible mining

Sustainabilty is not high on the agenda of mining TNCs, and the world is hardly awash with mining companies with good records. Roger Moody points out: 'Even where a mine proves profitable over decades, rather than years, the profits of transnationals tend to be deployed in opening up new prospects rather than consolidating existing ones.'[42] But people affected by mining plans are making their voices heard. In Australia's Northern Territory, for example, a new uranium mine, the Jabiluka, is being blocked by local Aboriginal landowners, who have made clear their opposition. In Costa Rica, indigenous peoples have made it clear to their government that they do not want mining – and there is no mining. In the Czech Republic where RTZ–CRA had been prospecting for gold on the banks of the Vitava river, local people strongly opposed the mining, fearing it would pollute their land and water. After vigorous campaigning:

RTZ was told to pack its bags by virtually all the local regional authorities, supported by the Minister of the Environment. If today's mining industry cannot even finance the clean-up of mining wastes from the recent past, what chance is there of safeguarding future generations against the even bigger wastes it is now planning to create.[43]

Moody points out that many of the new deposits are to be found in countries such as northern Russia, Lao, Kalimantan, West Papua and Samiland, 'many of whose indigenous inhabitants understand the threat posed by large-scale mining and are enlisting rising global consciousness of their natural and territorial rights'.[44]

Africa's general lack of environmental safeguards excites the interest of the TNCs. 'Mining TNCs go to Africa because no one cares about the environment', believes Thomas Akabzaa of Ghana. 'Governments make decisions about mining without even considering the environment.' But Africans are also showing resistance. In Ghana, the TNC, Goldfields South Africa, which acquired the State Gold Mine at Tarkwa, 'is making frantic efforts to evict people from their land, amid strong resistance', says Akabzaa. The company has been reluctant to pay farmers compensation, he alleges, and is considering bringing trained dogs from South Africa to protect the mine.[45]

The future is set for a big expansion of TNC mining activity. Health issues could become a factor in whether expansion goes ahead virtually unchecked. The *World Health Organisation 1996 Annual Report* warns that a disease called leishmaniasis, which is spread by sandflies, occurs in 88 countries, and that it is spread by activities such as mining, road building, dam construction, and other development programmes 'that bring more people into contact with the sandflies that submit the causative parasite'.[46]

Communities in would-be mining areas are likely to probe and challenge new activities, and to show that mining can be stopped if it operates in a way that harms local people and their environment. But the companies will fight hard to maintain their interests and profits.

Responsible mining would take care not to trespass on the land of indigenous peoples; it would seek their democratic consent before mining began. The World Bank and the International Monetary Fund are ill-advised to give loans for mining operations unless local peoples have been consulted. An international code of conduct on mining is necessary to ensure land and labour rights, and strict environmental standards. But it would need independent monitoring. The world may need the materials that mining produces, but the people in mining areas should not be expected to pay for them with their lives.

CHAPTER 7

Manufactured Goods: Poverty amid the Glitz

Toys, shoes, clothes, chemicals, electronic equipment and transport equipment are among the main manufactured goods that are produced by TNCs, their affiliates and their sub-contractors in developing countries. In some countries, TNC affiliates account for over half the total output of manufactured goods. This is especially the case in the fastest-growing developing countries. TNCs in Thailand, for example, account for 49 per cent of total output of manufactures, 89 per cent of the country's output of electrical and electronic equipment, 80 per cent of output of mechanical equipment, 72 per cent of chemical output, 60 per cent of the manufacture of transport equipment, and 46 per cent of textile, apparel and leather output.[1]

Even figures like these can underestimate the involvement and influence of the transnational corporations. In particular, statistics 'do not capture the impact of new forms of contractual arrangements, where TNCs extend their influence across boundaries', say Evers and Kirkpatrick. Sub-contracting is one such arrangement. 'TNCs are often involved in the production, design and planning of a developing country enterprise', they point out.[2] This type of arrangement has become more common; TNCs like it as they can exercise control for a minimum stake – without risking their money, without a direct financial investment. During the last decade there has been a huge growth in the practice of TNCs sub-contracting to small firms in Asia and Latin America, and this also 'appears to be on the increase in parts of Africa'.[3]

With commercial sub-contracting, a product is made to the specification laid down by a TNC and then sold under the corporation's brand name. Sub-contracting tends to depress the level of wages 'as sub-contracts tend to be made with small firms where relatively low wages predominate', concluded a study of Fiji.[4] The problem is universal. Low wages, often lower than a country's official minimum level, long hours and poor working conditions are common in the factories in developing countries that have been sub-contracted to make toys, garments and footwear for TNCs. Many of these goods are top-quality brand names that fetch high prices in the shops. But the practice can result in a high degree of exploitation, with the people who make the goods seeing little benefit.

Competition between companies involved in manufacturing in developing countries is often ruthless. We are seeing what Korten describes as 'a race to the bottom. With each passing day it becomes more difficult to obtain contracts from one of the mega-retailers without hiring child labour, cheating workers on overtime pay, imposing merciless quotas, and operating unsafe practices.'[5] The use of child labour in manufacturing units in developing countries – in both domestic and TNC-owned companies – to help make goods for the West, is a particularly obnoxious practice. It was highlighted in the early 1990s by disclosures about young children being employed in rug-making factories in India, Pakistan and Nepal (see below, p. 111). According to a 1996 International Labour Organisation (ILO) report, about 250 million children under the age of 14 are working in developing countries, 153 million of them in Asia.[6] Assuming that no children under five are employed, this means that about a quarter of children aged between five and 14 in developing countries are working. Many of them work in plantations, some in factories making high-value toys, footwear and garments for TNCs. Most are sent out to work by their parents who often do not earn enough to feed them.

Toys

Toys are big business for TNCs. Consumer demand is high and increasing with affluence. Children in the USA receive, on average, toys to the value of around US$300 every year. In 1994, world retail toy sales totalled an estimated US$31 billion.[7] Most leading toys are made by TNCs or by companies that have been sub-contracted to produce them. The largest toy transnationals are Mattel (USA), makers of Barbie, Fisher-Price and Disney; Hasbro (USA), makers of Sindy, Action Man and Monopoly; Bandi (Japan), which makes Power Rangers and Star Trek toys; Lego (Denmark), which makes Lego and Duplo; Nintendo (Japan), which produces Game Boy, NES and Ultra 64; and Toys R Us (USA), a retailer with some of its own brands.

The 1990s witnessed some phenomenal growth in toy company profits. Mattel, for example, increased its profits in 1994 by 88 per cent to US$256 million on a turnover of US$3,205 million. By 1998, however, there were signs that profit margins were coming under pressure, caused by fierce competition. The industry is constantly changing, with bids for rival companies and takeovers rife, as the corporations jostle to consolidate their positions in a growing market. In October 1996, for example, Toys R Us bought a rival Baby Superstore for US$403 million in order to expand an operation called Babies R Us, which had opened earlier in the year. A month later, Mattel, having failed in a bid to take over Hasbro, announced an agreement to buy Tyco Toys for US$755 million.[8]

Most of the toy TNCs sub-contract out some of their work to developing countries, especially to Asia: 'Attracted by cheap labour and weak enforcement of wage and safety laws, some of these companies depend heavily on subcontracted production in China, Thailand, Malaysia, Taiwan, Hong Kong, South Korea and the Philippines.'[9] According to the International Confederation of Free Trade Unions, about 75 per cent of the toys sold in the UK are made in Asia. Some of the most popular toys are made for poverty wages 'in working conditions which often fail to meet even basic internationally agreed standards', according to three NGOs that have campaigned for higher standards.[10] Their researchers visited factories where toys are produced for some of the world's largest toy makers.

In Thailand, Mattel sub-contracts work to a huge Bangkok factory, Dynamic, which employs 4,000 people. When a World Development Movement (WDM) researcher visited this factory in 1995, workers told her of low wages, forced overtime and unsafe conditions. For the minimum wage of 148 baht (about 42 pence) a day, the workers were expected to make 60 or more dolls (such as Lion King and 101 Dalmatians) a month. 'The management always say they are not forcing us to work overtime, but we have to do it otherwise we would be dismissed', alleged one worker. Working conditions are hot and sticky: 'I get dizzy and it's hard to breathe', maintained another. A women who was pregnant had a miscarriage; the doctor's certificate said it was because of the paint she was using.[11] Out of their meagre wages, the workers have to buy their own scissors and uniforms – which are compulsory.

About a quarter of Dynamic's workers are dismissed every 118 days, alleged another worker, and then re-hired. In this way, it seems that the firm gets around Thai laws which say that people who work for more than 120 days are entitled to benefits such as sickness and redundancy pay. According to one worker: 'The factory isn't safe. There was a fire in February – one building burnt to the ground and we're very worried there will be another ... the way out is so small.' A trade union leader, Arunee Situ, claimed that about 1,000 people were killed or injured in Thai factories in 1995. In May 1993, 188 people died in a fire at a

Bangkok toy factory, Kader, that had blocked firedoors, and had no fire alarms or sprinklers.

A Mattel spokesperson pointed out that the company produces more than 75 per cent of its products in its own plants and:

> employs strict safety standards. With respect to sub-contract manufacturers, we conduct business only with reputable suppliers. ... We expect Mattel suppliers to maintain a safe working environment. ... We have informed suppliers that we will withdraw business from any company not strictly adhering to Mattel requirements.[12]

Over one-third of Mattel's sales are Barbie Dolls, 90 per cent of which are made in two Chinese factories, employing 8,000 workers between them. Little is known of pay and conditions in these factories. Following pressure from voluntary groups in South East Asia, concerned about conditions in the toy factories, and also from WDM members in the UK, the International Council of Toy Industries agreed, in May 1996, to adopt a Code of Conduct that sub-contractors will have to keep to. The Code aims to ensure that toy companies accept responsibility for conditions in factories where their toys are made. Member companies of the council are now committed to purchasing toys only if they have been produced under reasonable conditions. The Code speaks of 'fair treatment and lawful compensation of workers ... no forced or under-age labour should be utilised to produce toys wholly or in part ... employees must not be put at risk of harm ... toys must be made in places that are well-ventilated and well-lit'.[13]

Factories must, in theory, adhere to this Code if they wish to sell to the British Toy and Hobby Association (BTHA) members. But there are serious doubts about its monitoring. David Hawtin, director-general of the BTHA, whose members account for most toys sold in the UK, is reported as saying there were too many factories for toy companies to monitor them properly. 'There is no way that an organisation like ours can even think about setting up inspectors. That is a job for governments to do.'[14] In the view of NGOs campaigning on the issue, however, it is a job that needs to be done independently. Unless the Code is independently and thoroughly monitored, it is of little value. Significant improvements in employment conditions and factory safety should be an urgent priority for the toy industry; a system of external independent verification of Codes of Conduct needs to be agreed (see also Chapter 12).

Footwear

Poverty amid the glitz is particularly noticeable in footwear. Production is labour intensive and mostly done in developing countries. According to a Christian Aid report: 'Shoe manufacturing is a key sector in developing countries. Not only does it generate jobs and money, but it is also a stepping-stone to building a manufacturing base.'[15] TNCs again have a considerable involvement, with sub-contracting playing a major role. A large part of the footwear industry today is sports shoes – 'trainers', as they are usually called. Only about 10 per cent of these shoes are actually used for sport. Leading TNC sports shoe companies include Adidas, Hi-Tec, Nike, Puma and Reebok. Some 99 per cent of branded athletic footwear is made in Asia. Tens of thousands of Asians are making high-value, highly regarded shoes for TNCs, but are working long hours for a pittance in poor conditions.

Under its company slogan 'Just Do It', Nike employs 8,000 people, directly, while a further 75,000 people make most of their shoes. These people work for their sub-contractors in Asia. Wages are much the same as in toy factories, ranging from 23 pence an hour in China to 46 pence an hour in Thailand. Conditions of work also appear to be rather similar. Most of Nike's sub-contracting is in Indonesia, with Korean and Taiwanese-run operations.

> In response to accusations by workers making shoes in Nike's 10 Indonesian supplier factories – accusations voiced sometimes by the workers but more often through international allies who do not have to fear for their jobs or safety – Nike adopted a voluntary code of conduct in 1992.[16]

The company also entered into 'memorandums of understanding' with each of its suppliers to ensure they uphold Nike standards. But Nike's activities in Indonesia in 1995 shows that the company and its suppliers 'frequently violate their most basic promises', claims Jeff Ballinger.[17]

Workers at Nike's supplier factories reported dangerous conditions, intimidation of employees and paltry wages, and it seems that most have yet to implement their 'memorandum of understanding'. Ballinger gives as an example a worker called Siti (not her real name) at the P.T. Pratama Abedi Industri (PAI) factory in Serpong, near Jakarta, 'who was physically abused by her Korean supervisor, Mr Kang', who, it is alleged:

> slapped her in the face and swatted on her behind. Siti had inadvertently scuffed a Nike shoe she was working on, rendering it unacceptable by the buyer. Kang, who had come to PAI from P.T. Nagasakti (NASA), another of

Nike's 10 Indonesian suppliers, brought over Mr Lee, another supervisor, to see her mistake. 'You are a dog!' he shouted in the only Korean words that the workers understand. Siti says she was too fearful to lodge a protest.[18]

The workers at PAI work 60-hour weeks with few breaks. 'The only rest you can get is after you collapse at your machine', said Siti. It happened to her recently. She nodded off and hit her head, after which she got a short rest in the infirmary. When asked if management excuses mistakes made by workers who toil to the point of exhaustion, Siti replied that her supervisors are very unforgiving. Physical attacks on workers occur often, she alleged. According to a friend of Siti's, Mr Kang recently slapped each member of a 14-person quality control team at PAI. Some of the 12,000 workers at the huge Nikomas plant, Nike's largest supplier in Indonesia, tell similar stories. Its workers say line supervisors demand unrealistic production targets which lead to serious injuries. 'A worker lost four fingers last week', claimed a worker. 'Workers go to dangerous machinery without even a week's training', alleged a Nikomas employee.[19]

Cheating on wages is also a problem, believe Nikomas workers. In 1994 the company delayed payment of a new minimum wage scheduled to begin at the start of April. The wage was to go from about US$1.35 to US$1.80 per day. In fact, the company did not begin to pay the increased wage until a massive strike was called in mid-July. Nikomas has dealt harshly with protesting workers. In March 1995 the company locked 12 workers, who expressed grievances, in an unused room on the factory premises for a week, keeping them under the watch of a uniformed member of the local military command. Since then, the workers have been suspended without pay in violation of the Indonesian labour code. 'Nike did not respond to questions about the 12 workers', claimed Ballinger.[20]

Labour unrest in Indonesia, in the mid-1990s, gave a modest boost to workers' bargaining strength, and forced employers to pay the government-set minimum wage. 'But to attract foreign investment, the minimum wage is set at just 6 per cent above the poverty line. In repressive Indonesia, prospects for more far-reaching improvements in working conditions appear dim in Nike supplier factories unless Nike sends a clear signal to its suppliers.'[21] Poverty wages contrast starkly with the huge amounts of money that sports shoe industry TNCs pay to celebrities each year to sponsor their shoes. Adidas, for example, 'recently paid £2 million to Paul Gascoigne to wear its boots. Michael Jordan reputedly earns $18–20 million a year from Nike. ... Nike's budget for funding athletes may be as high as five to seven per cent of the company's total revenues, which for the year ending 1994 was US$3.8 million.'[22] 'It is unacceptable that these firms make huge endorsement deals with sports stars and market themselves as progressive, while short-changing the Asian workers who make the shoes', said Martin Cottingham of Christian Aid.[23]

In September 1996, the chairman of Reebok, Paul Fireman, called on Nike to join Reebok in fighting 'abusive workplace conditions in factories around the world'. Reebok claims to have established its own production standards in 1992. 'With Nike's leadership in size, the combined share strength of our brands and Reebok's own experience in human rights, a collaboration could be awesome', he pointed out.[24]

In November 1996, Nike, Reebok and other TNCs met in London and drew up an industry-wide Code of Practice. This concentrated mainly on child labour, rather than on improving working conditions as a whole, but following continuing poor publicity, and consumer pressure, Nike and other leading companies agreed to a new Code of Conduct in April 1997 which does cover working conditions, and also includes provisions for outside monitors. The companies agreed that 60 hours should be the maximum working week and that no worker should be under 14 years of age.[25]

These initiatives are welcome, but the big question is whether they will lead to improvements in the Asian factories. The companies now have to prove that their concern goes beyond window-dressing. Nike, especially, has so far failed to convince. A report prepared for Nike in 1997 by Ernst and Young, one of the world's largest accountancy firms, detailed a number of unsatisfactory working practices at one of its factories in Vietnam. These included inadequate safety equipment, and exposure to chemicals, noise, heat and dust.[26] Although Nike said it had taken steps to improve these working conditions, it was named by *Multinational Monitor* magazine as one of the ten worst corporations of 1997.

Clothes

'Why I'll never buy a pair of Levis again' was a *Mail on Sunday* headline in November 1994 which focused attention on the conditions for workers in Bangladesh who make the jeans. The paper interviewed, among others, a 14-year-old girl who, it seemed, worked from 8.00 am till midnight for a company called OPEX (in a complex employing 3,000 people) for about £2 a week until she was allegedly sacked for being off sick for one day. The company makes garments for the US-based TNC Levi Strauss, and other companies, under sub-contracting arrangements. It produces half a million garments a year, half of them Levis. Unskilled workers at the factory earn around £8 a month, and can work up to 14 hours a day. The work was described by one employee as 'intense, monotonous and unrelenting'.[27] In response to the newspaper article, Levi Strauss said it would send a representative to Bangladesh to investigate.

Levi Strauss has a reputation for progressive management and for being the leader among garment TNCs in its social concern. The disclosures were therefore all the more disturbing. But sub-contracting is again the norm. Only about 3,000 of the company's 38,000 directly employed workers are based in developing countries. In June 1996, Levi Strauss was reported to be 'giving every member of its global workforce a year's extra pay'.[28] Contract workers would presumably not qualify.

Jeans are made from cotton, and the demand for jeans has led to a big increase in the demand for cotton and to land under the crop. Some estimates suggest that cotton now occupies around 5 per cent of the world's cultivable land area, some 34 million hectares. The problem with cotton is that pests find it very attractive. More pesticides have to be sprayed on cotton than on any other crop – about 25 per cent of all pesticide applications. For people who live close to cotton fields, this has often caused considerable health problems. TNCs could help reduce these toxic applications by using organically produced cotton to make their jeans. But they have shown little interest in this.[29]

The garment industry is notorious for low wages. Even in countries such as Mexico, bordering the USA, garment workers earn around only one-fifth to one-tenth of the hourly rate paid in the USA. But contracting-out is again the norm. Many of the clothes sold in Europe and North America are made in developing countries on the basis of a TNC contracted-out deal with local manufacturers. Clothes-shop TNCs, including some of the most prestigious names in European shopping malls, are selling clothes which are made for a pittance. The corporations involved sometimes even give the impression of knowing little about how the clothes they stock are produced.

But TNCs have been faced with concerted attempts by NGOs to act responsibly. The Clean Clothes Campaign (CCC), a Dutch-based NGO, was set up in 1989 to support the struggle of women workers in garment-producing units – factories, sweatshops, homes – in developing countries and in Europe. In its campaign for an improvement in labour conditions, the CCC has drawn up a Fair Trade Charter for Garments, a code of conduct for retailers selling clothing in the Netherlands. According to Janneke van Eijk of the CCC: 'The central idea is that retailers, as sub-contractors and buyers, are responsible and, through their policy, capable of realising better working circumstances and conditions.'[30] In 1996 the CCC reached agreement with the Federation of Dutch Trade Unions, the aid agency Novib, MITEX (a retailers' association) and FENECON (Federation of Dutch Garment Producers). The agreement states that a Fair Trade Foundation will be set up to promote the signing of the Charter by garment retailers. Clothes that have the Fair Trade Charter shopmark should now be increasingly available for consumers.

Companies who sign the Charter will guarantee that the clothes they sell have been produced in manufacturing units which meet ILO standards, give workers freedom to associate, a living wage, no forced overtime, healthy working conditions, and do not use child labour. In cooperation with an Amsterdam-based research organisation, SOMO, and also the Center for Research on Multinational Corporations, the Clean Clothes Campaign is setting up a European-wide campaign, particularly aimed at involving Belgium, the UK, France and Germany.

Following media disclosures and a campaign by Oxfam, the privately owned Dutch retail chain C&A announced in 1996 that it would 'transform' its buying operation to 'end the use of sweated labour' by some of its suppliers.[31] But it is not only in developing countries where workers are being exploited. In the UK, some workers in garment factories in the East End of London are earning only £1 an hour. Globalisation and fierce competition 'is causing downward pressure on labour standards in the North as well as in the South'.[32] In October 1996 C&A said that it was willing 'to take the lead' in eradicating poor working conditions in the clothing industry in the UK. It called for a forum of retailers, manufacturers, local authorities and government to improve working conditions.[33] There is a strong case for such a forum, not only at national, but also at the international level.

A report published by the US Labour Department in October 1996, claims that clothing factories in Central America, making goods for American companies and shops, have significantly reduced their use of child labour, following pressure from US retailers, consumers and labour groups, including the adoption of Codes of Conduct by retailers. But the department called on the retailers to adopt better monitoring practices to make sure their codes are implemented.[34]

At the beginning of November 1996, a ban on the use of cheap child labour came into force in Bangladesh's garment industry, again chiefly because of consumer and retailer pressure from the USA, which imports 60 per cent of Bangladeshi garment exports. Factories will be open to international inspection and could lose their export licence if they violate the ban. But again the question is whether the ban will be implemented as planned. Codes of Conduct and government legislation are needed to remove injustices in the workplace, but are worthless unless they are implemented.

Carpets: child labour

India, Pakistan and Nepal produce two-thirds of the world's woollen carpets. Around a million children are involved in their manufacture – 300,000 in India, 500,000 in Pakistan and 200,000 in Nepal. Almost all the carpets they make are exported, many of them to Europe. Some of the children are only six years old. Often they work long hours for little pay, and in many cases they virtually live at the looms. Their wages can be reduced and even cancelled to pay for food and 'lodging'. By the time they are adults, the children's eyesights are ruined because of the close work, and lung disease is common, caused by the dust and fluff from wool. Anti-Slavery International describes their plight as a form of 'debt bondage ... common, if illegal, in the industry, throughout South Asia'.[35]

In India, since the mid-1980s, there have been moves to end this exploitation. The ILO has called on the government of India to enforce its own laws and stamp out the illegal practices. In February 1993, Indian NGOs, UNICEF, a number of carpet exporters and the Indo-German Export Promotion Council set up a project to devise a label called 'Rugmark' that manufacturers who did not use child labour could attach to their carpets. This led to the setting up of the Rugmark Foundation in October 1994. Exporters wishing to use the Rugmark must register their looms with the Foundation, pledge not to use child labour, pay a certain level of wages to adults, and add 1 per cent to the value of their carpets to be paid into a UNICEF fund for child development and welfare programmes.

The Indo-German Export Promotion Council has helped to develop outlets for the carpets with the Rugmark label in Germany. These have now made big inroads into the market, accounting for 'about 20–30 per cent of the German import trade', estimates David Ould of Anti-Slavery International. The Rugmark label, and the bad publicity that India attracted, spurred the government of India to launch a label called 'Kaleen' which all exporters of carpets will have to use. 'Under the system now being introduced', it stresses, 'no carpet would be exported without the hallmark of commitment, a label to be given to exporters by the Carpet Export Promotion Council, indicating non-use of child labour'.[36]

The Kaleen label system will be regulated by the carpet industry in

India, including exporters, and monitored in a similar way to the Rugmark label. In June 1996, the US government proposed extending the Rugmark labelling system to the clothing industry and to other economic sectors where child labour is a problem.

In toys, garments and clothing, the brief history of voluntary Codes of Conduct is one of TNCs being dragged into them with little enthusiasm and not very much willingness to comply unless they have to – although of course, they stoutly maintain the opposite. Government regulation and independent monitoring of Codes are vital, and so also is consumer pressure. It is consumers who have the power to refuse to purchase goods from corporations who do not act to end injustices (see also Chapter 12).

Exporting processing zones

To try to maximise the export of manufactured goods, over 70 developing countries have set up export processing zones (EPZs). Also known as free trade zones, these have become more common as a result of globalisation. Usually located on industrialised estates situated near a sea- or airport, they offer inducements to TNCs to bring in their know-how to make manufactured products and to train local people in the necessary skills.

A 1998 International Labour Organisation report said that EPZs now employ 27 million people and 'had increased from a handful just a few decades ago to over 850 today'. The report noted that for increasing numbers of developing countries, 'EPZs are a vital entry point into the global manufacturing economy, providing a valuable source of investment, employment and technological know-how, but with widely mixed results'.[37] Wages in EPZs are usually low, working conditions are often poor, trade union rights restricted and any skills acquired tend to be specific and of limited use in other activities.

The USA is the most active EPZ operator and the largest numbers of zones (320) are in North America. Asia has 225 and the zones are rising rapidly in developing regions such as the Caribbean (51), Central America (41), and the Middle East (39). 'The figures are likely to increase throughout the world', says the ILO report. The Philippines, for example, currently has 35 EPZs operating but has approved plans for 83. China has 48 technological, economic development areas and hundreds of new zones, many on the scale of full-sized urban and industrial developments, complete with community infrastructures such as schools, transport links and social services. Bangladesh, Pakistan and

Sri Lanka have extensive EPZ strategies. In Africa, there are 47 EPZs, 14 of which are in Kenya. In Mauritius, the entire country has been zoned for export processing.

Jobs in the zones typically represent no more than 5 per cent of total employment in the manufacturing industries of developing countries and are tiny compared with the estimated 300 million people who work in the 'informal sectors'. Yet governments of developing countries have nonetheless allocated substantial amounts of scarce funds to attract companies into the zones. A country might typically offer companies a free building, a five-year 'tax-free' holiday, low-wage labour and other perks. To develop an EPZ at Bataan, in the Philippines, for example, the Filipino government offered companies 100 per cent ownership, permission to impose a minimum wage lower than in the capital, Manila, tax exemptions on imported raw materials and equipment, exemption from export tax, low rent for land, plus other inducements.[38] The first six months of employment at Bataan are a probationary period, paid at 75 per cent of the 'minimum' wage. 'Some plants terminate employment after this period has elapsed and replace workers by fresh trainees', reveals an ILO survey.[39]

Export processing zones have generally proved disappointing. 'Apart from a few notable exceptions', says the ILO survey, 'the process of export-orientated industrialisation continues to be of rather minor significance ... despite the fact that a substantial share of available infrastructure and investible funds have been swallowed up by export-orientated production.'[40] And the zones have led to little diversification of economies. The survey notes that EPZs 'continue to demand overwhelmingly unskilled and semi-skilled workers' and that skills acquired on the job 'are often limited and mostly unusable outside the plant'.[41]

The zones have led to increased exports and more jobs for a small number of developing countries. In Latin America (where the zones are known as *maquilas*), most of the employment gains have gone to Central America and the Caribbean. In Asia, where most countries have EPZs, the gains are spread more evenly, with zones in Hong Kong, Malaysia, South Korea, the Philippines and Sri Lanka attracting a large share of the available global investment. While goods can usually be moved in and out of EPZs free of customs duties, they are subject to the same Western-country barriers as goods made outside the zones. Mauritius is an example. Often cited as an EPZ success story, almost 90 per cent of EPZ investment in Mauritius went into textiles, chiefly sweaters and shirts. Most of the country's exports go to France, Germany, the UK and the USA.

Wages in the Mauritius EPZ are only about a quarter of those in

Hong Kong, making it particularly attractive to investors. But when woollen garments from Mauritius began to capture a sizable share of the European market in the early 1980s, the country was asked to 'voluntarily' restrict its exports. This meant cutbacks rather than expansion. An IMF Working Paper noted that 'expenditure for EPZ-related infrastructure will be a substantial long-term burden on the budget without guarantees for a positive return', and that 'losses in economic welfare cannot be completely ruled out'.[42]

Organised labour is beginning to rebel against EPZs. 'The trade union movement is particularly concerned about the increasing number of zones where millions of workers, mainly young women, are employed in grossly repressive conditions', pointed out the International Confederation of Free Trade Unions in a statement to the UN Commission for Social Development in May 1996. Two Canadian-based organisations, CoDevelopment Canada and Trade Union Group, are working with women's groups in four Latin American countries to reform the *maquilas*, where the workforce comprises mostly young women who work for long hours and are forced into overtime with no pay.

But the expansion continues. One of the latest countries to create an EPZ is Cuba, which, in September 1996, introduced a law governing its new zones. As the law foresees two categories of investors, national and foreign, the door lies wide open for the TNCs. EPZs are also growing fast in Africa, with countries such as Kenya, Mozambique and Senegal developing zones.

As governments spend resources on EPZs, they foresake the opportunity 'to create more jobs for the same amount of money by investing in and supporting small enterprises serving the local market'.[43] EPZs require government funds which could be used elsewhere for projects that directly help the poor. Their growth is coming at the expense of the poor. Whether they operate inside or outside such zones, TNCs involved in manufacturing have not helped most developing countries to improve the decline in their terms of trade, neither have they provided the poor with an escape from poverty.

CHAPTER 8

Energy: No Force for the Poor

We are moving from a trust-me to a show-me world (John Jennings, Chairman of Shell)

Damming

Every year, from the mid-1980s to the mid-1990s, around four million people were displaced from their homes because of large hydro-electric dam schemes. These schemes usually created huge reservoirs which flooded homes, forests and fertile land. The people who lived on that land were often the last to be told of projects that would force them to move elsewhere and profoundly disrupt their lives. Some moved into forest areas and cut down trees in a desperate bid to survive. Since the electricity generated by the dams was intended to power factories and houses in urban areas, few of the rural poor benefited from such schemes. Many big dam projects have turned out to be huge disappointments in economic terms, even leaving aside the wider environmental, social and human costs.

In addition, many of the projects that have displaced people have been funded in part by foreign aid from the World Bank and other donors. Less well-known is the close involvement of the world's largest international construction companies. For construction TNCs, aid-funded big dam schemes are manna from heaven; most of the money given under such aid projects ends up in their bank accounts. The hoardings at the entrances to dam schemes around the world often read like a roll-call of the world's biggest and most powerful construction TNCs.

These corporations are a vital link in the 'big dam' chain. Their experience of such projects means they can provide an expertise that national companies usually lack. Without the TNCs, the big aid-funded dam schemes of the last 40 years could not have gone ahead with such confidence. The schemes give the TNCs security of payment, as the money is coming mostly from foreign aid, and the opportunity to make good profits at low risk – if costs soar they can usually be passed on.

Dams often cost more than the original estimates, leaving governments of developing countries to pick up an extra bill.

The Victoria Dam

The Victoria Dam in Sri Lanka, for example, was allocated £100 million in British aid when it began in 1980. At the time, this was the UK's largest ever aid allocation for a single project. Victoria was then expected to cost £137 million, of which the Sri Lankan government had to find £37 million. By the time the dam was completed, in 1984, the cost had soared to £240 million. The British government gave Sri Lanka a little more aid to compensate, some £13 million, but the government of Sri Lanka had to find the remainder – in all, £127 million instead of £37 million. Ultimately, it was the Sri Lankan people who had to find this difference. Fifteen British companies received almost £200 million for building the dam (which generates electricity for industrial and urban areas), including Balfour Beatty Construction, Edmund Nuttall and Costains. As the dam flooded a large area, around 50,000 people had to be uprooted from their homes; they were given land in another part of the country, often in forested areas which they first had to clear in order to grow food.

Victoria is one of four huge dams in Sri Lanka's Mahaweli River development scheme. Canada, Germany and Sweden provided aid for the other three, which also suffered from escalating costs. In 1977, the whole scheme was expected to cost around £700 million, of which £400 million was coming in foreign aid, leaving Sri Lanka to find £300 million. By 1984, costs had escalated to over £2,000 million, leaving the host country with £1,600 million to find – over five times more than was originally expected.

The construction of the Mahaweli River scheme effectively witnessed an enormous transfer of wealth from people in one of the poorest developing countries to some of the world's largest TNCs. 'We are a poor country', said a critic of the scheme, 'we cannot afford this kind of aid.'[1] Only minimum compensation was paid to people who were displaced, and again the poor suffered most. Displaced people who had money of their own, in addition to the compensation money, had greater means to adapt to the new circumstances. People without money were not so fortunate.

People displaced by big dam schemes often receive little or no compensation for being moved, sometimes hundreds of miles away. The Kaptai Lake Dam in Bangladesh is an example. Funded by the USA, the dam was built to provide electricity for industrialisation, but it destroyed

40 per cent of cultivable land in the area. 'The human suffering and unrest caused by the dam was on a massive scale', says Andrew Gray of Oxford University.[2] Some 100,000 people had to be relocated and, even though they were promised compensation, over half of them received nothing. Those who gained compensation received three acres of land instead of the six they owned before the dam was built.

The World Bank estimates that India's Narmada Dam, now under construction, will displace 250,000 people but human rights activists believe that the livelihoods of two million people will be affected. The Bank also says that the Three Gorges Dam on China's Yangtze river will displace 1.3 million people; its reservoir would stretch over 350 miles. Construction of the Three Gorges Dam began in 1994 and is expected to take 20 years, but problems with funding are already being felt. Citing environmental concerns, the Export–Import Bank in Washington DC, refused, in May 1996, to issue letters of credit to companies that wished to take part in the project.

The Pergau Dam

An attempt by the British government to use aid funds to finance the Pergau Dam in the north of Malaysia was blocked by Britain's law courts in November 1994 following a campaign by the World Development Movement (WDM). The UK wanted to provide £234 million in aid for the dam, but two High Court judges declared the government's decision to be illegal and stopped all further payments from the aid budget. Almost £30 million in aid had already gone to help build the dam, and about 200 British companies were working on it when the decision was made.

The WDM mounted the legal challenge because it believed that funding for the Pergau Dam contravened the UK's 1980 Overseas Development and Co-operation Act. The Act says that the primary purpose of aid is the economic benefit of a country or the welfare of its people. The High Court said that the granting of aid to Pergau was 'fatally flawed' because the project was economically unsound and did not promote the development of a country's economy. Environmental groups in Malaysia were among those who opposed the dam.

The UK had agreed to give aid for Pergau in 1989 as a sweetener for securing a £1.3 billion arms deal with Malaysia. In 1991, Sir Timothy Lankester, a former permanent secretary at the Overseas Development Administration, the British government department which then administered the aid budget, opposed aid for the dam, saying he believed it was neither economic or efficient. He was over-ruled.

Again, the cost of building the dam had escalated. The House of Commons public accounts committee expressed 'astonishment' that British companies involved in the Pergau project increased their price from £316 million to £397 million within two weeks of The British government's approval of the scheme. Malaysian officials accused British companies of trying to rip off their government on large contracts. The Pergau Dam has gone ahead without British aid funds; it will cost around £450 million and supply about 600 megawatts (MW) of electric power.

The Bakun Dam

No sooner had the controversy over the Pergau Dam scheme subsided, than another big dam scheme in Malaysia came in for strong criticism from the country's environmental groups. They were incensed about their government's decision to go ahead with the Bakun hydro-electric dam project in Sarawak, Malaysia's easterly state. Much larger than Pergau, the Bakun Dam was expected to cost US$5.4 billion and supply about 16,000 MW of power within ten years – making it the largest dam in Southeast Asia. Sited in the northwest of Sarawak, along the Rajang river, it was planned to be almost twice the height of the Aswan Dam in Egypt and flood nearly 270 square miles, an area about the size of Singapore. Some 69,640 hectares of rainforest would have to be cleared for the dam. Again, the poor would suffer, with around 9,500 people belonging to the native tribes of Kenyah, Kayan, Lahanan, Ukit and Penan being uprooted. Transnational corporations would naturally be heavily involved in the dam's construction.

Friends of the Earth Malaysia alleged that the overall human and environmental cost of the Bakun Dam would be colossal and that the hydro-electric output of the dam would only last 30 to 50 years, possibly even shorter. There was a danger, it said, that the large reservoir (to be constructed as part of the scheme) would act as a trap for sediment (river dregs), clogging up the dam, and giving it a short lifespan. This is a classic problem affecting large dam schemes. The group was also concerned that rocks on one side of the proposed dam site would not be able to bear the pressure of water coming out of the new reservoir. It pointed to a warning by a German geologist that if the rocks did not hold the pressure, there could be an earthquake.

The tribespeople who would be displaced by the project live in traditional longhouses – large communal houses. Friends of the Earth Malaysia alleged that these people were not consulted about the dam, and nor were any proposals put forward regarding resettlement. Forest tribes also see the dam as a threat to the graves of their ancestors. FOE Malaysia warned that people in the dam area could expect a significant drop in the water level, which would threaten their water supplies, if the dam is built.[3]

Malaysian Prime Minister, Dr Mahathir Mohamad, described the dam as vital for the country's energy needs. He admitted, on launching the project, that it may destroy some trees and animals and displace some people, but that to get the 'desired achievement of wellbeing' of the people later on, a price had to be paid. The Malaysian government said that the studies it has conducted suggest that the economic gains of the project far outweigh the environment impact. Yet earlier, in June 1990, it had decided to scrap the idea of Bakun Dam. Dr Mahathir then pointed out that the government's decision was 'proof we care for the environment. ... Malaysia has made a big sacrifice for the environment.'[4] In September 1994, Dr Mahathir performed the ground-breaking ceremony for the dam that was rejected only four years earlier.

But within three years the Bakun Dam was again to be rejected. A Malaysian company, Ekran Berhad, was awarded the contract to manage the project. Ekran is headed by a Malaysian billionaire, Mr Ting Peck Khiing, and is one of a new breed of Malaysian TNCs with projects in a number of other developing countries, including China, Iran and the Philippines. When prospective British investors visited the Bakun Dam site in November 1995 they were met by indigenous people from the longhouses who handed them a letter saying that they did not want to be resettled: 'Should the Bakun project go ahead, we the poor people of Bakun, who make up the majority of the community, will die with this our ancestral land.'[5]

The economic viability of the dam came in for questioning by a University of Dortmund (Germany) specialist on dams, Dr Weillou Wang, who believed that Bakun's annual earnings could be only about half the projected figures. According to FOE Malaysia, the government was relying on selling electricity to neighbouring countries to make the dam pay. The group warned, however, that demand from Malaysia's neighbours could be small, given the problem of distance: 'It appears the only way for Bakun to be economically viable is for the government to raise electricity tariffs. ... Consumers may have to pay more with Bakun.'[6]

The poor would again be the hard hit. The contract to construct the dam was awarded, in 1996, to a consortium led by Asea Brown Boveri (ABB), voted Europe's 'most respected company' that year.[7] But in a letter to the chief executive of ABB, 129 NGOs and 30 Members of the European Parliament expressed 'grave disquiet' over the technology of

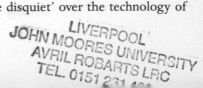

the dam and the lack of consultation. They claimed: 'There is a growing consensus in the development community that large dams represent an outdated, inefficient, uneconomic and environmentally and socially destructive technology.' The letter also alleged that the Malaysian government violated the country's environmental law in approving the dam. The company's chief executive responded by saying that the dam would be built with 'maximum respect for the environment'.[8] Prime Minister Dr Mahathir was reported as saying that he was confident the dam would be finished on schedule in 2002, 'despite legal complications and opposition from environmentalists'.[9] But in December 1996, Malaysian Mining Corp, the country's leading mining company and a member of the consortium, pulled out on the grounds that it would not have enough say in the project's management, a decision that seemed to reflect a concern that the risks associated with the project were too great.[10] In 1997 the dam was postponed indefinitely when ABB pulled out. But the Malaysian government is to continue with its resettlement scheme, moving people out of their forest homes, presumably to make their land available for logging and plantation TNCs. Bakun may never be built, but its shadow will long affect the lives of some of Malaysia's poorest people.

Coal-fired and gas-fired power plants

The construction of coal-fired and gas-fired power plants for electricity can also cause problems for the poor. A North Carolina, US-based TNC, Cogemtrix, plans to build a 1,000-megawatt coal-fired power plant in Dadshina Kannada, in the Indian state of Bangalore, for example. Listed by the United Nations as 'a valuable biodiversity area', Dadshina Kannada boasts 'richly forested lands, a wealth of plant and animal species, and a coastline which provides a livelihood for 400,000 fishermen'.[11] The company claims that the plant will be 'the cleanest in India', but local NGOs, especially fishers' groups, have spoken out against it, voicing concern that the plant would pollute their fishing grounds.

In the Indian state of Maharashtra, the world's biggest gas company, Enron, wants to build a US$2.8 billion 2,015-megawatt gas-fired power plant, a hundred miles south of Bombay. Villagers claim that effluent from the plant would destroy their fisheries, and coconut and mango trees. 'Why not remove them before they remove us?', asked one villager. In June 1995, soon after state elections, the incoming government cancelled the deal, saying that it acted to prevent Enron from making huge profits off 'the backs of India's poor'.[12]

Oil

Petroleum TNCs figure prominently on the list of the world's largest companies. The Royal Dutch/Shell Company was by far the most profitable TNC in 1998.[13] British Petroleum, Exxon and Mobil were also high on the list. Shell has interests in over 3,000 companies and operations in more than 100 countries; more Shell petrol is sold around the world than any other brand. Yet the mammoth oil TNCs appear to have become involved in activities that bring little credit to the industry.

The corporate development of oil resources in developing countries has led to huge social and environmental costs, affecting the livelihoods of millions of the poor. A great deal of such 'development' has taken place in remote areas populated by indigenous peoples, and has been done in an unplanned way with little apparent thought for its adverse local effects. The traditional livelihoods of many local communities have been fundamentally changed and often severely damaged as 'oil towns', and crime and prostitution have mushroomed with the introduction of an alien way of life.

The physical environment has also come under considerable pressure. Oil companies discharge toxins such as hydrocarbons, heavy metals and bactericides etc. into the environment. They pollute the areas where they operate with routine contaminations, often caused by badly run and badly monitored facilities, and also through accidents such as large discharges of oil. Many companies have traditionally flared into the sky the gas which comes with oil. This flaring is a serious pollution problem for people living close to a refinery and a sheer waste of the country's energy sources. It also damages the ozone layer and is a contributory factor to global warming.

Local people often gain little or nothing from the activities of the oil TNCs and may end up substantial losers. The experiences of people in the Niger Delta of Nigeria and the Oriente region of Ecuador are examples.

Niger Delta

Nigeria's Niger Delta, which has rainforests and mangrove habitats, has been described as one of the world's most fragile ecosystems. Shell has operated in the delta since 1958. Certain areas are densely populated, including the Ogoni region which houses some 500,000 people in a 404-square mile area – four times the population density of Nigeria as a whole. Of significance to Shell in the 1960s was the Ogoni region's rich oil reserves. In a joint venture with the Nigerian National Petroleum

Corporation (NPC) and with the oil companies, Elf Aquitaine and Agip, Shell's subsidiary, Shell Petroleum Development Company (SPDC) had the capacity to produce around a million barrels of oil a day from Ogoniland. Even for a company as large as Shell, this was viewed as an important source of revenue.

Since the beginning of its operations in the Niger Delta, alleges a Greenpeace report, Shell has wreaked havoc on local communities and the environment. The company's high-pressure pipelines pass 'above ground through villages and crisscross over land that was once used for agricultural purposes, rendering it useless'.[14] In total, some 2,100 kilometres of pipelines have been laid. Inevitably there have been spillages. The communities in the delta are said to be 'groaning under the perennial destruction of their property and environment by oil spillages'.[15] According to a record of Shell's spillages from 1982 to 1992, 1.626 million gallons of oil were spilt by the company's Nigerian operations in 27 incidents. In 1983, the Inspectorate Division of the NPC reported: 'We witnessed the slow poisoning of the waters of this country, and the destruction of vegetation and agricultural land by oil spills.'[16] But no concerted attempt was made by the government or the oil companies, it says, to control such environmental problems.

Flaring has been a huge problem. 'Nigeria's oil fields are better described as gas fields with oil', says the Ecumenical Committee for Corporate Responsibility.[17] From some of its sites, Shell has been flaring gas every hour of the day for more than 30 years. In total, the company releases 1,100 cubic feet of gas daily in Nigeria, about a tenth of all the gas flared worldwide. This huge waste not only contributes to global warming, but has a devastating effect on land close to the flaring sites. Even by Shell's own reckoning, the flaring will continue until 2008. According to Ken Saro-Wiwa, the deceased president of the Movement for the Survival of the Ogoni People (MOSOP):

> The flaring of gas ... has destroyed wildlife, and plant life, poisoned the atmosphere and the inhabitants in the surrounding areas, and made the residents half-deaf and prone to respiratory diseases. Whenever it's raining in Ogoni, all we have is acid rain which further poisons water courses, streams, creeks and agricultural land. Acid rain gets back into the soil, and what used to be the bread basket of the delta has now become totally infertile.[18]

There is also the waste problem. Open and unlined pits for storing drilling waste are reported to litter the area (which has 96 oil wells, two refineries and a petrochemical complex) but local communities feel powerless to prevent such practices. Independent researchers found that the level of oil effluents in drinking water in Ogoniland was 680 times higher than permitted levels in Western Europe.

Protests in Ogoni, over the summer of 1993, about the alleged damage done by the oil industry led to a series of suspicious and brutal attacks on Ogoni villages, resulting in the deaths of hundreds of villagers and to thousands being made homeless. The Nigerian government claimed that the attacks on Ogoni were the outcome of disputes between neighbouring communities. However, the sophistication of weapons used, and the fact that all Ogoni police were removed from the area prior to the attacks, implies that the military were responsible. The Ogoni claim that, in all, 27 of their villages came under attack, resulting in more than 2,000 deaths and the displacement of 80,000 people. At one time the Ogoni region was effectively sealed off by military checkpoints.

MOSOP urged Shell to halt 'the ecological war' it had waged over 35 years and to clean up the mess it had made. In April 1994, Shell ceased its operations in Ogoniland but argued that 60 per cent of oil spills were caused by sabotage. This was refuted by Professor Claude Ake of the UN World Commission on Development and Culture who called it 'irresponsible propaganda'. While some US$30 billion worth of oil was produced in Ogoniland between 1960 and 1994, the total cost to people and their environment may never be known. The Ogoni people say they have received nothing in return for the oil, except a blighted countryside, a land of polluted streams and creeks, and rivers without fish – in short, an ecological disaster.

Shell, however, denied that it caused environmental damage in Ogoniland. 'The whole of the land we occupied in Ogoniland was only about seven square kilometres in over a thousand square kilometres', claims Mark Moody-Stuart, a Shell managing director. Shell Nigeria's 1996 report admits, however, that in the Niger Delta as a whole, 'operational spills are increasing', but it claims that there has been a 36 per cent reduction 'in the volume of spills due to corrosion'.[19] It also claims to have spent US$36 million in 1996 providing infrastructure and welfare for communities in the Niger Delta, including those in Ogoniland.

In October 1994, Ken Saro-Wiwa and MOSOP were awarded the Right Livelihood Award. Saro-Wiwa was in a Nigerian jail at the time, charged with inciting youths to murder four Ogoni politicians. Amnesty International adopted him as a prisoner of conscience, saying that the accusation against him was unfounded, that he had neither used nor advocated violence, that his detention was solely because of his campaign against environmental damage and the inadequate compensation by oil companies operating in Ogoniland. In November 1995, Saro-Wiwa was executed by the Nigerian authorities.

A number of Shell shareholders had earlier asked the company what it was doing to save him from the gallows. They were told it was company policy not to become involved in the politics of the country where it operates. 'Ken Saro-Wiwa and his co-defendants were accused of a criminal offence', said a Shell press release, 'a commercial organisation like Shell cannot and must never interfere with the legal process of a sovereign state.'[20]

Shell's way of operating in Ogoniland has received massive publicity, especially since the death of Ken Saro-Wiwa. It was named as one of 1995's '10 Worst Corporations'.[21] The conflicting views of Shell and the people of Ogoniland about the amount of environmental damage in the region cannot easily be reconciled. It comes down to a question of who is to be believed – the people who live there, or a company that works there. The differing views point to the need for external, independent verification of a company's work performance. 'The way in which Shell conducted its business in Ogoni is an indication of the way in which Big Oil operates abroad without proper policing', said Greenpeace.[22] In the oil industry as a whole, Shell's practices hardly seem exceptional.

Oriente

The Oriente region in eastern Ecuador provides a further example of the adverse impact of oil companies on indigenous peoples and poor communities. Oriente, known as the Ecuadoran Amazon, spreads over 13 million hectares of tropical rainforest. It has an indigenous population of 95,000, but the development of oil has attracted 250,000 immigrants since the first discoveries in 1967. A consortium of companies, including Texaco, Gulf and Elf Aquitaine, developed oil resources in an unplanned manner in the late 1960s and early 1970s, against the background of scanty infrastructure. Huge social and environmental problems have resulted.

The oil companies promised jobs to local people but generally for only short periods of time as unsecured contract or casual labour, without benefits or guarantees and with poor safety conditions. Oil towns mushroomed and brought with them attendant problems of crime and prostitution. Refineries tended to be sited in poorer more distant regions, and once a contract was finished, people were left with nothing. As their farms had been neglected they had little to harvest.

Pollution is now severe. Ecuador's oil operations were discharging 4.3 million gallons of toxic wastes into the environment every day, alleged a report in 1991. A later report by the New York-based Center for Economic and Social Rights said that these wastes 'created a potential health catastrophe', with the toxic contaminant levels in drinking water reaching 1,000 times the safety standards recommended by the United States Protection Agency.[23]

Much of the waste crude is generated by exploration and well-cleaning activities every six months. The waste is dumped into open, often unlined, pools in the forest, and leaks into ground water. Heavy rains also flush out the oil into the rivers. An oil company official admitted that the impacts of routine contamination are much higher than the more dramatic spills.

People bathing in the rivers and drinking the river water have been affected with severe rashes and stomach upsets. Animals have died from drinking contaminated water from the waste pits. Fish have died, leaving people without a vital food source, while fish eggs are killed by very low levels of hydrocarbons. According to Helena Paul, who has studied the plight of indigenous peoples in the region: 'I have seen people living in conditions where they are afflicted with air, soil and water pollution and suffer noise pollution 24 hours a day caused by oil company activities.'[24]

The World Bank has described the region's socio-economic state as 'calamitous'.[25] Indigenous peoples cleaned their contaminated lagoons themselves in the absence of any help, but the contamination took place in an important forest which is the ancestral territory of these groups. Many of them have been largely dispossessed of their lands and livelihoods. 'At least one group, the Tetetes, has completely disappeared in the wake of Texaco's activities, and the Cofan population has been reduced from 15,000 to about 300 people.'[26]

Food brought into the oil exploration areas is Western-style and expensive, and many people have exchanged a diet of fruit, vegetables and fish for a diet of poorer quality foods. Few of the returns from oil exploitation are ploughed back into the affected communities. People in the oil boom towns have demonstrated against the lack of facilities, and this has helped to bring together outsiders and Indians in a common cause.

Texaco left the region at the end of their contract in 1992, leaving behind ageing facilities and long-term contamination, but being forced into a clean-up 'which needs careful monitoring if it is to be effective', says Helena Paul.[27] The company denies that its operations have damaged the region, saying 'we have international standards to which we hold ourselves responsible'.[28] It points out that oil revenues now account for about half the government of Ecuador's total revenues. In November 1993, a US$1.5 billion lawsuit was filed against Texaco in a

New York court on behalf of 30,000 Ecuadoran plaintiffs, alleging health and environmental damage.

Undaunted by damage to the environment, the government announced plans, in January 1994, to double the amount of rainforest subject to oil exploitation. This led to national and international protests. Says Helena Paul: 'Populations eager for work and prosperity close their eyes to the evidence of the realities and welcome this expansion, yet there is no evidence to show that oil exploitation can ever be anything but damaging to ecosystems and perhaps above all, to cultures and societies affected.'[29] Underlying many of these problems 'was the lack of integration of the petroleum activities into the local scene', an International Labour Organisation report pointed out: 'The problems included inadequate physical and social infrastructure, drugs, prostitution and tensions between the relatively well-off petroleum workers and the rest of the population.'[30]

Lack of care with the oil exploitation again emerges as a primary factor in a development that went wrong. The problems have now spread to Peru, because Oriente's contaminated rivers eventually flow through Peru. In December 1994, a lawsuit was filed (in New York) against Texaco on behalf of 25,000 Peruvians 'who complain of similar damages related to Texaco's former Ecuador operations'.[31]

There are other examples of oil TNCs appearing to abuse their power. In Burma, oil companies have been accused of directly supporting the illegal regime, and benefiting from the exploitation of indigenous peoples who are used as slave labour to build roads and installations. Burma's democratically elected government-in-exile has filed a lawsuit in the United States against the TNC oil company, Unocal, charging it with widespread human rights violations in connection with the construction of a gas pipeline in the country – a joint venture with the French oil company Total and the Burmese military regime.[32] The lawsuit alleges that tens of thousands of people were forced to work on the project and that villages were destroyed in the pipeline region. Unocal claims that no forced labour was used, but the Burmese military regime had a clear financial interest in cooperating with TNCs on the project – the annual income from the pipeline could be US$400 million a year, an amount larger than any other earner of foreign currency for Burma.

Colombia's rich oilfields in the Casanare region are witnessing scenes which have been described as a late twentieth-century version of the Wild West, an equivalent of the California gold rush. The fields are viewed by oil companies as potentially the most lucrative since Alaska in the 1970s – they could hold reserves of 2,000 million barrels. British Petroleum, Occidental and Total have been active in developing the fields, which are expected to produce a million barrels of oil a day for export.

But the behaviour of British Petroleum (BP) in Colombia was compared by Richard Howitt, a Member of the European Parliament, with Shell's behaviour towards the Ogoni peoples in Nigeria. Although Colombia may have huge oil reserves, it is also the scene of armed conflict, with the government battling against drug interests – the so-called narco-guerrillas – and left-wing guerrilla groups. The oil companies appear to have been given government protection, at a price. 'BP pays the military a $1.25 a barrel war tax (on each barrel of oil produced) and another $5.6 million in a 3-year voluntary agreement of cooperation.'[33] In return, government forces keep the guerrillas away from the company's installations. In October 1996, BP was accused in the European Parliament of colluding in gross violations of human rights by the Colombian army and of wanton environmental damage in pursuit of profit. A report by a high-level Human Rights Commission had alleged that BP passed photographs, video and intelligence about strikers to the army, and that this led to beatings, murders and disappearances. It also alleged that the company caused 'grave damage' to protected forest, polluted a river and damaged bridges and the only road available for locals to take their produce to market.[34] BP initially dismissed the allegations, but later urged the Colombian government to investigate claims that some of its staff had collaborated with the army. The role of Occidental and Total is also controversial. One tribe in Colombia, the U'wa, have threatened to commit collective suicide if Occidental persists in seeking to explore for oil on their ancestral lands. Total was accused by Richard Howitt of acquiescing in 'massive human rights violations' by the Colombian army.[35]

The overall impression given by the powerful and profitable oil corporations is that they appear to be insensitive to the livelihoods and needs of families who happen to live where oil reserves are being tapped, and who will live there long after the oil is gone. Most of these people number among the world's poorest and most vulnerable. But when local people are in the way of TNC profits, they seem to be expendable pawns on the corporate chess board.

CHAPTER 9

Tourism: The Great Illusion

Tourism is cultural prostitution (Haunani-Kay Trask of Hawaii)
TNCs ... account for a substantial part of international tourism transactions (UN report)

Tourism is the second largest foreign currency earner for developing countries (next to oil) and one of few economic sectors that is thriving. It is the only major sector of the international trade in services in which there have been consistent surpluses. The developing world's balance of trade in tourism rose from US$6 billion in 1980 to US$62.2 billion in 1996, according to the UN Conference on Trade and Development.[1] But while tourism promises much, especially for governments of countries with natural resources that might attract foreign holiday-makers, the promise is an illusion. Most of the foreign exchange that developing countries appear to earn from international tourism goes to transnational corporations, through their ownership of hotels, airlines and tour operators, and while TNCs reap the benefits, the industry often harms the environment and the poor in the countries that play host to the tourists.

Many developing countries have viewed tourism as a growth sector which is an attractive way of diversifying the economy and escaping from a dependence on traditional exports. Tourism does not have the problems that surround 'traditional' exports such as coffee and tea, with their low and unstable prices. Whereas people in Western countries do not normally increase their consumption of goods like coffee and tea when their incomes rise, they often do spend more on holidays, and are likely to travel further, perhaps to Africa, Asia, Latin America or the Pacific. Tourism also avoids the tariff and quota barriers that Western countries employ to keep out the manufactured goods of developing countries. Tourism now earns developing countries over 10 per cent of their total earnings from exports of goods and services, and over one-third of their earnings from services (shipping and nationals working abroad are the other major service sector currency earners).

Asian countries, which are experiencing greatly devalued currencies in the wake of the region's financial crisis, are set to be more attractive to foreign tourists, although as one of the effects of the crisis is lower growth worldwide, people may have less money to spend on tourism. In the summer of 1998, the number of Japanese travelling abroad fell to its lowest level for 18 years.[2]

Economic desperation has played a part in the rise of the Third World's tourism industries. Faced with crippling debt burdens, worsening terms of trade and declining aid, developing countries have hardly been in a position *not* to develop their tourism potential, especially as tourism seems to offer nothing but positive benefits, not least an ability to repay foreign debts. 'Tourism development is often seen as a relatively quick and simple solution to the problems of economically under-developed regions, as the use of the natural attributes of an area can provide a quick economic return', points out tourism specialist Veronica H. Long.[3] But the negative aspects of the industry are considerable and rarely calculated. Most of the price that Western tourists pay for their holidays in developing countries is for airfares and hotels, and is likely to go to Western-based TNCs. 'The main actors in the industry (tourism) are transnational corporations from developed countries', says the UN Centre on Transnational Corporations.[4] When tourists visit their shores, developing countries are often left with less than a third of the money the tourists pay, and it can be less. M. Thea Sinclair of the Tourism Research Centre at the University of Kent points out: 'A major issue related to tourism in developing countries is ... the distribution of the revenue obtained from tourism between firms and individuals in destination and origin countries.'[5] The benefits and costs which developing countries derive from international tourism arrivals 'are related to the contractual relationships that exist between tourism enterprises in developing and industrialised countries'.[6]

Three branches

Tourism TNCs are defined by the World Tourism Organisation as 'foreign enterprises providing services for movements of persons with direct investment or other forms of contractual arrangements in one or more receiving country'.[7] While the main actors want to effectively control key sectors of the industry in developing countries, such as large hotels and restaurants, they often prefer not to invest their money directly. Many have learnt to exercise power with a minimum financial stake. An Australian, Harvey Perkins, who has studied the effects of international tourism, estimates that 13 TNCs dominate the tourism industry: six from the USA; four from France; and one each from Australia, the UK and Canada. He estimates that four of them operate 97 per cent to 100 per cent of their hotels outside their country of origin, and nine have more than 50 per cent outside.[8]

The attractions of the tourist industry for TNCs are understandable. As tourism is one of the world's fastest-growing industries, the corporations are eager to get into growth markets and exploit new opportunities.

> Many kinds of TNCs can be found in the international tourism industry ... The most important are airlines, hotel and restaurant chains, tour operators and travel agencies. They account for a substantial part of international tourism transactions.[9]

A close web of inter-locking relationships characterises the different branches of the industry. The majority of tourists, having purchased their tickets from travel agents or tour operators based in industrialised countries, use an airline based in that country and stay in a hotel that is part-owned or managed by a TNC hotel group. Some tourist enterprises have a vertical structure – tourists book their holiday through a travel agent which is part of the same corporation as the tour operator, the airline and the hotel where they stay.

Airlines

Airlines move over 80 per cent of international tourists. But the role of airline companies in international tourism cannot only be gauged by their shares in passenger-revenue volumes. Many of the major airlines have subsidiary tourism operations, including direct investment and contractual arrangements with hotel and restaurant chains, tour operating companies, catering and travel agencies. British Airways, for example, owns a tour operator and is reported to be planning expansion into travel insurance 'and to team up with global rail, sea and hotel partners'.[10] Many airlines also have affiliates in developing countries, covering activities such as catering, insurance, computer services, technical services and shipping.

Changes of policy by international airlines, over which developing countries have no control, can drastically affect receipts from tourism. In 1988, for example, Japan Airlines and Continental withdrew from Fiji's international airport, adversely affecting arrivals of tourists from Japan, Canada and the USA. For developing countries, the trade can be high risk.

Table 9.1 The world's top ten airlines, 1995 (by turnover US$ million)

1. American Airlines	(USA)	16,910
2. Japan Airlines	(Japan)	15,026
3. United Airlines	(USA)	14,943
4. Lufthansa	(Germany)	13,904
5. Delta Air Lines	(USA)	12,194
6. British Airways	(UK)	12,143
7. All Nippon Airways	(Japan)	10,031
8. Northwest Airlines	(USA)	9,085
9. Air France	(France)	7,957
10. US Air	(USA)	7,474

Source: Euromonitor, *World Tourism*, 1997.

Tour operators

Tour operators are the wholesalers that put together the various elements of a tour or travel package, 'thus achieving significant price reductions to pass on to consumers'.[11] While they have a significant role in the UK and Japan, they are much less important in France, Germany and the USA, partly because domestic tourism is more popular. Tour operators of one country tend to serve only the residents of that country, which means they are smaller and less well known internationally than hotels and airlines.

Some operators are part of TNCs that include hotel chains and airlines. They normally prefer to use the airlines of Western countries, not least because tourists prefer these airlines. They sell their tours through travel agents, sometimes in the same group, and make use of persuasive advertising that presents an idyllic image of a developing country, but does little or nothing to show what it is really like.

Hotels

Of all the activities that make up the tourism industry, hotels have probably the biggest impact on developing countries. The overwhelming majority of the largest hotels worldwide are owned, operated or managed by, or are affiliated to, TNCs. Such hotels account for 'a considerably higher percentage of the total number of rooms in many developing countries than in developed countries'.[12] They operate in different ways – one United Nations study indicated that in Asia, 60 per cent of hotels affiliated to transnational hotel chains were linked by management contracts, 23 per cent by franchise and 15 per cent by equity shares.[13]

Table 9.2 The world's ten leading hotel operators, 1995 (by number of hotels)

1. Hospitality Franchise Systems	(USA)	5,010
2. Best Western International	(USA)	3,462
3. Choice Hotels International	(USA)	2,902
4. Accor	(France)	2,379
5. Holiday Inn Worldwide	(USA)	2,096
6. Marriott International	(USA)	1,036
7. Forte	(UK)	926
8. Promus	(USA)	669
9. Société du Louvre	(France)	453
10. ITT Corporation (Sheraton)	(USA)	412

Source: Euromonitor, *World Tourism*, 1997.

The growth of tourism has given local hotels in fast-growing regions such as Asia more bargaining strength *vis-à-vis* TNC hotel chains, for example, enabling them to negotiate management contracts on more favourable terms. In Asia, the proportion of hotel rooms affiliated to TNC chains ranges from 44 per cent for the Philippines to 10.4 per cent in Thailand. In Kenya, one of Africa's chief tourist destinations, there has been considerable investment by tourism TNCs: 'By 1988 there was foreign direct investment in approximately 78 per cent of major hotels in coastal areas, 67 per cent in Nairobi, 66 per cent in lodges in national parks and reserves.'[14] The world's largest hotel networks are mostly USA-based; only one Third World-based hotel chain is among the top 15 – New World Renaissance of Hong Kong (see Table 9.2 for the world's ten leading hotel operators). Other, comparatively smaller, hotel chains are based in developing countries. The India-based Oberoi chain of hotels, for example, has hotels in nine other Third World countries, including Nepal, Egypt, Saudi Arabia and Indonesia.

A hotel connected to one or more of the big chains can be found in almost every country in the world. The largest hotel chain, Hospitality Franchise Systems, includes Howard Johnson and Days Inn hotels; it franchises Ramada Hotels in the USA and Canada. In developing countries, the hotel chains swarm like bees round a jam jar. In India, where the government has declared hotels 'a high priority area' for foreign investment, at least eight of the hotel corporations listed among the top 15 are collaborating with local interests either to manage or to franchise hotels. Accor has a joint venture agreement with Oberoi for the setting up of the Novotel brand of hotels in India. Days Inn has a franchise agreement 'with a Bombay-based group for eight mid-market hotels, four of which are operational. ... Holiday Inn Worldwide has entered a joint venture agreement ... to set up 70 mid-market hotels over the next ten years', according to an Economist Intelligence Unit report.[15]

Transnational corporations usually prefer not to own hotels abroad, or even to have a direct financial stake in them. Hotel chains make most of their money either managing hotels 'or simply charging very high fees for the use of their brand name', points out Koson Srisang, Executive Secretary of the Ecumenical Coalition on Third World Tourism.[16] Management agreements and franchising dominate the industry, accounting for over 90 per cent of TNC-associated hotels in developing countries.

Under management agreements, a TNC undertakes the operation and management of a hotel in a developing country which is owned by local interests. These are popular with TNCs – they give them a large measure of control over a hotel's finances without the risk of expropriation. TNCs 'have increasingly been disinvesting themselves of hotel properties and concentrating their energies on securing management contracts', says Srisang.[17]

Franchising allows a local company to use the name, trademarks and services of the TNC hotel chain in return for a sizable fee (usually a fixed sum plus a percentage on rooms). The hotel is then promoted as a member of the TNCs group of hotels. An example is the use by local hotels of the Hilton or Holiday Inn trade names. If anything goes badly wrong – severe economic downturn, for example – it's the local firm that can go bust. The TNC bears no risk.

There are some cases of vertical ownership under which the TNC owns everything – airline, travel agent, tour operator and hotel. An example is the International Thomson Organisation's ownership of Thomson Holidays, Portland Holidays, Skytour Operators, Britannia Airways, Orion Airways and Lunn Poly travel agents. There are also some joint ventures, where ownership of hotels is shared by the TNC and a local interest in a developing country – where a joint venture may be preferred as it lessens TNC dominance.

Boosting business

For tourism TNCs, cutting costs and boosting business is the name of the game and they are quick to spot bottlenecks that are impeding growth. When, for example, the US-based finance corporation, American Express, discovered that tourism industry personnel in Latin America often receive no formal training, it offered an NGO called

Partners of the Americas funding for training courses. The Dominican Republic was chosen as a test site, and the industry was subsequently given a boost. According to Kathleen Agena:

> Better trained tourism personnel has meant improved service for American Express credit card and travellers cheque customers, and the surge in tourism in the Dominican Republic has brought indirect benefits to all credit card and travellers cheque companies, including American Express.[18]

The most recent attempt by airline TNCs to cut costs and boost profits involves switching much of their office work to developing countries. In July 1995, for example, Swissair's ticket accounting, computer entry queries and discount schemes were switched to an office in Bombay. 'Ticket bookings will stay in the country of the passenger,' predicts Stuart Howard of the International Transport Workers Federation, 'other functions can be located anywhere.'[19] Lufthansa, British Airways and American Airlines have transferred some of their data processing to countries with low wage costs, and Lufthansa is reported to be doing some of its ticketing in India and Ireland.

The corporations involved in tourism are constantly on the look-out for new destinations and opportunities. A report about Asia says that 'secondary destinations like Phuket in Thailand and Cebu in the Philippines have become tourism's lifesavers'.[20] It notes that hotels are moving up-country, where labour costs are lower, to take advantage of new opportunities.

Based in the UK

British Airways (BA) controls over 80 per cent of the international traffic from the UK; it is the world's sixth largest airline by turnover, but is the number one carrier in terms of passenger miles flown. In 1997, it was the UK's 37th largest company with a turnover of £8.36 billion and profits of £640 million. BA has a stake in a number of airlines outside the UK and has a package holiday subsidiary company, British Airways Holidays Ltd. In late 1996 it announced plans to link up with American Airlines to create a giant operation. The link-up was approved by the European Commission in July 1998, on condition that the two airlines gave up some landing and take-off slots. This caused the airlines to go cool on the deal and they decided to phase it over 4 to 5 years. In September 1998, BA and American Airlines nonetheless announced the formation of a five-airline alliance – with Canadian Airlines, Cathay Pacific and Qantas. United Airlines, Lufthansa and SAS airlines are also planning an alliance, again creating a huge operation.

These link-ups smooth the path for TNCs, the most lucrative airline customers, making for easier travel plans for TNC employees, helping them to conduct more business in other countries.

Among tour operators, charter airlines and travel agents, TNCs dominate. The Thomson Travel Group, part of Canada's Thomson Corporation, includes an airline, a tour operator and a chain of travel agents, and is the UK's largest tourism company, after BA, with sales in 1997 totalling £1.78 billion and profits of £112.4 million – up from £82m in 1996. It is closely followed by Airtours (1997 sales of £1.72 billion, profits of £86 million) and First Choice (previously known as Owners Abroad). All have their own in-house airlines – Britannia, Airtours International and Air 2000 respectively. Thomson Tour Operations, Airtours and First Choice sell around 60 per cent of the ten million charter-based package holidays arranged from the UK – up from 25 per cent in the late 1980s. This is set to rise to 80 per cent by 2000. Thomsons and Airtours are linked with High Street travel agents – Thomsons with Lunn Poly (the UK's largest travel agent with over 750 shops), Airtours with Going Places. The large groups have opened over 1,000 new branches since 1992, while 500 independent agents have either gone bankrupt or sold out to the big operators. Tourism TNCs based in the UK are therefore gaining ground at the expense of smaller companies. The tourism industry is moving more and more into corporate hands.

The TNCs sell most of the holidays to destinations in developing countries. Their activities raise a number of questions. For example, do they give any thought to their impact on people in developing countries? Are the corporations, because of their power, getting a deal in developing countries which gives them a good bargain but leaves the host country with very little? Are they aware of the downside of their activities, the negative impacts they can cause in tourist locations? Are TNCs prepared to help spread the benefits of tourism to enable developing countries to benefit more?

Foreign exchange

Net foreign exchange earnings for developing countries are 'often much lower than the income figure might lead one to believe', says a UN report.[21] The difference is due to 'leakages' – the percentage of the tourist's money which does not stay in the county being visited, but which goes instead to the foreign-owned airline, tour operator and hotel. In the Caribbean, leakages range from 30 to 80 per cent of nominal inflows of foreign currencies. A leakage of 77 per cent has been estimated for 'charter operations' to the Gambia.[22] A study published in 1978 by the Economic and Social Commission for Asia and the Pacific estimated the leakage was between 75 and 78 per cent when both the airline and the hotel were owned by foreign companies, and between 55 and 60 per cent in the case of a foreign airline but locally owned hotel. These figures are significant. They show that a great deal more foreign exchange stays in a country when hotels are locally owned.[23]

To estimate the percentage of tourists' spending which is received by Kenya, and the percentage 'leaked' to foreign tour operators, travel agents and airlines, M. Thea Sinclair looked at the data in brochures for 235 package holidays to the country. Different types of holidays, including beach and safari, offered by nine tour operators were considered, including Thomsons, Airtours and Thomas Cook. The prices paid by tourists were assessed and disaggregated into estimated amounts received by hoteliers in Kenya, by suppliers of local ground transportation, national parks and game reserves, airlines and foreign tour operators. Estimates for the provision of accommodation and food were made by calculating the differences between a sample of the prices which tour operators charge for an additional night's accommodation and food, obtained from brochures, with the revenue received by hoteliers (provided by interviews with hoteliers). It was found that a considerable percentage – often between 30 and 50 per cent – of the total price charged for accommodation and food was retained by tour operators. The survey discovered that with beach holidays the total foreign exchange leakage attributed to the overseas tour operator and airline range between 62 per cent and 78 per cent for the 14-night holidays which are most common. The leakage is lower in the case of safari holidays – 34 to 45 per cent – as more is spent on ground transport and on entrance fees to game reserves. In money terms, Kenyans therefore fared much better from safari than from beach holidays.[24]

Employment

In some countries, in parts of the Caribbean for example, tourism employs over half the labour force. Most of the jobs in the industry are unskilled or low-level skilled and poorly paid, even though less privileged groups, such as women and young people, are often not employed. An International Labour Organisation report said that 'in many parts of the world, the renumeration of employees in hotels and restaurants seems to be at the lower end of the salary spectrum'.[25] In Uruguay, in 1987, for example, the average hourly salary for a waiter was 171 pesos compared to 573 pesos for a calculating machine operator. Working hours tend to be longer than in other economic sectors. In Bangladesh, the weekly hours of work are 56 in the hotel and catering sector, and 45 in banking, construction, printing and other sectors. While working hours in hotels in most countries are normally not more than 48 hours (a six-day week is common), said an ILO report, in Thailand they are 54 hours.[26] Workloads in hotels tend to be irregular. The report speaks of 'extreme irregularity in the workload (in hotels and restaurants), combined with the physical and nervous fatigue of having always to provide a courteous and friendly service'. While most countries have legislation governing working time and other conditions, the weakness of trade unions in most developing countries means that standards are not always adhered to.

Tourism TNCs can help to upgrade skills (for example, computer skills in the case of hotels), which in turn can help the host country's economy. There can also be spin-off effects in that jobs are created in local industries which serve the tourist sector, and also in the informal sector, where women are more likely to seek employment. The jobs are a mixed bag, including washing clothes for tourists, petty trading, cooking or looking after the children of other women officially employed in the tourism industry 'or providing other services such as massage on the beach or sexual services', says Anne Badger.[27] Prostitution apart, a woman who earns money in her own right from a TNC hotel activity, either through direct employment or in indirect ways, can improve her status in the family and community. But her working hours may be considerably lengthened, as she may still be expected to carry out her domestic duties as before. Tourism has the potential to both 'degrade and improve women's status'.[28]

While new jobs may be created by hotels, there can be a serious downside for employment. A tourism development may displace local people from work they have done all their lives – fishing communities, for example, often rank among the biggest losers from the tourism trade. Most hotels in developing countries are built close to beaches. Although local fishers may have made their living from a base on a beach, it is common for them not to be consulted about new tourist complexes, but to be cleared away with no compensation. At one location in the Philippines, local fishers were forbidden to fish within 25 miles of a new hotel complex.

Again, while jobs are created in new tourism complexes, they may not go to local people. When a Sheraton Hotel opened in 1988 in Santa Cruz on Mexico's Pacific coastline, the qualifications needed for front-desk jobs 'included 100 per cent English fluency; maids needed to be 80 per cent fluent. The vast majority of community members in Santa

Cruz would not qualify.'[29] Employment was effectively restricted to educated outsiders. Trained workers from other parts of Mexico soon dominated the labour market. The types of job created by tourism are also questionable. Waiting on affluent Northerners in restaurants and bars, cleaning their rooms, caring for their every whim, may do nothing to advance people's dignity and sense of worth.

The impact on a country's wider employment situation is also questionable. In some cases, very few jobs have been created and little economic development is occurring in tourist areas. In Kenya, for example, tourism's new jobs have by no means solved the unemployment problem, but have led to even larger numbers of jobless people migrating to tourist centres.[30]

But is it development?

According to a UN Centre on Transnational Corporations report:

> Tourism TNCs generate numerous linkages with the local economy. Some of the linkages have a significant impact – both negative and positive – on local infrastructure. Some of the business practices of tourism TNCs may impose additional costs on the host country.[31]

In most developing countries there is little evidence that tourism has helped development.

While the industry has the potential to stimulate other economic sectors, in practice it does not usually develop sufficient positive links with them, nor does it benefit a country's development as a whole. The beneficial 'spin-offs' are often few and the costs higher. Economies have to be adapted to suit tourists' needs; land, beaches, water etc., have to be reserved and infrastructure, hotels and holiday complexes built. New feeder roads will usually be needed, services have to be laid on. The cost of providing the infrastructure may have to come from host country budgets, causing other items of government spending to be postponed. 'Development' is hardly advanced.

The tourism industry tends to buy its wares from *outside* developing countries. It would not be unusual, points out Lorine Tevi of the World Council of Churches, who has studied the effects of tourism in the Pacific, for a Pacific island hotel to buy its furniture from Sweden, office machinery from the USA, lighting from Holland, vans from Germany, curtains from France, and its food from Australia.[32]

The growth of tourism has led to a mini-construction boom in some Pacific Island countries, like Fiji, Tonga, Vanuatu and Western Samoa. Capital from Australia, Japan, the USA, New Zealand and Southeast

Asia is heavily involved in the construction of new hotels and facilities. The mini-boom seems to have chiefly benefited Western-based construction and hotel supply companies.

Food output and farmer incomes in the host countries can be stimulated if hotels buy their food locally. But this often does not happen. In Gambia, the manager of one hotel admitted importing virtually all the food that was placed before the hotel's guests.[33] Tourism TNCs can be very choosy about the sources of food.

> Local partners may be obliged to obtain supplies of particular products from specified third party or from the franchiser. McDonald's, for example, insists that a certain kind of potato be used for its French fries; if the need arises, the potatoes have to be imported.[34]

People who live in Third World tourist areas often have little or no power over an industry which can critically affect them. They can lose their homes, their land and traditional means of livelihood; survival becomes dependent on serving the wealthy tourists whose demands have upturned their lives. Women living near large hotels often bear the biggest burden. In India's Goa resort, 'massive quantities of water are transferred to the resort (luxury hotels) from some water resource of another. This results in the lowering of the water table and the wells running dry', says Albertina Almeida of a Goan's women's collective. She also alleges: 'Hoteliers are known to drill water within 500 metre of the high tide line, utterly disregarding the fact that this results in irreversible saline water intrusion, which again means longer distances, more work and bad health for women.'[35] Some of the daily tasks that a woman normally performs are therefore made harder by the industry's presence – collecting water, for example. The big demand for water by tourist hotels can mean that village water wells and taps run dry, or become polluted or saline. Local farmers may be left with less water and this can reduce their food output. Tourism can therefore affect local food supplies for local people.

Culture

Tourists often go to a developing country to experience its culture, and possibly its heritage and cultural sites. Yet their presence, and the infrastructure needed to service their visit, contributes to the destruction of the things that attract them. Turning sacred local sites into tourist attractions diminishes the sacredness the tourists come to experience. But it is the overall cultural impact of tourism which has aroused criticism. 'Tourism is cultural prostitution', believes Haunani-Kay Trask, professor of American studies at Manoa University on Hawaii. 'It is violence against us.'[36] Hawaii's culture has suffered acutely from tourism. With a local population of around one million people, Hawaii receives around seven million tourists each year and their impact is enormous. 'Tourism as it exists today is detrimental to the life, well-being and spiritual health of native Hawaiian people. If not checked and transformed, it will bring grave harm', read a statement by the Third World Ecumenical Coalition on Tourism after a conference in 1993. Tourism 'perpetuates the poverty of native Hawaiian people', it said.

Huge hotel development has put severe strains on water supplies. Reefs and fishing grounds have been destroyed because of hotel sewage runoff and gold course irrigation. 'Tourism is cutting the ties between native Hawaiians and our land, culture, tradition and lifestyle', warns the Revd Kaleo Patterson, a local pastor. Writing of tourism's impact on people who live near Malindi, a popular resort on the Kenyan coast, anthropologist, Robert Peake says: 'To the elders and the Western concept of leisure it represents, is the opposite of everything that is proper and wholesome in society ... tourism threatens the social relationships that form the basis of traditional Swahili society.'[37]

One of the worst human and cultural aspects of tourism is that it has led, in a number of destinations, to a big increase in prostitution. This is especially evident in countries such as Thailand and the Philippines. Two out of every three Japanese tourists to the Philippines are men on package tours with 'built-in' sex. An estimated one million children in developing countries are caught in the slavery of child prostitution, mostly prompted by the tourist trade. A Christian Aid report estimates that around 200,000 children work as prostitutes in Thailand and probably 60,000 in the Philippines. Some 200,000 Nepali girls have been sold into slavery in Indian brothels. In Sri Lanka around 2,500 boy prostitutes, so-called beach boys, earn their living from male tourists.[38] These children are the most tragic losers of international tourism. TNC tour operators based in Europe as well as Japan have been involved in this business.

Environmental damage

As the number of tourists increase, so also does the environmental damage. In some countries, tourists are in danger of destroying the very environment that attracts them. Examples are many. Hotel chains in Mexico have burnt down parts of the forest in order to construct new complexes for tourists. Unplanned tourism development in the country's resort of Acapulco has resulted in a polluted bay and a large squatter settlement. Some of East Africa's game parks have been turned into dustbowls by tourists' vehicles. Indonesia's head of tourism planning has warned that traditional life on the island of Bali is threatened by environmental damage caused by investment in tourism. In Ladakh, Kashmir, hotels have mushroomed, overloading the fragile ecology of Lak town. In Goa, the discharge of sewage from a large number of hotels along the sea front has polluted the ocean and damaged sea life. While the ITT Sheraton hotel group donates to conservation schemes, reports say that a new 204-room five-star hotel in the Cook Islands, built on tribal land, sacred to local people, 'left a bill of over US$1 million for environmental destruction'.[39] 'If no measures are taken to conserve the environment, pollution and damage to natural reserves will eventually reduce tourist flows', says a UN report on Asia and the Pacific. 'On the other hand, conservation measures will hinder tourist growth.'[40] But in parts of the developing world where tourism is causing serious environmental damage, measures that 'hinder tourist growth' could be welcome.

Golf courses, constructed partly for tourists, are expanding rapidly in Asian developing countries, putting severe strains on water supplies, and also on land and forests. In the early 1980s the region had few courses outside Japan. Now there are 'about 160 in Thailand, 155 in Malaysia, 90 in Indonesia, 80 in the Philippines and many more are planned', points out Chee Yoke Ling of the Asia Pacific Peoples' Environment Network, which started the Global Anti-Golf Movement (based in Malaysia) to draw attention to the problems. Some of these courses have been funded with Japanese aid money.

The world's biggest golf course operator is the US-based TNC, the American Golf Corporation. A standard 18-hole golf course uses 6,500 cubic metres of water a day – an amount that could meet the needs of 60,000 villagers. Building golf courses in tropical areas can mean that forests have to be cleared, coastal areas bulldozed, mountain tops lopped off and swamps are drained.[41] Course maintenance usually requires large amounts of chemicals such as fertiliser and fungicides which can pollute water and cause health hazards. Like tourism as a whole, golf courses can affect local food supply, sometimes by taking over land which once grew food. In May 1998, farmers in the Philippines planted rice on a golf course in Manila, in a protest about the way the land was being used.

Eco-tourism

Transnational Corporations have not been slow to jump on the bandwagon of 'eco-tourism'. While this is the fastest-growing sector in international tourism, the eco-tourism label can mean little or nothing. In countries such as Costa Rica and Thailand, NGOs allege that unscrupulous developers and politicians are building massive resorts in the name of eco-tourism. Costa Rica has become one of the world's top eco-tourism destinations. But here, as elsewhere, there are doubts about whether local people are having any say in its development.

In 1991, tourism TNCs belonging to the World Travel and Tourism Council set up the World Travel & Tourism Environmental Research Centre (WTTERC) 'to monitor, assess and communicate effective environmental strategies, objectives and programmes for world travel and tourism'. Until then the industry had done little to consider environmental impacts. Yet 'moving, housing, feeding and entertaining hundreds of millions of people every year has an evident environmental impact', say WTTERC officials.[42] The centre points to a huge potential for the industry to achieve environmental improvements worldwide. 'However, in 1992 it was apparent that little was being done to realise this potential.'[43] The 'key environmental issues', dealt with by the Centre's 1994 review, are global warming, the ozone layer, acid rain, water resources and natural resources. The effects of the industry on people are absent. The section on water resources omits any discussion of the demand of tourists for water and the impact on local water supplies.

The threat of regulation is encouraging tourism TNCs to at least consider the environmental impact of their business. In July 1994, the World Travel and Tourism Council launched 'Green Globe', which it says is:

> A programme to help companies improve their environmental performance and to communicate these improvements to clients. ... The plain facts are that if companies do not develop programmes to manage their environmental performance they face increasingly costly and complex regulation.[44]

Small-scale, participatory tourism is well placed to make a contribution to sustainable development. Alternative tourism is now on offer in, for example, Senegal and Sri Lanka, with visitors staying with local people rather than in hotels. Participation of local people is a key factor. In Zimbabwe, a project called CAMPFIRE (The Communal Areas Management Programme) began in 1989 and now involves local people in 12 rural areas in the management of their own lands. In many of these areas money is earned from tourism. Local Zimbabweans are involved in analysing tenders from safari operators to run tourism ventures, and are helping to build tourists' accommodation in the villages.

The chief international agreement affecting tourism is the General Agreement on Trade in Services (GATS) which was signed in April 1994 in Morocco, in the aftermath of the Uruguay Round of the GATT. GATS sets up a legal and operational framework for the gradual elimination of barriers to international trade in services, including tourism. Trade restrictions currently affect corporations in a number of ways, including: their ability to move staff to a foreign country; the use of trademarks; their ability to create and operate branch offices abroad; and the repatriation of profits. When the GATS is fully operational, these restrictions will be swept away. For the hotel sector, GATS will facilitate franchising, management contracts and licensing. TNCs will be eligible to receive the same benefits as local companies, and they will be allowed to make international payments and transfers without restriction. GATS is good for the industry but hardly for developing countries. While revenues from tourism may increase, GATS could limit the sovereignty of host governments to control the activities of tourism TNCs. GATS increases the power of TNCs at the expense of governments.

Regulation

If they are trying to make sustainable development a central plank of their overall policy, governments may need to reconsider their policy on tourism, and be prepared to regulate the activities of tourism TNCs. The corporations have limited time horizons; their concern is to make profits in the short term. The WTTERC has shown little sign that tourism TNCs are changing their practices to ensure that their activities contribute to a country's long-term sustainable development. Sustainability can only come if TNCs agree to safeguard local environments and people.

Governments of developing countries that want to attract tourists are competing with each other for the business. But unless they regulate TNCs, it may not be a trade worth having, and it can have a detrimental impact on the lives of many people. 'Governments must accept that the tourism industry is unlikely to regulate itself. It is up to governments to regulate the industry in the way they feel is necessary', says Tricia Barnett of Tourism Concern.[45] Governments need to ensure that their tourism industry operates in a way that can be sustained, with fair regulation of foreign interests, and not in a manner that damages local peoples, cultures and environments. In countries with democratic voting systems, the negative effects of tourism on local people could lead to a backlash at the polls. To get a grip on the industry, governments should do the following:

1. Consult local people, women as well as men, at the design stage of

a tourism project. In the case of a tourism complex in Mexico, 'the resort was designed and the social impact mitigation plans were made by tourism industry professionals far away from the actual resort site … [and] superimposed upon a small, low socio-economic, indigenous community'.[46] Such a lack of consultation is basically unjust to local people and makes for poor tourism development.

2. Examine their country's planning laws, and ensure that an independent assessment is completed for any tourism development scheme.
3. Make a human and environment assessment of any planned project. Consider costs and benefits from the widest possible angle.
4. Employ local architects, engineers, project managers and other technical staff in the construction of hotels. Construction materials for hotels can also be sourced locally. This will foster the development of sub-contracting industries and strengthen linkages in the economy.
5. Encourage in every way possible the development of indigenous tourist facilities.
6. Not invest in tourism to the detriment of other sectors of the economy.
7. Make use of the policy of Western countries and impose 'quotas' on foreign tourists, limiting the number that are allowed in. Impose 'tariffs' such as room taxes and higher airport taxes.
8. Charge hotels for water use to encourage its conservation.
9. Cooperate with other countries in the region to exercise effective control over tourism TNCs.
10. Urge Western countries to pass legislation that makes it a criminal offence for their nationals to exploit children abroad, in, for example, sex-tourism.

Some governments are showing a willingness to rethink their plans to build five-star hotels and encourage indigenous tourism facilities rather than TNC-led tourism. The Gambia, for example, asked Tourism Concern to rewrite a tourism plan that had been developed with the aid of the United Nations Development Programme. The plan's weakness – especially its emphasis on mass tourism – had become clear. A seminar on alternative tourism in 1995 gave birth to a cooperative venture called DEEGOO (which means cooperation and understanding). Tourism Concern, Voluntary Service Overseas, an NGO called Afrikan Heritage, and small-scale business people are involved in this venture which is now trying to market small hotels run by local people.[47] This is an important alternative to TNCs. The right kind of tourism can generate profits for local people rather than the corporations.

CHAPTER 10

Health: The Poor Take the Corporate Pill

Drugs are not just any products, they must be surrounded by more ethical and moral principles than other products (Fredrik Hedlund of Sweden)

The legal drug scene is nothing short of scandalous (Susan George)

Along the streets of towns and cities in developing countries, one shop frequently stands out for its bright and shiny appearance – the pharmacy. Look carefully at the products for sale and the vast majority have been made by pharmaceutical corporations based either in Europe or the USA, or by their affiliates and subsidiaries in developing countries. The health budgets of their countries may be declining, but High Street pharmacies are booming, with people flocking to them in huge numbers. Instead of tackling the root cause of the illness that makes them seek medicine, they have been persuaded by slick advertising on television and billboards to seek a 'cure-all' in a packet or a bottle. Moved by such advertising, the poor are prepared to pay a sizable proportion of their earnings for that hoped-for cure.

The pharmaceutical TNCs have developed drugs which benefit millions of people. But NGOs concerned with health matters also allege that the same companies engage in practices which can damage the health of the poor. Specifically they allege that the corporations:

- sell products in developing countries that are withdrawn in the West;
- sell their products by persuasive and misleading advertising and promotion;
- cause the poor to divert money away from essential items, such as foodstuffs, to paying for expensive, patented medicines, thereby adding to problems of malnutrition;
- sell products such as appetite stimulants which are totally inappropriate;
- promote antibiotics for relatively trivial illnesses;

- charge more for products in developing countries than they do in the West;
- fail to give instructions on packets in local languages;
- resist measures that would help governments of developing countries to promote generic drugs at a low cost;
- use their influence to try to prevent national drugs policies;
- give donations of drugs in emergencies which benefit the company rather than the needy;
- use their home government to support their operation with threats if necessary, such as withdrawing aid, if a host government does anything to threaten their interests.

These allegations form part of a largely unpublicised struggle which is taking place in developing countries about the health of its four billion plus people. The outcome of the struggle will determine the health not only of present generations but of many millions more in the years ahead. It is a struggle for scarce resources, with pharmaceutical TNCs competing for all they are worth for the limited amounts of money that most governments and people have available to spend on health care. Frequently it takes the form of TNCs struggling to prevent the host government from bringing in legislation that will curb their business in favour of generic drugs made by local companies.

Medicine for the poor is big business for the rich. The global market for pharmaceutical products is worth nearly US$300 billion a year, and the industry spends between 15 and 20 per cent of its annual turnover on marketing – more than it spends on developing new drugs. In many poorer countries, 20–30 per cent of the health budget is spent on drugs, most of them made by pharmaceutical TNCs. Some are banned or have been withdrawn in Western countries because they are considered unsafe. In the Third World, however, they may be labelled 'safe', and people will buy them in the hope that their pain will be removed and their health restored. In reality, the drugs might kill them.

The pharmaceutical TNCs are growing 'at an unprecedented rate. In the 1996/97 financial year, Merck grew by 19 per cent, Pfizer by 16 per cent, Astra by 16 per cent and SmithKline Beecham by 10 per cent'.[1] By mid-1998, it seemed that sales in Asian countries were being hit by the region's financial problems.

The size and annual budgets of the major companies in relation to most developing countries put them in a position of considerable power to influence both government health policy and customers. For most people in developing countries the industry is often the major source of information on drugs. This places a moral responsibility on the

Table 10.1 The ten largest pharmaceutical corporations, in drug sales, 1997 (US$ billion)

Merck (USA)	13.5
Glaxo Wellcome (UK)	13.1
Novartis (Switzerland)	9.7
Bristol Myers Squibb (USA)	9.7
Pfizer (USA)	9.2
Roche (Switzerland)	7.9
Johnson & Johnson (USA)	7.6
Eli Lilly (USA)	7.4
American Home Products (USA)	7.3
SmithKline Beecham (UK)	7.3

Source: Lehman Brothers, July 1998

companies to give accurate information, to present the full facts to the customer. However, this responsibility is often abused.

Promotion

The methods used by the corporations are highly controversial. Making use of advertising that is inexpensive in comparison to what they pay in industrialised countries, the drug TNCs use the most persuasive, not to say unethical, methods to persuade the poor to buy their wares. Extravagant claims are made that would be outlawed in Western countries. A survey, in the *Annals of Internal Medicine*, found that 62 per cent of the pharmaceutical advertisements in medical journals 'were either grossly misleading or downright inaccurate'.[2] Neither do the diseases of the poor have much priority. According to a UN report:'In the case of pharmaceutical products, the bulk of promotional efforts by TNCs in developing countries is directed towards the relatively expensive goods, originally designed for markets in developed countries.' Personal care products are also promoted 'frequently of doubtful medical value, instead of the relatively simple and inexpensive preparations needed to cope with illnesses most common among poorer populations'.[3]

Also, 'there is widespread availability in the Third World of many drugs on the UN consolidated list of products whose consumption and/or sale has been banned, withdrawn or severely restricted', according to Zafrullah Chowdhury, who developed Bangladesh's National Drugs Policy.[4] He lists, for example, tonics: 'an ordinary tonic, with 17 per cent alcohol content, marketed in the UK by Squibb as Verdivition was promoted in India as a brain tonic'. An UNCTAD study of Nepal, in 1980, 'found that out of 2000 products in the drug market, 733 – or more than a third – were tonics'.[5]

A huge double standard is being practised. In Francophone Africa, a drug containing meclozine is advertised for nausea and vomiting in pregnancy, yet in France, prescribers are warned not to use meclozine during pregnancy because of insufficient evidence of safety. One study of the Philippines found that the more reliant doctors are on commercial sources of information, the less appropriately they prescribe.[6] When products are withdrawn from European markets, and manufacturers accept they should stop making them, it would seem that the Third World is a useful place to unload surpluses and so reduce losses.

Chowdhury alleges that 'the pharmaceutical industry is as corrupt as it is powerful'. 'As Australian criminologist Professor John Braithwaite has shown, it has a worse record of bribery and corruption than any other industry and a disturbing history of criminal negligence in the manufacture of drugs and of fraudulent practice in the area of safety-testing.'[7] The first investigation into a pharmaceutical market in a developing country was carried out by a committee set up by the government of India in 1974. One of its chief conclusions was that brand names were responsible for 'the large number of unnecessary and often irrational formulations on the market'.[8]

Doctors are usually the first target of drug industry promotions. Promotional spending on doctors is huge. In the Philippines, for example, promotion accounted for 22 per cent of income from drug sales in 1987, according to the Drug Association of the Philippines. 'Most of this is spent on promotion to doctors. Many scientific studies have shown the impact of drug marketing on doctor's prescribing patterns.'[9]

Doctors are persuaded, sometimes by bribes or sweeteners, to recommend products made by the drug companies. An alliance therefore comes about between TNC drug companies, Western governments (which protect the interests of their companies) and local doctors and medical establishments. Doctors can be won over in different ways. A report in the *Journal of the American Medical Association* has revealed that doctors who accept fees for speaking at conferences, free meals or other perks from a drug company are more likely to recommend the company's products. Doctors who add drugs to hospital stocks seem to have the strongest links with the TNCs.

Antibiotics

Antibiotics have saved more lives than any other class of medicine, but, ironically, their over-use is now leading to serious health problems, with the developing world chiefly at risk. These drugs work by killing or slowing down the growth of bacteria, and, as such, are a very powerful intervention. A 1987 report said that the use of antibiotics 'has set in motion the biggest intervention in population genetics seen to date on this planet'.[10] Such a colossal intervention in nature could, however, be expected to have risks.

Heavy promotion of antibiotics by the international drug companies, and their use to treat comparatively trivial illnesses, means that millions in developing countries have become resistant to them. When people do contract a serious disease, antibiotics may not work. Taking too many can render antibiotics useless; this has huge consequences for health.

Some bacteria are now becoming resistant to antibiotics. Professor Stuart Levy, director of the Centre of Drugs Resistance at Tufts University, Boston, points out: 'Society is facing one of its gravest public health problems – the emergence of infectious bacteria with resistance to many, and in some cases, all, available antibiotics.'[11] Resistance to antibiotics has now reached epidemic proportions in many countries 'and multi-drug resistance leaves doctors with virtually no room for manoeuvre in the treatment of an increasing number of diseases', says Professor Jacques Acar, Chairman of the World Health Organisation Working Group on Monitoring and Management of Bacterial Resistance to Antimicrobial Agents.[12] The poor may therefore be denied a life-saving drug when they desperately need one.

The most vulnerable people could be the hardest hit. A bacterium called *Shigella dysenteri*, for example, 'is now the cause of most African cases of dysentery, a principal cause of death of young children. The bacterium is resistant to all available antibiotics.'[13] According to Dr Graham Dukes: 'We are faced with a return to a medical dark age in which antibiotics no longer work against a vast range of infections, some created by antibiotics, some perhaps epidemic and deadly.'[14] The problems have been known about for some time, however.

> In September 1989, more than 500 cases of typhoid were reported from Shrirampur in Maharashtra, India. In 83 per cent of the cases the bacteria causing the typhoid were resistant to chloramphenicol, the life-saving drug that has been the mainstay of the treatment of typhoid in India.[15]

But their promotion goes on, with pharmacists again given particular encouragement to promote the drugs. In Peru, for example, pharmacists are offered television sets and other prizes if they gain enough points by selling medicines produced by three companies. Some of the highest points are offered for selling antibiotics.

Antibiotics are now commonly being misused to treat viral infections such as non-bacterial diarrhoea, respiratory tract infections, including coughs and colds, and other common infections. The drug company Laboratories LAFI, for example, recommends a combination antibiotic in Bolivia, says Health Action International (a network of consumer, health and development NGOs) 'for babies and children with commonly occurring acute respiratory infections'. But HAI says that although the indication is for 'bacterial infections' many of the infections listed are 'commonly viral. The overall emphasis of the ad is to use this product in many circumstances.'[16] In Latvia, Eli Lilly produced a 1996 calendar for doctors advertising an antibiotic for children. This mentions flavour and dosage, etc., but contains 'no information on indications for use, contra-indications, warnings or adverse effects'.[17]

People with limited incomes, who are induced by advertising, doctors and pharmacies to divert their scarce funds away from other purposes to buying antibiotics, are affected in two ways: they face the possibility that they will have no resistance when they contract a serious disease; and buying these products means they have less disposal income for more essential goods and services.

Vitamins and stimulants

The promotion and sale of vitamin pills is widespread in developing countries, with the pharmaceutical TNCs again in the lead. Once more the poor can be persuaded to pay for costly substances. In 1991, the drug company Abbott advertised in the Caribbean one of its products, called Paramettes, as a 'high quality, well-balanced vitamin/mineral formulation for the whole family. Helps to prevent or correct nutritional deficiencies. Helps promote proper growth in children.'[18] The best source of vitamins, however, is food. If children eat enough food of the right kind, they do not normally need vitamin pills. The British Medical Association has said, for example, that most people: 'obtain sufficient quantities of vitamins in their diet and it is therefore unnecessary in most cases to take additional vitamins in the form of supplements'.[19]

In developing countries where malnutrition is widespread, advertising may persuade people to buy the solution in a packet, rather than buy nourishing food. The widespread promotion of vitamins also helps to 'medicalise' hunger, points out Andy Chetley, 'so that the economic and social cause of malnutrition are not tackled'.[20] There are even dangers for health in the use of some vitamin substances. 'Excessive use of one or more vitamins may cause relative deficiencies of other essential micronutrients. Large doses (of minerals and vitamins) are toxic.'[21] According to Chetley: 'Misuse of vitamins can distort national health priorities, drain limited national economic resources, waste limited individual and family financial resources, encourage incorrect and harmful beliefs about the nature of health, and encourage ineffective and harmful practices.'[22]

The persuasive promotion of appetite stimulants can also be a drain on scarce family resources. Loss of appetite is a common symptom of illness but is usually temporary and does not require medicine. It can be due to a shortage of food. 'In extreme cases of malnutrition ... the use of appetite stimulants may be dangerous.'[23] Yet in some developing countries, TNCs widely advertise these stimulants. In Pakistan, for example, an antihistamine is advertised as an appetite stimulant for children with malnutrition. Sedation is listed as a side effect, but doctors are told: 'This is beneficial for nervous and restless children.' But, in any case, 'malnourished children need food not appetite stimulants', stresses Health Action International.[24] In 1991 appetite stimulants were Pakistan's fourth largest category of drugs.

Donations

Donations of drugs by TNC pharmaceutical companies to developing countries may seem a wholly good thing. Since 1988, Merck has donated drugs to treat onchocerciasis (river blindness), a disease that affects millions of people in West Africa. SmithKline Beecham announced in January 1998 that it would donate several billion doses of a drug to treat elephantiasis (a swelling of limbs and genitals), a disease that affects as many as a billion people.[25] Donations give the companies good publicity but the health of people in developing countries might be better served if they lowered the prices of such drugs instead.

In emergency situations, donated drugs have often turned out to be useless. According to the World Health Organisation:

Experience in emergencies over the years has shown that drug donations often prove to be more harmful than helpful. They may not be relevant to a particular emergency situation, or may not comply with local drug policies and standard treatment guidelines.[26]

In the Bosnian town of Mostar, for example, some 340 tons of donated drugs were estimated to be stored in warehouses in late 1995. The people of Mostar had been badly hit by the civil conflict and they urgently needed drugs of the right kind. But most drugs in the stores were old and dangerous: 'After a thorough sorting, less than 5 per cent was found useful. The rest was so dangerous it had to be burnt as rubbish, needing special treatment.'[27] In 1995, one container of antibiotics had the label 'must be used within June 1962', and was probably produced in the 1950s. The drugs had come from TNCs in European countries. The Mayor of Mostar called them 'drug rubbish … a serious health hazard' and warned that it would take three months to burn them.

'The largest one-time pharmaceutical donation ever' was how the Indiana, US-based drug company Eli Lilly described the gift of an antibiotic called CeclorCD to Rwanda during the country's refugee crisis in 1994. The company sent enough for 1.3 million people. But the antibiotic is not on the World Health Organisation's list of essential drugs for the treatment of refugees. Nor is it on the treatment schedules of any countries in Central Africa. Médicins sans Frontiéres (Doctors without Borders), a leading relief group, said 'it would never prescribe such medicine in the camps'.[29] Doctors in Rwanda believed the antibiotic was too risky. In 1996, the problem for the Rwandan authorities was how to dispose of six million pills, many of them past their expiry date. For a country with enough problems in the aftermath of civil conflict, the disposal of unwanted drugs was one it could have done without. While Eli Lilly conceded that the tablets donated were excess stock nearing expiry date, they 'felt it was the right thing to do'.[30]

Non-governmental organisations have cooperated with the distribution of donated drugs. In 1995, a US-based aid agency sent nearly 100,0000 anti-diarrhoeal drugs to Eritrea a month before the expiry date. Such drugs did nothing to combat dehydration, the major cause of death from acute diarrhoea. In April 1996, a Kansas, US-based NGO, Heart-to-Heart International, airlifted into Calcutta US$10.5 million worth of medicines for the poor that had been donated by more than 30 pharmaceutical companies, based in Europe and the USA. Health Action International alleges: 'Only 9 of the 57 types of medicines were essential drugs; another 7 were "borderline", and 41 – or 95 per cent of the value of the consignment – were non-essential. Most had expired or were due to expire in less than a year.'[31] A Calcutta-based NGO, the Community Development Medicinal Unit, described 'the whole contingent of antihistamines and the lion's share of the antibiotics and anti-inflammatory drugs and cough remedies' as 'not worthy of donation'.[32] It calculated that the drugs would only have cost a fraction as much had they been purchased on the Indian market. A local doctor said that the consignment did not appear to be 'need-based'.[33]

Therefore although drug donations may seem pure altruism, they can sometimes harm rather than help the victims of emergencies. However, they nearly always help a company's balance sheet. European and USA-based TNCs receive substantial tax benefits when they give donations. For gifts to the needy, US tax regulations allow a write-off for tax purposes of up to twice the production costs.

There may be a place for donated drugs that are appropriate for people in need, but donations of the wrong type waste the time and resources of people in developing countries. The World Health Organisation has adopted guidelines for drug donations which are based on four 'core' principles: (1) the donation should benefit the recipient to the maximum extent possible; (2) a donation should be given with full respect for the wishes and authority of the recipient, and support existing government policies; (3) there should be no double standards in quality – if the quality of an item is unacceptable in the donor country, it is also unacceptable as a donation; and (4) there should be effective communication between the donor and its recipient.[34]

Generic drugs

Pharmaceutical TNCs have hindered attempts by developing country governments to provide people with safe, effective, low-cost generic drugs. A drug's generic name is the pharmacological name of a compound (aspirin, for example), usually assigned by the World Health Organisation (WHO). Although generic drugs have been in existence since the 1890s (patent medicines had begun to proliferate earlier in the nineteenth century), they started to become more prominent in the 1950s. They have the great advantage of costing much less than branded goods and are usually just as good. For the poor, this is crucial. But TNCs have waged 'a strategic marketing war against low-cost generic name products', alleges Chowdhury. Their vast armies of sales representatives have spread the rumour that generic drugs were produced 'by insanitary, incompetent and inexperienced cottage industries, and that they were impure, contaminated or ineffective'.[35] By the mid-1960s, however, TNCs could see that their attempts to discredit generics were unlikely to succeed, and they began to move into the generic market themselves. The companies have continued, however, to thwart national drugs policies.

Bangladesh was the first developing country to introduce, in 1982, its own national drugs policy. This took the form of a health strategy based on the manufacture of a relatively small number of generic drugs, and the restriction of some patented goods. As Bangladesh is one of the world's poorest countries, its citizens have only limited ability to purchase brand-name goods, but the TNC drug companies nonetheless kicked up a huge fuss about the policy and put every effort into trying to stop it.

Soon after independence in 1971, Bangladesh had begun to purchase generic drugs from Eastern European countries. Cost was the major factor – these drugs were cheaper than drugs from TNCs. But the corporations were 'predictably hostile to this approach', maintains Chowdhury, 'and embarked on a campaign of misinformation among the medical profession and elite consumers. ... They began to spread rumours about the dubious quality of drugs from Eastern Europe.' The US government was also displeased about Bangladesh's trade links with socialist countries. 'This led ultimately to the withholding of wheat exports from the USA during the 1974 famine in Bangladesh when several hundred thousand people died.'[36]

In May 1981 the World Health Assembly of the WHO adopted an Action Programme on Essential Drugs, urging member states to adopt essential drugs lists, generic names, tougher drug legislation, strategies for reducing drug prices and a code of drug marketing practice.

Bangladesh, under the military rule of General Ershad, was the first country to take up the challenge. A year later, in May 1982, the Council of Ministers in Bangladesh approved a National Drug Policy report. Under the policy, 1,742 out of 4,340 branded drugs were considered 'inessential or ineffective', and were banned. It recommended that 150 essential drugs and 100 specialised drugs be prescribed by specialists and consultants; 45 of the essential drugs were to be manufactured and sold only under their generic names. TNC drug companies would no longer be allowed to manufacture simple products like common analgesics and vitamins. These were to be made exclusively by local firms. In June 1981, a people's health centre, Gonoshasthaya Kendra, which was set up ten years earlier, started Gonoshasthaya Pharmaceuticals (GPL) to manufacture and market low-priced generic drugs.

The new policy threatened only a quarter of the business of US-based pharmaceutical TNCs, but it unleashed a storm of protest, with the US companies leaning on their government to use its influence to get the policy revoked. Within days of the report being approved, the US Ambassador in Bangladesh was trying to convince the government that 'as the policy was unacceptable to the USA it should not be implemented'.[37] 'TNCs started mobilising the Bangladesh Medical Association and elite public opinion', says Chowdhury. At a public hearing 'they [the TNCs] insisted that generic drugs policies had failed all over the world'. But the chairman of the hearing concluded that 'the TNC's campaign was based on total falsehood and that they were simply wielding their power in defence of their commercial interests. He recommended that the policy should immediately be given a legal framework.'[38]

The drug companies continued their campaign against the new

policy, however. They placed advertisements and feature articles in newspapers and

> encouraged doctors to see the policy as a curb on their right to prescribe and an infringement of their clinical freedom. ... They pulled other strings too. British, Dutch and West German Ambassadors called on General Ershad to express their dismay at the proposed drug policy.[39]

The US Secretary of State instructed the US Embassy in Bangladesh 'to express concern over the drug policy at the highest government level'. What worried the TNCs was that if the Bangladesh government pursued its policy, which it did, despite the enormous pressure, then other countries would follow suit. 'Their fears were justified; on July 23rd 1983 the Indian government banned the manufacture and sale of 25 drugs with immediate effect.'[40]

By 1992, Bangladesh was enjoying substantial benefits from the new drugs policy. Essential drugs had increased from 30 per cent to 80 per cent of local production, and drug prices had increased by only 20 per cent compared with an increase of 178.8 per cent in the consumer price index. For the poor, this was a life-saver. The drop in price, in real terms, made essential drugs much more affordable. The National Drugs Policy also meant that Bangladeshi companies increased their share of local production from 35 to 60 per cent. It saved the country around US$600 million of foreign exchange on imported drugs and also improved the quality of drugs available – the proportion of drugs found to be substandard fell from 36 per cent to 9 per cent.

Transnational corporations, backed by their governments, nonetheless kept up the pressure for changes and gained some concessions. In June 1992, for example, Pfizer won an appeal decision to get two drugs that had been banned in 1982 back on to the market. 'The groups which have opposed the drug policy since its inception continue their efforts to undermine it', says Chowdhury. 'TNCs and local producers alike, backed by the World Bank, are pressing for deregulation and liberalisation.' While parts of the 1982 policy are still in place, there has been 'a gradual erosion' of the basic principles on which it is based.[41]

Support from the WHO for the country's policy has been muted and low-key. When WHO chief Dr Halfdan Mahler visited Bangladesh in September 1982, five months after the National Drug Policy had been put in place, he praised the government for its commitment to the WHO programme 'Health for All by the Year 2000', but did not comment on the drugs policy. More forthright support from the WHO would have been a morale booster for the initiative, but the muted support may have occurred because the WHO did not want to offend its largest donor, the USA. The US role throughout the drama was a blinkered and one-sided view of its corporate interests. Yet US behaviour in Bangladesh was not unlike its behaviour in the Philippines. When the Philippines announced a national drugs policy in 1987, the US Ambassador in Manila warned the Philippine health minister that the policy would discourage foreign investment.

In 1974, when a severe cholera epidemic gripped Sri Lanka, the country's State Pharmaceutical Corporation (SPC) asked the US-based TNC, Pfizer, to produce tetracycline capsules 'with raw materials which had been imported from Hoechst. ... Pfizer refused to comply with the SPC's request.' The US Ambassador called on the Sri Lankan Prime Minister and 'indicated that the supply of food aid from his country would be in serious jeopardy if any action were taken against Pfizer'.[42] The drug companies have never hesitated to use the power of their own governments to get their way.

In Pakistan, it seems to have been the power of high-profile people from finance and economic backgrounds that persuaded the government to weaken its national drugs policy, which had been drawn up in line with WHO recommendations. The policy promised 'universal access to essential drugs, self-sufficiency in the manufacture of drugs through transfer of technology and the import of only those drugs by TNCs that are allowed free sale in their home countries'.[43] Following pressure from TNCs and financial interests, the government dropped the clauses that the corporations did not like, saying they were in conflict with the country's economic liberalisation policies. Once again the power of the TNCs had proved too strong for a supposedly sovereign government. The incident also showed that liberalisation hinders a country's ability to take independent action.

Discrediting critics

The pharmaceutical TNCs are probably the world's most powerful corporations, in terms of the influence they wield, and they have carefully thought-out strategies about how to deal with their critics. Andy Chetley recalls how in the early 1970s the United Nations set up a Committee of Eminent Persons to enquire into the high profits of the pharmaceutical and chemical companies. 'A small subcommittee of at least 6 Swiss companies (including Ciba-Geigy, Sandoz and Roche) was established to weaken the impact of the enquiry,' alleges Chetley,

> and avoid the introduction of an international code of conduct for TNCs. During one meeting the companies outlined a five-point strategy for dealing with critics:

1. The critic is identified as an opponent of the system and thus discredited as a discussion partner.
2. Dubious motives are attributed to the critic: ideological or nationalistic prejudices, envy, stupidity, ignorance and lack of experience.
3. When criticism is global or circumstantial: the contrary is 'proved' by means of isolated instances (for example, a description of an individual project).
4. When criticism is indisputable (for example, in the case of ITT in Chile), emphasis is put on the fact that it is an individual case, and that it is still under investigation.
5. In any case, it should be said in public that defending free enterprise is in everybody's interest. Therefore, it should be shown, especially in the mass media, that criticism of multinationals is basically criticism of free enterprise and that behind it are the enemies of the free world, whose view of life was based on Marxism.[44]

Despite corporate attempts to discredit them, NGOs are having successes. In Germany, for example, the BUKO Pharma Campaign, part of a network of 200 NGOs, is urging the TNCs 'to withdraw non-essential and irrational drugs and change their marketing strategies'.[45] The campaign successfully lobbied the German parliament and a law was passed tightening controls on drug exports.

Conclusion

The record of the pharmaceutical TNCs in developing countries is one of putting the pursuit of profit before peoples' health, even when that profit is tiny compared to their overall profits. Greed for every cent they can get has pushed TNCs to irrational behaviour and arguments. It is what these TNCs are omitting to do, as well as what they are doing, that is of concern. A materially poor parent whose child is sick should be able to buy a locally produced, inexpensive medicine. In many developing countries, she or he does not have the choice of doing that because the TNCs have persuaded governments that locally produced drug are not necessary. Choice has been denied the poor because of what is effectively a corporate veto.

Patented medical substances can of course be used to good effect. When properly prescribed they can save lives. But they are open to many abuses, abuses in which some of the major pharmaceutical TNCs are involved. The mistake that most governments have made is to believe that the corporations have the answers to the health problems. But as Roberto Lopez of the Peru-based NGO Accion Internacional poor la Salud points out: 'You cannot solve problems caused by poverty with pills.'[46] The corporate pill is especially hard to swallow.

CHAPTER II

The Corporate Persuaders

*They hired counsellors to work against them [the people] and frustrate
their plans (Book of Ezra, chapter 4, verse 5)*

*If business wants to influence what happens in government, a guy
like me can be helpful (Derek Draper, political lobbyist)*

Transnational corporations have the highest access to the most senior
policy-makers; they can call presidents, prime ministers and heads of
key international agencies to put their case, and their call will be put
through. They also know that government ministers can often be persuaded more easily of a TNC's claims if palms are suitably oiled when
the need arises. While the large corporations have the money to do
this, developing countries are often broke. In a poverty-stricken country,
especially, ministers may not be averse to a deal that gives them a
degree of personal security.

Bribes

In Nigeria they are known as 'dash', in Malaysia as 'money politics',
in other countries as 'sleaze'. Whatever they are called, bribes are an
ugly but common fact of business life. Corruption has become a
widespread global problem, with TNCs sometimes paying huge bribes
to win business. But the losers are ordinary people, for large-scale
corruption does enormous damage in developing countries. A bribe,
typically between 10 to 20 per cent of the cost of a deal, may be paid
to government ministers and officials and added, at least in part, to its
cost. A TNC may win the contract, and a tiny number of people in a
developing country will gain from the bribe, but the country as a whole
pays more than it should. This means that less money is available for
other purposes, such as health care and education.

Big money is involved – bribes of as much as US$20 million can be
paid on a single deal. On armaments deals, says George Moody-Stuart,
a former chairman of Booker Agriculture, bribes of around US$3 billion

a year are being offered and accepted. Money has been 'stripped out of the economies of developing countries', he says. 'In many cases it has been largely responsible for the burden of foreign debt.'[1] But as big as the money is, 'even more significant is the damage that bribes do to decision making. Once a decision maker has a personal interest in placing an order with a firm that is willing to pay a bribe, his judgment goes out of the window'. This means that priorities get distorted. Goods and services may be purchased that are not needed (armaments are a classic case) and a project which has attracted a large bribe may get priority over others, which are possibly more useful. This can lead to projects going ahead that make economic nonsense.

Opportunities for bribery and corruption can come through the sale of capital goods, major civil engineering projects, ongoing supplies or consultancy services 'usually in that order of attractiveness to the beneficiaries', points out Moody-Stuart. And what used to be a problem in only a small number of countries, 'has now become a major South-wide problem, with tremendous deterioration in the last 10 to 15 years'. Grand corruption has become 'the general rule rather than the exception in major government-influenced contracts in the South'. Those who receive the big money, receive it indirectly and have the protection of numbered Swiss bank accounts.

Not all TNCs are involved in bribery and corruption, and the ones that are involved would of course deny it. They do it carefully, working through agents so as not to be found out. For TNCs, image is all-important and they pay a lot of attention and money to ensuring that they have a good image. While their influence is with policy-makers, in government and in the United Nations and its agencies, the image-making is also for the public.

Influencing the United Nations

At the Earth Summit in Rio de Janeiro in 1992 – the United Nations Conference on Environment and Development – it seemed curious that the regulation of TNCs was absent from the agenda. But it was hardly surprising. The corporations had used their considerable influence to see that their role was played down. But then the evidence suggests that the policies of the United Nations and its agencies have been profoundly influenced by TNCs. In the months before the Rio Summit, the International Chamber of Commerce and its members, many of whom are TNCs, urged that the Agenda 21 document for sustainable development (to be agreed by leaders at the summit) contained no references to the corporations or to their regulation. All references in an original draft were duly dropped, (see also below, p. 164, on PR companies).

TNC influence over the United Nations stretches over many years. It was highlighted in 1978, when a Swiss-based organisation, Association pour un Developpement Solidaire, published excerpts from internal files which showed how the corporations operate in the UN system. The files showed that TNCs have succeeded in 'subversively infiltrating the UN and its agencies and neutralising them as a potentially countervailing force, or even utilising them for the corporation's own purposes'.[2] During the late 1970s and the 1980s, the corporations killed off a proposed code of conduct for TNCs, which was then under discussion at the UN.

The United Nations Centre on Transnational Corporations (UNCTC) – set up in 1974 to serve as the UN Secretariat's focal point on matters related to TNCs – had tried to draw up a code to 'establish standards for the conduct of TNCs from all countries to protect the interests of host countries, strengthen their negotiating capacity and ensure conformity of the operations of TNCs with national development objectives'. Also, to 'set standards for the treatment of TNCs by countries to protect the legitimate interests of investors … .and create a climate for foreign direct investment which is beneficial to all parties in the investment relationship'.[3] TNC influence was supreme, however. Western countries urged in the negotiations that developing countries should encourage TNCs and protect their investments. Developing countries stressed the need for the companies to adhere to their development objectives – they wanted a code that would pinpoint the responsibilities of TNCs to their economies, people and environments. But this aspect of the code received far less attention in the discussions than the issue of how governments of developing countries treated the companies.

When, in the late 1980s, a growing number of developing countries removed barriers to trade, and began to offer guarantees about the protection of TNC investments, so Western countries, influenced by their TNCs, began to lose interest in the code. In 1992, the negotiations were abandoned, and the UNCTC was down-graded and renamed 'The Transnational Corporations and Management Division'. The Centre's inability to finalise a code of conduct on TNCs underlined the deep influence that the corporations have in the UN system and over governments. It was TNCs, not governments, which made the running. The TNCs used their power to influence the UN agenda to the point that negotiations over the code were for the corporate benefit. They scored a huge coup – they effectively turned the UNCTC into a centre *for* TNCs rather than *on* TNCs.

With the UN's largest specialised agency, the Food and Agriculture Organisation (FAO), the corporations have enjoyed a 'special status' through the FAO's Industry Cooperative Programme (ICP), points out Zafrullah Chowdhury. Through this programme, they have had 'a strong influence' on FAO policy, he says, quoting Professor Eric Jacoby who worked for FAO for many years:

> Through their representatives on the Central Committee of FAO/ICP ... the TNCs have gained valuable information on forthcoming investment opportunities. Ever since ICP has become an integral part of the UN System, FAO actually functions as an agent for the transnational corporations in the underdeveloped world.[4]

This is an important criticism, even if not all the FAO's work helps TNCs (its work on integrated pest management in Asia, for example, could lead to a reduction in pesticide sales). But its link with industry was again evident at the World Food Summit in November 1996, when the FAO issued a media kit bearing the name 'New Holland. Agricultural machinery worldwide'. New Holland is a leading Dutch-based manufacturer of farm machinery.

Some of the policies of the World Health Organisation suggest an unwillingness to upset TNCs, even if they try to prevent Third World governments introducing the kind of policies that the World Health Organisation (WHO) supports. In 1978, the World Health Assembly of the WHO officially recommended an Action Programme on Essential Drugs (see Chapter 10). Only in 1981 was the programme instituted by the WHO, and not until 1988 did the World Health Assembly adopt ethical criteria for medicinal drug promotion.

Likewise the WHO has seemed reluctant to offend TNCs that are selling unhealthy products. It has given smoking control a very low priority in its work, even though smoking is the biggest single cause of preventable disease. In the 1980s, when it was proclaiming the goal 'Health for All by the Year 2000', the WHO employed just one part-time person on its smoking control programme. This inevitably gave the impression that the organisation was serving the interests of TNCs rather than the health of the poor, for it must have been obvious to the WHO that until smoking ceases, 'Health for All' would never be achieved. The TNCs – together with the USA and a number of European governments – appear to have persuaded the WHO to give only a low priority to such a huge matter for human health. However, in July 1998 Dr Gro Harlem Brundtland took over as WHO director-general with the campaign against tobacco as one of her priorities. Anything less than a full WHO assault on tobacco smoking in the late 1990s and early years of the twenty-first century would again be seen as a sign of caving in to industry pressure.

With aid budgets declining, UN agencies are under increasing pressure to accept funds from TNCs. Organisations such as UNICEF and WHO might even be offered funds from tobacco and milk companies. For the companies, the acceptance of such funds would be a public relations triumph. For health, it would be a disaster.

The taming of UNCTAD

Established in 1964 following a resolution at the 1961 UN General Assembly, expressing concern for the Third World's trade prospects, the United Nations Conference on Trade and Development (UNCTAD) has become another corporate scalp. UNCTAD's mandate was to help poor countries with their trade and development efforts, and it initially came up with ideas for stepping up foreign earnings from primary commodities, such as copper and coffee, and to enable poor countries to earn more from the export of their processed foodstuffs. Meeting for a major conference every four years, UNCTAD's work has produced little, although until recently it was seen as an organisation on the side of the poor. One of the few achievements of UNCTAD conferences was the establishment of a Common Fund for Commodities, following UNCTAD IV in 1976. In theory, UNCTAD remains the chief UN agency concerned with the primary commodities that are of key importance to most developing countries.

In the early 1990s some Western governments were intent on closing down UNCTAD unless changes were made. The organisation was even given some perks, such as taking over responsibility for running the UN Commission on Transnational Corporations from the defunct UNCTC. Following the setting up of the World Trade Organisation in 1994, Western leaders recommended that UNCTAD's role be reviewed; this review effectively took place at the ninth UNCTAD conference in 1996. UNCTAD remains in business although with a very different mandate. Its chief task now seems to be one of smoothing the path for TNC investment in developing countries.

UNCTAD's support for TNCs is seen in a section of its *World Investment Report, 1995* headed 'The Role of Transnational Corporations in Restructuring in Asia'. This focuses, for example, on what is called the 'positive contributions' of TNCs, 'not possible negative ones, such as the displacement of local entrepreneurs, market domination and sociocultural impacts'.[5] In statements like these, UNCTAD is no longer seen to be defending the poor and living up to the ideals of its mandate.

Rather, it has been turned into a pro-industry organisation, a corporate poodle.

At UNCTAD IX in 1996: 'UNCTAD signalled its profound shift towards companies with global reach. It lauded enterprises not only for creating jobs and promoting technological change but also for contributing to broader social and economic objectives, such as reducing poverty and accelerating structural adjustment.'[6] The communiqué issued by the Group of Seven (G7) Western leaders, following their summit in France in June 1996, said that at UNCTAD IX 'we succeeded in reforming UNCTAD's intergovernmental machinery and refocussing development through trade and investment'. Western governments and TNCs had got the UNCTAD they wanted.

The World Trade Organisation

With trade a key area for TNCs, so they have developed close links with trade policy-makers. In negotiations for a world trade deal, the corporations were active between 1986 and 1993 in trying to influence the outcome of the GATT Uruguay Round of talks. During the talks, 'representatives from TNCs staffed *all* of the 15 advisory groups set up by the Reagan administration to draw up the US position', points out Kevin Watkins.[7] TNC representatives 'supplied drafts of the critical TRIPs (Trade Related Intellectual Property Rights) agreement'.[8]

'In the US, the Department of Commerce International Trade Administration identifies its primary aim to be ... dedicated to helping US businesses compete in the global market place', says Myriam Vander Stichele. The Brussels-based Union of Industrial and Employers' Confederations of Europe – comprising 33 industry and employers' federations from 25 countries – 'has frequent contacts with the European Commission either via phone calls or visits made by officials. It closely monitors the EC's initiatives in trade.'[9]

The Uruguay Round ushered in an era of freer trade and led to the setting up of the World Trade Organisation (WTO). While it is ministers and their officials who conduct business at WTO meetings, representatives from major corporations are often there to lobby for decisions which help their business, and they may even be part of the official delegation. 'The enormous role TNCs can play in a nation's economy can make their host government a very accommodating and attentive audience', says Stichele; the corporations have 'much more access to WTO decision-makers than citizens groups and NGOs'.[10]

Transnational corporations can even be powerful enough to turn WTO member applications to their own advantage, urging that a developing country wanting to join the WTO should not be allowed in unless it does more to liberalise its economy. A corporation that is barred from selling its goods to an aspiring WTO member country may urge, for example, that it lifts the ban on those goods before it can join. What is clear is that lobbying by TNCs has secured new international trade rules that are intended to create 'a world order moulded in the image of multinationals', believes Watkins.[11]

As governments have retreated and cut back on their economic and social role in recent years, so the role of TNCs has grown. Corporations that offer employment to large numbers of people in industrialised countries have to be listened to. But the question is whether the TNCs, by their sheer power, count more than the views of the public, who do not have such access to policy-makers.

Against a background of declining official aid budgets, TNCs are also trying to cast themselves as economic benefactors which are capable of aiding poor countries. This was seen, for example, when a representative of Enron, the US-based energy TNC, told a US Congressional Committee:

> Private parties, like our company and others, are now able to develop, construct, own and operate private infrastructure projects in these countries. ... [They] are able to achieve the 2 things which US foreign assistance efforts have long been trying to achieve:
>
> 1, the projects are serving as action-forcing events that are getting the host countries to finally implement the legal and policy changes long urged upon them;
>
> 2, as an adjunct to these polices, to win local support, the private developers are installing substantial amounts of medical facilities, schools and the like to alleviate current problems in these countries.[12]

The notion of privatised 'action-forcing' aid is another example of a TNC strand of thought which runs – 'we know what's best for you poor people; you will have to change along the lines we like'. It raises again the question of sovereignty itself.

Relations with the public

In place of higher TNC standards have come public relations. Instead of changing policies and doing something to remove the causes of the problems they are causing, TNCs have turned instead to PR people. The corporations have their own public relations office, staffed by people who are paid well for putting across the image in the best possible way. But coming under greater scrutiny as they are, the transnational corporations also feel a need for outside help. So they hire public relations companies to get their message across, and can afford to spend enormous sums to establish a favourable climate for their business. PR people will often react to criticisms, for example, by making statements to explain the effort the company is making to comply with the regulations and codes. Their ambition is to calm public fears over babyfoods, toys, shoes, garments and other product lines.

By the late 1990s, the public relations business had become one of the fastest-growing sectors in the global economy. Many PR companies advise TNCs that are active in the developing world. The point of PR, says a Mobil Oil Company executive 'is getting people to behave the way you hope they will behave by persuading them that it is ultimately in their interest to do so'.[13]

The larger PR companies are themselves TNCs. Burson Marsteller, the world's largest public relations firm, has 63 offices in 32 countries. Renowned for its 'crisis management' for Union Carbide after the Bhopal disaster (see Chapter 3), and for Exxon after the Valdez oil spill, it also appears to have played a key role in keeping discussion of TNCs off the Rio de Janeiro Summit agenda. In 1997, Burson Marsteller helped European biotech companies to create a successful PR strategy for the European biotech industry. This led to the passing, in July 1997, of a European parliament directive which permits the patenting of animals and plants. A Burson Marsteller strategy document (leaked to Greenpeace) on how bio-industries can win public acceptance for bio-products shows how the weak and the strong points of a product are identified and played on. This revealing document admits, for example, that 'public issues of environmental and human health risk are communications killing fields for bio-industries in Europe. ... All the research evidence confirms that the perception of the profit motive fatally undermines industry's credibility on these questions.'[14] The biotech industry was recommended to organise media campaigns on the 'environmental and economic benefits' of biotechnology. The document shows the extent to which powerful corporations try to manipulate the debate.

Shandwick, the second largest PR company, describes its business as 'global reputation management'. Clients include ICI, Monsanto and Shell. Its Brussels office adopts an approach 'which mirrors the structure of the EU itself', says the company's publicity material. Hill & Knowlton, the third largest PR company, was hired by Nestlé in the 1980s to send publicity material to church ministers and religious bodies to try to dissuade them from boycotting a leading Nestlé product (see Chapter 4).

Soon after the World Health Organisation adopted a code on the marketing of breastmilk substitutes in 1981, says Judith Richter, 'TNC's became concerned about the global power of citizens. They had ... exposed publicly what they considered to be harmful business practices and used consumer boycotts to influence corporate practices.'[15] In August 1980, Nestlé's then vice-president, Ernest Saunders, wrote in a secret memo to the company's general manager:

> In view of the overall propaganda campaign now being mounted through IBFAN, and the professionalism of the forces involved, it is always possible that we could even win a battle in the US and lose the war as a result of determined pressure on Third World governments and medical authorities. It is clear that we have an urgent need to develop an effective counter-propaganda operation, with a network of appropriate consultants in key places, knowledgeable in the technicalities of infant nutrition in developing countries, and with the appropriate contacts to get articles placed.[16]

It seems ironic for an NGO activity to attract the phrase 'the professionalism of the forces involved' when the corporation has the means to employ vast numbers of people and every professional force possible to combat NGOs which often employ a mere handful of people! The 'counter-propaganda operation' was mounted when Nestlé set up a 'Coordinator Center for Nutrition' to improve the company image and deflect criticism.

Corporations will try to keep controversial issues hidden from the public gaze, says Richter, but if this fails they will use 'a mix of four strategies to influence public debate – delay, depoliticise, divert and fudge'.[17] They might, for example, announce a voluntary code of conduct to delay tougher regulation of their activities, try to shift the debate from political to technical issues, divert attention from the main issue on to secondary issues, and finally, they will fudge, as Richter believes Nestlé did over the code on breastmilk substitutes.

On some issues, however, a TNC will use direct methods to try to persuade the public of its case. In June 1998, Monsanto (see Chapter 3) launched a £1 million PR campaign in the UK to try to persuade people that genetically modified food was good for them. Full-page advertisements in broadsheet newspapers, over a three-month period, tried to soften opposition. With limited funding, NGOs fought back to highlight the weakness of the case for genetically modified foods.

In 1998, the tobacco industry in the USA launched a huge US$40 million, eight-week radio and TV advertisement campaign to defeat a tobacco bill in the Senate that would have obliged them to pay US$516 billion in damages to victims of smoking. Five major tobacco companies purchased time in 30 to 50 markets each week and on CNN. They also placed large advertisements in major national newspapers, including

The Washington Post. The idea was to intensify pressure on wavering senators, mostly Democrats. Republican Senators needed little convincing; many have received millions of dollars in tobacco contributions in recent years. 'The ad. blitz has far surpassed other campaigns to defeat congressional action'.[18] President Clinton attacked the ads as 'a bunch of ooey' and said that the industry was attempting to distract attention from its complicity in misleading the nation about the dangers of smoking. The Senate defeated the bill; the industry won.

But then big industry usually wins. It has the money to win and will use every cunning device to win. The tide turns, however, when people become aware and angry about how much they are being manipulated. TNCs can be stopped if people care enough to stop them. For their part, the world's poor will never be clients of a PR company, but rather its victims, often of a 'double-whammy' – the link-up of product TNC and public relations TNC. Although not a conspiracy against the poor, it has much the same effect.

CHAPTER 12

Tackling the Power

(STRATEGY)

> *Did you ever expect a corporation to have a conscience when it has no soul to be damned and no body to be kicked? (Edward, 1st Baron Thurlow)*
>
> *They encourage each other in evil plans ... but suddenly they will be struck down (Psalm 64, verses 5 and 7)*

Transnational corporations have used their money, size and power to influence the policies of governments and change the rules of the game in their favour. They have pushed the idea of privatisation and taken over much of the economic role that government once played. They have used their position to influence international negotiations and their muscle in different ways to effectively cause hardship for the poor – the invisible in corporate eyes. And they have used the power of public relations to assure us that all is well. In some cases they have even been funded by aid schemes.

But although TNCs are powerful, their power is to some extent limited by rivalry between them and they cannot force people to play their game. They depend on people using their technologies and buying their products. They depend on the market they promote and on the governments they try to influence. They depend on keeping the support of the shareholders who own them and the loyalty of their staff. Control of TNC activity is ultimately up to governments and citizens of both developed and developing countries.

Regulation

The attempt in the United Nations to regulate the corporations with a general international code of conduct came to nothing (see Chapter 11). Western governments backed the TNCs in the negotiations rather than the developing countries. Such is corporate power that it seems most unlikely that a general code of conduct on TNCs could ever be agreed – or implemented if it was agreed. It is also doubtful whether the poor would gain anything from more years of negotiations with TNCs and the governments that are virtually their puppets. Talk in the 1990s of international regulation was still largely in terms of protecting TNCs rather than developing countries – like, for example, the Multilateral Agreement on Investment (see Chapter 2).

There is, however, scope for specific, product codes of conduct at the international level. The code on the marketing of breastmilk substitutes has helped to curb some of the worst abuses of the industry's practices, although the milk companies have still found loopholes. Codes on toys, rugs and garments are now emerging, but they need independent monitoring to ensure they are implemented. Consumers want proof that the codes will be put into practice and are not just a marketing ploy. In a report on the monitoring of business practices, an independent research institute, the London-based New Economics Foundation, said that monitoring systems should incorporate 'verification by bodies that are demonstrably competent and fully independent from the companies involved and their agents'.[1]

There is also scope for national codes of conduct for TNCs, which lay down certain standards that must be kept, the level of wages that must be paid, etc. The experience of Guatemala shows that such codes can be helpful. Workers who had been fired from a factory in Guatemala City, in contradiction of a code, were reinstated following pressure from retailers who were buying its products. Independent investigators played a key role.[2]

Governments can incorporate both international and national codes into their legislation. Some countries have already done this for certain products. India, for example, has passed legislation on the marketing of babymilks in line with the World Health Organisation (WHO) code. Companies and their executives can be prosecuted if they violate this law; offenders can be sent to prison for up to three years.

Governments have a duty to their citizens to legislate and regulate TNCs so that they act in a responsible way. Such legislation can also be used to raise funds for specific purposes – a profits tax on TNCs can be levied, for example, and used for training local people. Overawed by corporate power, however, many governments of developing countries have been reluctant to take regulatory measures for fear of frightening away investors. In some cases, regulation only happens if TNCs agree. The result is that regulation of foreign investment is unsatisfactory in most developing countries. But standing firm in the face of pressure from the companies can be done. As shown earlier, the Namibian government's robust policy on fishing has encouraged the right kind of investment and kept the activities of TNCs under control; the Filipino government eventually stood up to the mining TNCs.

Third World governments could exercise control over TNC activities by employing a small number of people who have recently worked for the corporations and who know the tricks of their trade. TNCs are often masters at getting around the rules and regulations they are supposed to keep; only insiders may know the game well enough to match them. Again, to check corporate power, a national code might stipulate that TNCs should not be involved in more than one economic sector. If, for example, a corporation is involved in the seeds sector, it should not also be involved in pharmaceuticals.

Regulation in Western countries can also be important. In the USA, pressure by the federal government, city authorities and states has influenced TNCs. As noted in Chapter 7, the US government brought pressure to bear on Bangladesh to stamp out child labour in its factories that make garments for export to the USA. The US city of San Francisco passed a law in 1996 which forbids companies that invest in Burma from bidding for contracts in San Francisco. The Motorola company, which was bidding to supply a new radio system to San Francisco and which also had investments in Burma, pulled out of that country. In October 1996, the Apple Computer company announced that it was withdrawing from Burma to comply with Massachusetts law, which also penalises firms that do business in that country. TNCs who try to take advantage of the low wages and repressive working conditions in countries ruled by juntas can therefore be checked by government authorities at different levels in their home country.

A new and quite sinister development to stop developing countries from regulating TNCs is seen, however, in the USA's African Growth and Opportunity Act, which was passed by the House of Representatives in 1998 but still has to get through the Senate. If approved, it would remove all restrictions on investment and effectively prohibit 'the regulation of commerce and factors of production' and even insist that countries join the World Trade Organisation.[3] Some countries have chosen not to join because they dislike its ethos. The Act would say to African countries: if you want foreign investment you have to surrender sovereignty, your right to run your country as you see fit. When US President Bill Clinton visited South Africa in March 1998, Nelson Mandela told him bluntly that the measure was not acceptable. Under the Act, the USA offers Africa the 'carrot' of buying more of its goods. But such deals are worth little in a world that is moving towards free trade and open borders.

If TNCs do not accept proper regulation, and if Western governments try to make regulation impossible, then developing countries are right to wonder whether they might be better off without foreign companies.

Producers

In the world's predominant industry, agriculture, farmers can lead the fight-back against the large TNCs. It is farmers who decide whether or not to use the products of the corporations. While the agrochemical TNCs claim that farmers need their seeds and chemicals to produce the food that is needed, such claims are essentially bogus. The mono-cropping (a large area under the same crop) that is encouraged by the corporations has been shown to be far less productive, in terms of yields, than multiple cropping – two or more crops on the same land.[4] Planting just one crop in mono-fashion increases the risk of disease and of damage from pests, and is the kind of agriculture that is less likely to be sustainable.

Disillusioned by the so-called 'green revolution' technology of TNCs, some farmers in developing countries have switched back to non-chemical or low-external-input farming. While a switch to these systems may cause an initial drop in yields, far more food can eventually be harvested from the same plot of land. Some farmers in India who have switched to permaculture ('permanent agriculture' that uses no outside inputs) are enjoying yields four times higher than they did under chemical agriculture. Producing more food from the same land, and doing it in a way that can be sustained, is surely what governments want from their agricultural sector. TNCs have not proved they can do that. Farmers have therefore no need to buy and to plant the patented seed of TNCs. 'The refusal [of farmers] to buy hybrid or patented seed … and the rejection of industrial monoculture is the beginning of resistance', says Kneen.[5]

The need for more jobs is a pressing concern in most developing countries. Methods of production and distribution which do not depend on TNCs can be encouraged, including alternative methods which put people rather than capital at the centre of economic policy. Subsidising the local economy, 'rather than transnational capital, could help to create huge numbers of jobs, through the renewal of cities, towns and rural areas and face-to-face caring work in health, education and community support'.[6] Small and medium-sized enterprises are alternatives to TNCs. They are usually much better placed to provide jobs and to make a contribution to overall development efforts.

In virtually every economic sector in the developing world, TNCs have introduced inappropriate, large-scale technology that has little relevance to the needs of the poor. If their technologies are inappropriate for the poor, so also are the large-scale corporations. Governments need to question whether TNC-type technology is appropriate for their country and its peoples, and whether it really is superior to local practices. They can, if they wish, choose to promote technologies and operational methods in which TNCs have shown very little interest because they do not yield a big profit for outsiders.

Producers in developing countries can identify the TNC's products that are being imported, and seek to make an alternative. In Mauritania, for example, a local diary product has enabled people to switch from buying imported milk to buying locally produced camel's milk, 'benefiting individuals' health and the capacity of pastoralist communities to maintain their livelihoods'.[7]

The issue is one of how a country uses its resources – in particular whether scarce resources should be used to attract TNCs and import their products. 'It remains an issue whether the sale of products and the fostering of lifestyles inaccessible to most of the population is an effective way of using scarce resources in developing countries', says the United Nations report *Transnational Corporations in World Development*.[8] The poor are unlikely to gain from a TNC's presence in their country, a presence which government resources have helped to facilitate.

Consumers

TNC profits depend on people buying their goods. It is consumers who decide which foodstuffs, beverages, clothes, toys, footwear and medicines to buy, and which holidays to take. Consumers can choose not to buy TNC goods and services which they believe are exploiting the poor. By doing this, they hit at the point where it matters – the company's balance sheet. Consumers can make it clear that corporate irresponsibility does not pay.

Growing consumer pressure in the 1990s was making retailers seek assurance from the TNCs making goods for their shelves that the items had been produced without exploitation. Many retailers are themselves transnational corporations. The aid agency Christian Aid has estimated that the UK's top ten supermarkets 'make more money in a year than the world's 35 poorest countries combined'.[9] But retailers are a bridge between the consumer and the usually larger TNCs involved in production.

Pressure from US retailers helped to reduce child labour in clothing factories in Bangladesh and Central America which are making goods for American shops (see Chapter 7). Retailers, however, need to adopt monitoring practices to make sure that codes are being observed. To try to offset pressure from consumer groups, some stores have drawn up their own code. Major supermarkets in the UK which buy and stock a wide range of goods from developing countries have been urged by Christian Aid to 'adopt a set of ethical principles for Third World purchasing; implement a code of conduct for all overseas supplies of own-brand products, [and] agree to independent monitoring of adherence to the code'.[10] As noted in Chapter 4, the Swiss-based retailer Migros undertook to continue importing pineapples from the Philippines, even if they became more expensive, because of a social clause the company had agreed to improve worker conditions. This again shows how consumer pressure is helping the poor.

About 3 per cent of the UK market for coffee has been gained by the fair-trade product Cafédirect. The coffee beans for Cafédirect are purchased from producers who grow coffee on small farms in Africa and Latin America. Paying them above the market price, Cafédirect has enabled small-scale producers to improve transport, provide scholarship funds, purchase agricultural equipment and make other community and social improvements. And it has given them an alternative to marketing through the normal corporate channels.

In November 1996, a newly established Dutch company, Agrofair, starting selling bananas from African, Caribbean and Pacific countries which give the producers 40 per cent more than the big traders pay. This can be done because the commodity traders' profit is eliminated.[11] As much as TNC activity concerns international trade, the continued growth of fair trade initiatives is vital. To be part of this growth market, TNCs would need to change their policies drastically.

Shareholders

TNCs are public companies that are owned by shareholders who in turn have a degree of power over corporate policies. In the late 1990s there were growing signs that shareholders are prepared to exercise that power. Shareholders who are concerned about their company's work in developing countries have made their voices heard at annual meetings since the 1960s. Some activists for a specific cause have bought a single share in a TNC, entitling them to attend its annual meetings and to table resolutions urging the company to put right an injustice and change its policy. In the late 1970s, for example, members of the World Development Movement bought shares in the tea company Brooke Bond and tabled resolutions urging the company to raise the wages of tea workers on its Asian estates. Barclays Bank, BAT, Nestlé and RTZ were among other TNCs that attracted similar activity. Although the resolutions were always heavily defeated, they gained considerable press publicity, highlighting the injustices that the activists were alleging.

The late 1990s witnessed an additional and more significant form of shareholder pressure. At the annual meeting of Shell in May 1997, 130 shareholders tabled a resolution which attracted the support of institutional shareholders in the form of managed pension funds. The resolution requested Shell to 'establish an independent review and audit procedure' for its environmental and human rights policies. This earned the support not only of NGOs such as Amnesty International, the World Wide Fund for Nature and Friends of the Earth, but also of a London-based organisation called Pensions and Investment Research Consultants (Pirc). Pirc advises pension funds on whether companies have sound records on the environment and human rights. Anne Simpson, a co-director of Pirc, pointed out that there was no commercial case against the resolution and noted that Shell had already taken action on the issues raised, although this seemed to vary from country to country. Although defeated, the resolution was backed by 18 pension funds with investment assets of between £25 billion and £30 billion. 'Shareholders should be telling a public company how to run its affairs because they are the owners', says Simpson.[12]

Following a highly publicised campaign by NGOs, and bad publicity about its activities in Ogoniland, Shell had announced plans, in March 1997, to consult environmental and human rights groups on sensitive projects. Even though the Shell board opposed the resolution, the company accepted the principle of external verification of the company's performance. Shareholder pressure therefore paid off; even huge companies cannot afford to ignore public opinion. Shareholders who are prepared to stand up and oppose what they believe are unethical practices by their company will gain publicity for their cause and may encourage the company to rethink its policies.

NGO activity

Protests from communities and non-governmental organisations in both South and North about TNC activity have been seen to influence corporate policy in a number of sectors. Alliances between Northern and Southern NGOs have helped groups in the South to resist transnationals such as Cargill, Shell and Rio Tinto. New means of communication, such as the Internet, allow a more rapid flow of information between groups and enable global link-ups and campaigns on specific issues. The Internet was important in helping NGOs to launch a successful campaign against the planned Multilateral Agreement on Investment. It is also making it possible for NGOs to know more about what TNCs are doing. For NGOs in both North and South, the Internet is proving an effective yet low-cost way of exchanging information – a way of using globalisation for the social good.

In some cases, local NGO action in developing countries has successfully thwarted the plans of TNCs. When, for example, the US-based corporation DuPont linked up with an Indian company Thapar to form Thapar–DuPont Ltd (TDL), to build a tyre manufacturing factory in the highlands of Goa, the company said it would act in an environmentally sound manner. What it did not say was that 'DuPont's contract with TDL exempts the US-based parent company from liability for environmental claims or a Bhopal-style industrial accident'.[13] But local activists intercepted a company message which acknowledged that control measures had not been taken on groundwater protection, waste water treatment, solid waste recycling and air pollution. Following protests in 1994 and 1995, the company decided to relocate the plant elsewhere. DuPont was named by *Multinational Monitor* as one of 1995's '10 Worst Corporations'.[14] Other examples of successful NGO pressure in the South have been considered in this book.

But although NGO campaigns on sports shoes, toys, garments, mining, foods, pharmaceutical products, baby foods, etc. have raised public awareness of the issues, and appear to be causing at least some of the companies to take notice, 'very little progress has been made in changing TNC behaviour'.[15] Changing such entrenched behaviour requires an enormous and many-sided public effort. The international trade union movement is in a position to contribute to that effort by persuading TNCs to introduce reasonable labour standards. But while the largest grouping, the Brussels-based International Confederation of Free Trade Unions, which claims to represent 126 million workers in 134 countries, has plans to influence TNCs, results have yet to be apparent.[16]

NGOs can also expose development aid that helps TNCs rather than needy people. In 1994, campaigners in the UK took their government to court because of its plans to aid the Pergau Dam in Malaysia (see Chapter 8). The court's ruling underlined the fact that a UK Act of Parliament says that the primary purpose of aid is the economic benefit of a country or the welfare of its people. It is not only funds for Pergau that seem to breach the Act. Public protests about aid that helps TNCs, and also about the privatisation of aid, could help to ensure that government aid is focused on overcoming poverty.

Farmer resistance, community and consumer resistance, shareholder pressure, local authority and NGO pressure have emerged as powerful ways to combat the behaviour of the large TNCs. There is room for a concerted, international network of these groups, and other concerned people, to resist corporate power, closely monitor their activities and their impact, and to publicise alternatives. The Internet makes such a network possible.

Corporate behaviour

These pages have shown how some of the world's most prestigious and profitable companies have become involved in practices that damage the livelihoods of the world's poor. The question is why do they do it, when it tarnishes their image, leads to boycotts of their products, and forces them to resort to clever public relations and statements that often bear little or no relationship to reality? Why do they pay out vast sums to polish their image, while seeing the poor suffer as a result of their work? Is the answer that these companies have no understanding of the world of the poor? That their policies are made in far-away foreign capitals, and their decision-makers are totally remote from the lives of poor in Third World communities?

The reality is more complex. The big TNCs often have people who scour even the remotest regions of the developing world in search of profits. They do have a glimpse into people's lives; they know something of how the poor live. The TNCs know the damaging effect of their policies on Third World peoples but nonetheless pursue those policies. This lends weight to the charge that TNCs have no conscience, even about the way they deal with the world's most vulnerable people. In a civilised society, the poor would be treated better. The best public relations that TNCs could practise is summed up in the word 'responsibility', especially to the poor.

However, recent developments in employment practices have served to increase the severity of the corporate impact on the poor. Many TNCs have sought to boost profits by axing many of their employees and by expecting more from those who remain. In the late 1990s, especially in the wake of the Asian economic crisis, this is putting TNC employees under enormous pressure to deliver – pressure to operate their part of the business as profitably as they can so that it makes the maximum contribution to the balance sheet. With the age of job security gone, if TNC employees do not succeed, then their jobs are on the line.

Inevitably this can lead to the employees cutting corners. It may lead them to make decisions without enough thought or care for the people they will affect. The poor, who cannot fight back, are particularly vulnerable. Double standards can creep in. A senior manager of an oil company confided: 'you cannot expect us to have the same high standards in developing countries as we do in Western countries'. In the West, governments insist on high environmental standards and TNC operations are carefully scrutinised. In the Third World, legal requirements are often lower and TNCs can get away with more. The employees are caught up in this exploitation, on pain of losing their jobs. Mr Tim Melville-Ross, the director-general of the UK's Institute of Directors, has admitted that most companies apply different standards to their operations in the developing world from those in their home country, but claims there is now a convergence.[17]

Can the larger TNCs, especially, ever change? Would they ever consult, for example, with local communities in developing countries to assess thoroughly the likely impact of their actions? If corporations are staffed with people who genuinely want their company to behave in a responsible way, who are not straining to get the last penny or cent out of their business in the Third World and who want to put people before profit and take a long-term view of where the company's interests lie, can they make enough money to satisfy their shareholders? If TNCs do not maximise their profits in the fairly short-term, there is something of a 'Catch 22' situation, for they may be seen by the financial markets as 'under-performing' and be vulnerable to take-over bids. 'A corporation that takes the long view of its profits and the broad view of its social responsibilities is in grave danger of being acquired by an investor group that can gain financially by taking over the corporation.'[18] Such investor groups are basically 'raiders' who seek to acquire an 'under-performing' corporation to maximise its financial efficiency. This may involve splitting up or selling part of the corporation. Profit is the only criteria. 'There are plenty of socially conscious managers', says Korten, 'the problem is a predatory system that makes it difficult for them to survive.'[19]

While the threat from predators will always hang over publicly owned companies, it is no reason why TNCs should not clean up their act. In some cases, quite small changes would help, with no significant impact on profits. It would cost Nestlé very little, for example, to abide by the WHO code on the marketing of breastmilk substitutes. A tiny number of TNC directors, usually of smaller companies, are showing distinct unease about corporate behaviour. Anita Roddick, founder and chief executive of The Body Shop, has spoken of the 'burning priority' to incorporate issues such as social justice, human rights and spirituality into management training. Ms Roddick is setting up a new business academy to promote this approach.[20] While The Body Shop is unusual among TNCs – it has its own trading charter, for example, which includes human and civil rights – it could be showing the way ahead for larger corporations.

Conclusion

The growing power of TNCs affects not just one region of the world but all of it. But in a world dominated by the large corporations, the wealthy have the money that allows them to buy choices. The poor are not so fortunate. We need only look at what is happening: how people in Bangladesh are unable to buy low-cost, locally made essential drugs because of the power of the pharmaceutical TNCs; how farmers in India are threatened by TNCs taking out patents on their crops; how the water supplies of people in tourist resorts are under threat because of tourism 'development'.

'Our challenge is to create a global system that is biased towards the small, the local, the cooperative, the resource-conserving and the long-term', says Korten.[21] The challenge is to create a system that is pluralistic not monopolistic, a system in which the poor matter. The key question is whether TNCs, answerable only to their shareholders, could ever be part of such a system. Unless they cooperate with codes of conduct and national regulations, TNCs will outstay their welcome in developing countries. There is an urgent need for their activities to be more open, democratic and accountable to people in developing countries as well as to shareholders in the North. This would mean their operations would at least be open to the possibility of change.

A judge in a Swiss Court said of Nestlé (see Chapter 4) that if the company wanted to be spared the accusation of immoral and unethical conduct, it would have to change advertising practices. Change 'advertising practices' to 'all business practices' and, for Nestlé, read transnational corporations, and this is the challenge facing TNCs at the start of the third millennium. If they wish to be a part of the future, they have to change more profoundly than they ever imagined.

Again, the question is whether they could do it. Brewster Kneen notes in his book on Cargill:

> Corporate ideology holds that the corporation is the fount of wisdom and the most competent body to plan global production and distribution; accordingly, Cargill now puts itself forward as the most competent agency to back the backward (un-industrialised) peoples of the world. ... TNCs deal in

volume, and there is a definite threshold beneath which a company like Cargill cannot function even if it wanted to. Therein lies the key to resistance and the pursuit of alternatives.[22]

New social organisations are emerging, he points out, 'communities that thrive on, and in turn generate, diversity and inclusivity. They share ... the identification of personal long-term well-being with the good of their community and of a society as a whole. It's hard to imagine a place for Cargill in such a community.'[23] It is hard to imagine a place for any large transnational corporations in such a community. Just possibly, smaller TNCs with *genuinely* responsible management, could have a place. But any TNC will earn or disqualify itself from such a place by its actions.

Notes

Preface

1. Turner, L., *Multinational Companies and the Third World*, London: Allen Lane, 1974, p. ix.
2. Korten, D. C., *When Corporations Rule the World*, London: Earthscan, 1995, p. 12.
3. Green, R. H., 'Transnational corporate responsibility and states, workers and poor people', *Churches and the Transnational Corporations*, Geneva: World Council of Churches, 1983, p. 119.
4. For a discussion of these companies, see *Handbook on Foreign Direct Investment by Small and Medium-sized Enterprises: Lessons from Asia*, New York and Geneva: United Nations, May 1998.
5. Hudson, E. (ed.), *Merchants of Misery: How Corporate America Profits from Poverty*, Maine: Courage, 1996.
6. *Transnational Corporations in World Development*, New York: United Nations, 1988, p. 219.
7. Chowdhury, Z., *The Politics of Essential Drugs*, London: Zed Books, 1995, p. xvi.

1. Introduction

1. Green, R. H., 'Transnational corporate responsibility and states, workers and poor people', *Churches and the Transnational Corporations*, Geneva: World Council of Churches, 1983, p. 110.
2. Figures from *World Investment Report 1996*, Geneva: UNCTAD, 1996.
3. See *World Investment Report 1994*, Geneva: UNCTAD, 1994.
4. *World Investment Report 1996*, op. cit.
5. *World Investment Report 1998*, Geneva: UNCTAD, 1998.
6. *Globalization and Liberalization.* New York and Geneva: UNCTAD, ECDC/PA/4/Rev.1., 1996, p. 242.
7. Independent Commission on International Development Issues, *North–South: A Programme for Survival*, London: Pan Books, 1980, p. 187.
8. *Transnational Corporations*, Vol. 3, No. 1, February 1994, Geneva: UNCTAD, p. 28.
9. Estimate of Richard Tapper, World Wide Fund for Nature, quoted in *The Guardian*, 8 May 1992.
10. *Transnational Corporations*, Vol. 3 No. 1, op. cit.

11. Dunning, J. H., *International Production and the Multinational Enterprise*, London and Boston: Allen and Unwin, 1981, p. 7.

12. Page, S., *How Developing Countries Trade*, London: Overseas Development Institute, 1994, p. 99.

13. *Transnational Corporations*, Vol. 3 No. 1, op. cit.

14. Evans, Tony, 'International environmental law and the challenge of globalisation', in T. Jewell and J. Steele (eds), *Law and Environmental Decision Making*, Oxford: Oxford University Press, 1998.

15. Dunning, op. cit., p. 368.

16. Ibid., p. 359.

17. *Human Development Report 1996*, New York: UN Development Programme, 1996.

18. *The Transnational Corporation and Issues for Developing Countries*, Newcastle, UK: New Consumer, 1993.

19. *Towards a New International Economic Order*, London: Commonwealth Secretariat, 1977, p. 61.

20. Kenneth Dadzie, in a speech to launch the *World Investment Report*, London, August 1994.

21. Lewis Pringle, quoted in *The Guardian*, 15 November 1995.

22. Dinham, B. and Hines, C., *Agribusiness in Africa*, London: Earth Resources Research, 1983, p. 112.

23. Lee Teng-Hui, quoted in *Adverse Impact of Export-Orientated Industrialisation on Third World Environment and Economy*, Walden Bello, Penang, Malaysia: Third World Features Network, January 1992.

24. Tsai, Pan-Long, 'Foreign direct investment and income inequality: further evidence', *World Development*, Vol. 23, No. 3, 1995, p. 480.

25. Green, op. cit., p. 118.

26. *World Investment Report 1994*, op. cit., p. 192.

27. Ibid., p. 209.

28. Green, op. cit., p. 117.

29. Dunning, op. cit., p. 370.

30. Kreye O., Heinrichs, J. and Frobel, F., *Multinational Enterprizes and Employment*, Geneva: International Labour Organisation, Starnberg Institute, 1988.

31. *Globalization and Liberalization*, op. cit., p. 242.

32. Brannon, J. T., James, D. J. and Lucker, G. W., 'Generating and sustaining backward linkages between *maquiladoras* and local suppliers in northern Mexico', *World Development*, Vol. 22, No. 12, 1994.

33. Ibid.

34. Ibid.

35. *Handbook of International Trade and Development Statistics, 1990*, Geneva: UNCTAD, 1990, p. viii.

36. Flanders, S., 'Banks and the wealth of nations', *Financial Times*, 7 October 1996.

37. Martin, Hans-Peter and Schumann, Harald, *The Global Trap: Globalization and the Assault on Democracy & Prosperity*, London: Zed Books, 1997.

38. *The Social Impact of the Asian Financial Crisis*, Geneva: International Labour Organisation, 1998.

2. Why poor countries 'want' the corporations

1. See, for example, 'Rubin urges S Africa to embrace globalisation', *Financial Times*, 15 July 1998.

2. Vandana Shiva, in reply to a question at 'The People's Summit', Birmingham, May 1998.

3. *Human Development Report 1997*, New York: UN Development Programme, 1997, p. 82.

4. Qureshi, Zia, 'Globalization: new opportunities, tough challenges', *Finance and Development*, Washington, DC: International Monetary Fund, March 1996.

5. Ibid.

6. Quoted in United Nations Non-Governmental Liaison Service 'Roundup', UN–NGO Liaison Service, Geneva, July 1996.

7. *World Investment Report 1993*, Geneva: UNCTAD, 1993.

8. *Global Economic Prospects and the Developing Countries*, Washington, DC: World Bank, 1996.

9. *Trade and Development Report 1997*, Geneva: UNCTAD, August 1997.

10. Dunning, J. H., 'Re-evaluating the benefits of foreign direct investment', *Transnational Corporations*, Vol. 3, No. 1, February 1994, Geneva: UNCTAD, p. 27.

11. *South Letter*, Vols 2 & 3, No 31, 1998, Geneva: The South Centre.

12. *Comparative Experiences with Privatization: Policy Insights and Lessons Learned*, New York and Geneva: UNCTAD, 1995, p. 111.

13. J. H. Dunning in conversation with the author, February 1996.

14. Whelan, R., 'Foreign aid: who needs it?', *Economic Affairs*, London: Institute of Economic Affairs, Autumn 1996.

15. Gelinas, Jacques B., *Freedom from Debt*, London: Zed Books, 1998, p. 34.

16. *Human Development Report 1997*, op. cit., p. 93.

17. Barry Coates, in a letter to WDM members, November 1997. London: WDM.

18. *Rainforest Action Report*, London: Friends of the Earth, Winter 1992.

19. Korten, D. C., *When Corporations Rule the World*, London: Earthscan, 1995, p. 166.

20. *World Bank News*, 19 September 1996.

21. Bernard Pasquier, quoted in *The Ecologist*, July/August 1996, p. 177.

3. The agri-corporations

1. Mooney, Pat Roy, 'The parts of life', *Development Dialogue*, Uppsala: Dag Hammarskjold Foundation, April 1998, p. 147.

2. *The World Seed Market*, Utrecht: Rabobank, 1996.

3. Mooney, op. cit., p. 148.

4. *State of the World's Plant Genetic Resources*, Rome: Food and Agriculture Organisation, March 1996.

5. Shiva, Vandana, 'Seeds of Discontent', *Multinational Monitor*, Washington, DC, June 1996.

6. *Patenting Plants: The Implications for Developing Countries*, London: Overseas Development Institute, 1993.

7. Emmot, S., 'The directive rises again', *Seedling*, Vol. 14, No. 1, March 1997, Barcelona: GRAIN.

8. See Sharma, D., *GATT to WTO: Seeds of Despair*, New Delhi: Konark, 1995.

9. See 'Rifkin fires first shot at W. R. Grace in battle against "Patents on Life"', *Diversity*, Vol. 11, No. 3, 1995, Bethesda, USA: Genetic Resources Communications Systems.

10. M. D. Nanjundaswamy, quoted in 'Indian farmers protest against company seeds', *International Agricultural Development* magazine, September/October 1993.

11. Quoted in *Intellectual Property Rights and the Biodiversity Convention*, London: Friends of the Earth, 1995.

12. See *Food? Health? Hope? Genetic Engineering and World Hunger*, Dorset: The Corner House, August 1998.

13. Vandana Shiva, 'The risks are not understood. And the livelihoods of millions of people in the Third World are threatened', *The Guardian*, 18 December 1997.

14. 'Monsanto reaps benefit of genetic engineering', *Financial Times*, 1 November 1996.

15. See 'Terminating food security?', *International Agricultural Development* magazine, May/June 1998, pp. 7–9.

16. Ibid.

17. Statement by Cargill and Monsanto, Monsanto web-site, May 1998.

18. 'The Benefits of Biodiversity: 100+ examples of the contribution by indigenous and rural communities in the South to the development of the North', RAFI Occasional Paper Series, Vol. 1, No. 1, Ottawa: RAFI, March 1994.

19. 'Conserving indigenous knowledge: integrating two systems of innovation', RAFI/UNDP report, quoted in the *Financial Times*, 28 October 1994.

20. Shiva, Vandana, 'Globalism, biodiversity and the Third World', in E. Goldsmith, M. Khor, H. Norberg-Hodge and V. Shiva, *The Future of Progress: Reflection on Environment and Development*, Green Books/ISEC, 1995.

21. Sharma, op. cit.

22. Dinham, B., 'Transnational corporations: in debt to the poor?', *Christian Action Journal*, Winter 1990.

23. *Export Taxes on Primary Commodities*, Commonwealth Paper No. 9. London: Commonwealth Secretariat, 1984.

24. Goldin, I., Knudsen, O. and van der Mensbrugghe, D., *Trade Liberalisation: Global Economic Implications*, Paris: Organisation for Economic Cooperation Development/World Bank, 1993.

25. Lang, T. and Hines, C., *The New Protectionism*, London: Earthscan, 1993, p. 35.

26. Clairmonte, F. and Cavanagh, J, *The World in Their Web*, London: Zed Books, 1983, p. 59.

27. Watkins, K., *Fixing the Rules*, London: CIIR, 1992, p. 38.

28. Kneen, B., *Invisible Giant*, London: Pluto Press, 1995, p. 206.

29. Speech by R. H. V. Cowley, Unilever's head of research, to a 'Business in Development' discussion meeting, London, April 1995.

30. Dinham, B. (ed.), *Growing Food Security*, London: The Pesticides Trust, 1996.

31. Weir, D. and Schapiro, M., *The Circle of Poison*, San Francisco: Institute for Food and Development Policy, 1981, p. 3.

32. Partow, H., 'The cost of hazards posed by pesticides in Kenyan export crops', *Pesticide News*, No. 29, September 1995, London: The Pesticides Trust.

33. Ibid.

34. *Say Yes to the Best – Justice for Banana Workers*, London: World Development Movement, July 1997.

35. See Benbow, S. J., 'The Bhopal legacy lingers on', *Pesticide News*, No. 26, December 1994.

36. Luesby, J., 'Treatment of Bhopal victims "immoral"', *Financial Times*, 10 December 1996.

37. Conversation with author, February 1994.

38. Ibid.

39. Conversation with author, June 1996.

40. *Prevention and Disposal of Obsolete and Unwanted Pesticide Stocks in Africa and the Near East*, Rome: Food and Agricultural Organisation, 1996.

41. *The Economist*, 16 September 1995.

4. Agri-commodities take their toll

1. 'Guatemala files lawsuit on tobacco', *Financial Times*, 13 May 1998.

2. 'US group spinning off Gallagher to cut links with tobacco', *Financial Times*, 9 October 1996.

3. *Tobacco: Supply, Demand and Trade Projections, 1995–2000*, Rome: Food and Agricultural Organisation, 1990.

4. World Health Organisation Press Release, No. 44, 30 May 1994.

5. Chapman, S., 'Tobacco trade in Africa: a bright future indeed', in D. Yach and S. Harrison (eds), *The Proceedings of All Africa Conference on Tobacco or Health*, Pretoria: 1994.

6. Aliro, O. K., *Uganda: Paying the Price of Growing Tobacco*, Kampala: The Monitor Publications, 1993, p. 23.

7. Chapman, S., with Leng, W.W., *Tobacco Control in the Third World: A Resource Atlas*, Penang, Malaysia: International Organisation of Consumer Unions, 1990.

8. Ibid.

9. 'Curiosities', *New Internationalist*, October 1996.

10. I am indebted to Dr Keith Ball, former chairman of Action on Smoking and Health, for this information.

11. MacKay, J., 'The fight against tobacco in developing countries', in *Tubercle and Lung Diseases*, London: Longman, 1994.

12. Paper given to the Fifth World Conference on Smoking and Health, Winnipeg, 1983.

13. Aliro, op. cit., p. 18.

14. World Health Organisation Press Release, op. cit.

15. Ibid.

16. Ibid.

17. Aliro, op. cit., p. 11.

18. *Tobacco and Food Crops Production in the Third World*, London: Economist Intelligence Unit, 1983.

19. Personal communication.

20. See 'Growing the golden leaf', *African Farming*, November/December 1996.

21. *Hunger and the Global Agenda*, London: Action Aid, November 1996, p. 6.

22. Taylor, P., *Smoke Ring: The Politics of Tobacco*, London: Bodley Head, 1984, pp. 252–3.

23. Goodland, R. J. A., Watson, C. and Ledec, G., *Environmental Management in Tropical Agriculture*, Boulder, CO: Westview Press, 1984, p. 56.

24. Wilkinson, J., *Tobacco*, London: Penguin, 1986, p. 125.

25. Watts, R., 'Crops to snuff out tobacco', *African Farming*, September/October 1993.

26. Watts, R., 'Tobacco profits go up in smoke', *African Farming*, July/August 1993.

27. Radio interview for *Deutsche Welle*, February 1996.

28. McCoy, R. S., 'So-called benefits of tobacco industry debunked', *Utusan Konsumer* (Penang), Mid-July 1996,

29. *The State of the World's Children Report, 1991*, New York: UNICEF, December 1990.

30. See, for example, 'EC frowns on dried milk's baby smiles', *The Daily Telegraph*, 8 April 1992.

31. 'Action now on baby foods', *New Internationalist*, August 1973.

32. Muller, M., *The Baby Killer*, London: War on Want, 1973.

33. See Palmer, G., *The Politics of Breastfeeding*, London: Pandora Press, 1988, p. 206.

34. Op. cit., p. 207.

35. Op. cit., p. 237.

36. UNICEF Executive Board resolution 1991/22, 1991.

37. *Breaking the Rules*, Cambridge: International Baby Food Network (IBFAN), 1991.

38. *Breaking the Rules*, Cambridge: IBFAN, 1994.

39. Letter to Baby Milk Action, Cambridge, 28 November 1994.

40. Letter to an organiser of the 1995 Nestlé-sponsored conference on business ethics, quoted in *New Internationalist*, January 1996.

41. Lewis, L., 'Charity seeks Beijing baby milk probe', *Financial Times*, 8 July 1996.

42. 'Boycott News', supplement to *Baby Milk Action Update* 22, June 1998, Baby Milk Action, Cambridge.

43. *Cracking the Code*. Report of the Interagency Group on Breastfeeding Monitoring, London, January 1997.

44. Interagency Group on Breastfeeding Monitoring, News Release, January 1998.

45. Thrupp, L. A., with Bergeron, G. and Waters, W. F., *Bittersweet Harvests for Global Supermarkets: Challenges in Latin America's Agricultural Export Boom*, Washington, DC: World Resources Institute, 1995.

46. Ibid.

47. 'Bean Counting in Chile', *The World Paper*, Boston, MA, December 1993.

48. Thrupp et al., op. cit., pp. 67–8

49. Ibid., p. 70

50. Ibid.

51. Ibid.

52. Francisco Morales, in conversation with the author, May 1994.

53. Ibid.

54. Thrupp et al., op. cit., p. viii.

55. Stewart, S., *Colombian Flowers: The Gift of Love and Poison*, London: Christian Aid, July 1994.

56. Watts, R., 'Nairobi Show confronts controversy', *African Farming*, July/August 1996.

57. *Modern Times: Mange Tout*, BBC Television, 27 February 1997.

58. Thrupp et al., op. cit.

59. *Philippines Development Briefing, No. 6*, London: CIIR, 1994.

60. Madden, P. and Orton, L., *The Global Supermarket*, London: Christian Aid, 1996, p. 26.

5. Extracting logs and fish

1. *State of the World's Forests*, Rome: Food and Agricultural Organisation, March 1997.

2. Fred Pearce, quoted in 'The global chainsaw massacre', *The Observer*, 29 September 1996.

3. Information supplied by the Rainforest Action Network, San Francisco, CA.

4. 'Business Day', *New York Times*, 11 May 1993.

5. Tom Fawthrop, writing in *The Nation* (Thailand), 15 December 1995.

6. Ibid.

7. Lochhead, James, 'Indigenous land rights in Malaysia', discussion paper, Simba (Singaporean Malaysian British Association), London: no date.

8. See *International Agricultural Development* magazine, November/December 1997.

9. Snow, D. and Collee, J., 'The rape of an island paradise', *The Observer*, 29 September 1996.

10. Quoted in Baird, N., 'Saying no to Asian loggers', *People & the Planet*, Vol. 5, No. 4, 1996.

11. Quoted in 'Asian loggers have begun to invade Amazon', *AGRA–Alimentation*, 22 July 1996.

12. Ibid.

13. Colchester, M., 'The New Sultans', *The Ecologist*, March/April 1994.

14. Information supplied by the Rainforest Action Network, San Francisco, CA.

15. The World Business Council for Sustainable Development is a Geneva-based group set up in 1990 at the request of Maurice Strong, Secretary-General of the UN Conference on Environment and Development.

16. José Luiz, in conversation with the author, 17–20 May 1992.

17. João Pedro Stedile, in conversation with the author, 17–20 May 1992.

18. Personal communication.

19. Carlos Alberto Roxo, in conversation with the author, 17–20 May 1992.

20. Manuel Carol Gomes, in conversation with the author, 17–20 May 1992.

21. *Earth Matters*, No. 36, Winter 1997, London: Friends of the Earth.

22. Tickell, O., 'Honduran chop logic', *The Guardian*, 14 February 1992.

23. Fred Pearce, quoted in 'The global chainsaw massacre', *The Observer*, 29 September 1996.

24. Lori Pottinger, quoted in 'Making Waves', *World Rivers Review*, July 1996, Berkeley, CA.

25. NGO coordinator, quoted in ibid.

26. Oliver Envor, quoted in ibid.

27. *Plunder in Ghana's Rainforests for Illegal Profit*, London: Friends of the Earth, March 1992.

28. Fairlie, S., Hagler, M. and O'Riordan, B., 'The politics of overfishing', *The Ecologist*, March/April, May/June 1995.

29. Le Sann, Alain, *A Livelihood from Fishing*, London: Intermediate Technology Publications, 1998.

30. I am indebted to Brian O'Riordan for information about Starkist and Kjell Inge Rokke.

31. See 'Fishing deals impoverish communities', *International Agricultural Development* magazine, May/June 1997.

32. Madeley, J., *Fish: A Net Loss for the Poor*, Panos Briefing Paper, London: Panos Institute, March 1995, p. 8.

33. Aliou Sall, in a letter to the author.

34. Brian O'Riordan, letter, 15 August 1997, addressed to the President of South Africa, reproduced in *Samudra* magazine, January 1998.

35. Brian O'Riordan, quoted in Madeley, op. cit., p. 8.

36. Quoted by Mukul Sharma in *Economic and Political Weekly* (India), 26 February 1994.

37. Burrell, Ian, 'The P&O port that no none wants', *Independent on Sunday*, 1 February 1998.

38. 'P&O's Indian harbour plans halted by protests', *Financial Times*, 27 November 1998.

39. Madeley, op. cit., p. 13.

6. Mining the poor

1. Moody, R., 'Mining the world, the global reach of Rio Tinto Zinc', *The Ecologist*, March / April 1996, pp. 46–52.

2. See 'Mining groups spend record sums', *Financial Times*, 23 October 1996.

3. 'Globalization picks up pace in the mining sector', *Financial Times*, 31 May 1996.

4. Moody, op. cit.

5. Ibid.

6. Woolf, M., 'South Africa's Gold Standard Bearer', *The Observer*, 13 October 1996.

7. Quoted in 'Apartheid in the mines', *Multinational Monitor*, June 1995.

8. See *Business Day* (Johannesburg), 3 June 1996.

9. Hawkins, Tony, 'Copper-bottomed pledge to sell-offs key to Zambia aid', *Financial Times*, 12 May 1988.

10. Moody, op. cit.

11. 'Deep appetite for deposits', *Financial Times*, 11 August 1993.

12. Bennett, G., Testimony to 1981 International Tribunal on RTZ, quoted in Moody, op. cit.

13. Moody, op. cit.

14. Jones, J. D. F., 'The price of a great African wilderness', *Financial Times*, 20 January 1996. See also 'Scheme banned on environmental grounds', *Financial Times*, 7 March 1996.

15. Address to Mining and Indigenous Peoples Consultation, London, 6–16 May 1996.

16. Melanesian Environment Foundation, 'Mining development, environmental pollution and social changes in Melanesia, Papua New Guinea'. Paper presented to Mining and Indigenous Peoples Consultation, London, May 1996.

17. From the Declaration of the Mining and Indigenous Peoples Consultation, London, 6–16 May 1996.

18. Tribal elder, quoted in 'The mining menace of Freeport McMoran', *Multinational Monitor*, April 1996.

19. Quoted in a World Development Movement brochure: *Protests and Profits: Mining in West Papua*, London: World Development Movement, 1994.

20. Tribal leader, quoted in 'The mining menace of Freeport McMoran', op. cit.

21. Moody, op. cit.

22. Perpetua Serero, quoted in ibid.

23. Ibid.

24. Wallace, J., *RTZ Mineral Sands Project*, London: Friends of the Earth, 1995.

25. '1995's 10 worst corporations', *Multinational Monitor*, December 1995.

26. Address to Mining and Indigenous Peoples Consultation, London, 6–16 May 1996.

27. Moody, R., *The Lure of Gold*, Panos Media Briefing, No. 19, London: Panos Institute, May 1996.

28. 'Action: Mining companies threaten Amerindian lands in Guyana', urgent action bulletin of *Survival International*, London: September 1996.

29. Emberson-Bain, A., *Labour and Gold in Fiji*, Cambridge: Cambridge University Press, 1994. See also review by Farnsworth, S., *Multinational Monitor*, June 1995.

30. Gooding, K., 'Gold miners prepare for output boom', *Financial Times*, 2 October 1996.

31. Simon, B., 'Jungle hideaway for salting operation', *Financial Times*, 7 May 1997.

32. Gooding, K., 'Conference told of bright future for African gold', *Financial Times*, 19 November 1996.

33. Sharma, A., 'Aborigines pitted against RTZ', *Spur*, September/October 1996, London: World Development Movement.

34. Ibid.

35. Mohideen, K., 'Women undermined', *Spur*, September/October 1996, London: World Development Movement.

36. Ibid.

37. Corpuz, C., Jr and Links, C., 'Mining standoff in the Philippines', *Spur*, November/December 1996, London: World Development Movement.

38. Ibid.

39. Luce, E., 'Mine groups warn on environment curbs', *Financial Times*, 19 September 1996.

40. Ibid.

41. Luce, E., 'Philippines reins in foreign mines', *Financial Times*, 22 October 1996.

42. Moody, op. cit.

43. Ibid.

44. Ibid.

45. Akabzaa, T., speech to Mining and Indigenous Peoples Consultation, London, 6–16 May 1996.

46. *World Health Organisation 1996 Annual Report*, Geneva: WHO, 1996.

7. Manufactured goods

1. *World Investment Report 1995*, Geneva: UNCTAD, 1995, pp. 230–1.

2. Evers, B. and Kirkpatrick, C., *New Forms of Foreign Investment in Developing Countries*, Bradford: University of Bradford Press, 1990, pp. 12–14.

3. Mayne, R., 'Adjustment and small businesses', *Appropriate Technology*, December 1995, London: Intermediate Technology Publications.

4. Evers and Kirkpatrick, op. cit.

5. Korten, D. C., *When Corporations Rule the World*, London: Earthscan, 1995, p. 229.

6. *Child Labour: Targeting the Intolerable*, Geneva: International Labour Organisation, November 1996.

7. Media briefing on the Toy Industry, Catholic Institute for International

Relations, the Trades Union Congress and the World Development Movement, 14 December 1995.

8. See 'Toys R Us buys rival for $403m', *Financial Times*, 3 October 1996, and 'Mattel to take over Tyco Toys for $755m', *Financial Times*, 19 November 1996.

9. 'Toying with workers', *Multinational Monitor*, Washington, DC, April 1996.

10. News Release, Catholic Institute for International Relations, Trade Union Congress, World Development Movement, 14 December 1995.

11. Ibid.

12. Personal conversation with the author, December 1995.

13. 'Code of conduct for toy makers', *Financial Times*, 4 June 1996.

14. 'Toy companies urged to monitor conditions at Asian suppliers', *Financial Times*, 26 July 1996.

15. Brookes, B. and Madden, P., *The Globe-Trotting Sports Shoe,* London: Christian Aid, December 1995, p. 4.

16. Ballinger, J., 'Just do it – or else', *Multinational Monitor*, Washington, DC, June 1995.

17. Ibid.

18. Ibid.

19. Ibid.

20. Ibid.

21. Ibid.

22. Brookes and Madden, op. cit., p. 8.

23. Martin Cottingham, quoted in Jury, L., 'Sports firms pledge to end child labour', *The Independent*, 28 September 1996.

24. Paul Fireman, quoted in ibid.

25. Usborne, D., 'Nike swears off slave labour', *The Independent*, 15 April 1997.

26. Lewis, William, 'Nike under fire on conditions in Vietnam', *Financial Times*, 10 November 1997.

27. 'Why I'll never buy a pair of Levis again', *The Mail on Sunday*, 27 November 1994.

28. 'Levi-Strauss offers £500m cash bonus to employees', *Financial Times*, 13 June 1996.

29. Ransom, David, 'Jeans: the big stitch-up', *New Internationalist*, June 1998.

30. Information supplied by Clean Clothes Campaign, Amsterdam, The Netherlands.

31. 'C&A to clamp down on sweated labour', *Financial Times*, 13 May 1996.

32. Mayne, R., 'Observatory', *The Observer*, 23 June 1996.

33. 'C&A calls for forum to improve working conditions', *Financial Times*, 4 October 1996.

34. See 'Use of child labour is diminishing', *Financial Times*, 22 October 1996.

35. Briefing Paper: *Campaign Against Exploitation of Child Labour in the Carpet Industry*, London: Anti-Slavery International, September 1995.

36. Press release, 'India launches label for carpet exports', Government of India, 9 June 1995.

37. *Labour and Social Issues relating to Export Processing Zones*, Geneva: International Labour Organisation, September 1998.

38. Bello, W., 'Behind the success of Asia's export-orientated industrialisation', *Third World Features Network*, Penang, Malaysia, January 1992.

39. Kreye, O., Heinricks, J. and Frobel, F., *Multinational Enterprises and Employment*, Geneva: International Labour Organisation, Starnberg Institute, 1988.

40. Ibid.

41. Ibid.

42. Alter, R., *Export Processing Zones for Growth and Development*, IMF Working Paper, P/90/122, Washington, DC: International Monetary Fund, 1990.

43. Weissman, R., 'Waiting to export', *Multinational Monitor*, Washington, DC, July/August 1996, pp. 12–16.

8. Energy

1. Personal conversation with the author, March 1983.

2. Andrew Gray, in a speech to the conference, 'Development Induced Displacement and Impoverishment', Oxford, January 1995.

3. Madeley, J., 'Second dam deal outrages greens', *The Observer*, 13 March 1994.

4. Ibid.

5. 'Indigenous groups lobby Bakun funders', *The Ecologist*, November/December 1995.

6. 'Bakun is not economically viable', *Utusan Konsumer* (Penang), mid-July 1995.

7. Quoted in *The Ecologist*, September/October 1996, from a *Financial Times* survey.

8. 'Northern NGOs urge Bakun consortium to withdraw', *Utusan Konsumer* (Penang), mid-August 1996.

9. 'Malaysia signs dam contract', *Financial Times*, 3 October 1996.

10. See 'Malaysian Mining quits Bakun team', *Financial Times*, 4 December 1996.

11. Vaughan, L., 'Indian power scheme nears final hurdle', *Financial Times*, 1 October 1996.

12. 'Enron's political profit pipeline' *Multinational Monitor*, December 1995.

13. 'FT 500', *Financial Times*, 28 January 1999.

14. A. Rowell, *Shell-Shocked: The Environmental and Social Costs of Living with Shell in Nigeria*, London: Greenpeace, July 1994, p. 10.

15. Ibid., p. 11.

16. Ibid., pp. 11–12.

17. Ecumenical Committee for Corporate Responsibility Newsletter, 15 November 1994, Banbury, UK.

18. Ken Saro-Wiva quoted in *Shell-Shocked*, op. cit., and 'Without Walls', Channel 4 TV, 14 November 1995.

19. *People and the Environment*, Annual Report 1996, Lagos: Shell Nigeria, May 1997.

20. Quoted in Christian Concern for One World Newsletter, March 1996. Banbury, UK.

21. Quoted in *Multinational Monitor*, December 1995.

22. *Shell-Shocked*, op. cit., p. 6.

23. Jochnick, C., 'Amazon oil offensive', *Multinational Monitor*, January/February 1995.

24. Helena Paul, in conversation with the author, July 1996.

25. Quoted in Jochnick, op. cit.

26. Ibid.

27. Helena Paul, in conversation with the author, July 1996.

28. Quoted in Jochnick, op. cit.

29. Helena Paul, in conversation with the author, July 1996.

30. International Labour Organisation report, quoted in *Transnational Corporations in World Development*, New York: United Nations, 1988, p. 224.

31. Jochnick, op. cit.

32. See 'Burma sues Unocal', *Multinational Monitor*, October 1996.

33. 'BP does a U-turn on rights abuses', *The Observer*, 10 November 1996.

34. 'BP accused of funding Colombia death squads', *The Observer*, 20 October 1996.

35. 'Oil giant in troubled waters', *Financial Times*, 6 November 1996.

9. Tourism

1. 'Developing countries could target tourism to boost economic growth', Press Release, TAD/INF/2755, Geneva: UNCTAD, June 1998.

2. 'Japanese make fewer visits', *Financial Times*, 10 July 1998.

3. Long, V. H., 'Government–industry–community interaction in tourism development in Mexico', in M. Thea Sinclair and M. J. Stabler (eds), *The Tourism Industry: An International Analysis*, Wallingford, UK: CAB International, 1991, p. 4.

4. *Transnational Corporations, Services and the Uruguay Round*, New York: United Nations Centre on Transnational Corporations, p 109.

5. Sinclair, M.T., Alizadeh, P., Atieno, E. and Onunga, O., 'Tourism development in Kenya', in David Harrison (ed.), *Tourism and the Less Developed Countries*, London: Belhaven Press/Halstead Press, 1992, p. 55.

6. Long, in Sinclair and Stabler, op. cit., p. 185.

7. *The Role of Transnational Tourism Enterprizes in the Development of Tourism*, Madrid: World Trade Organisation, 1985.

8. Harvey Perkins: information presented at the conference on Tourism and Third World Peoples at Bad Boll, Germany, March 1986.

9. *Transnational Corporations, Services and the Uruguay Round*, op. cit., p. 92.

10. Walters, J., 'Being an Airline is not enough, so BA plots world domination', *The Observer*, 4 May 1997.

11. *Transnational Corporations, Services and the Uruguay Round*, op. cit., p. 95.

12. *Transnational Corporations in International Tourism*, New York: United Nations Centre on Transnational Corporations, 1982, p. 9.

13. *Services in Asia and the Pacific: Selected Papers*, Vol. 1, New York: United Nations, 1990, p. 372.

14. *The Tourism Industry: An International Analysis*, op. cit., p. 188.

15. *EIU Travel and Tourism Analyst*, No. 2, London: Economist Intelligence Unit, 1995.

16. Koson Srisang, quoted in *Contours* magazine, September 1991, Thailand: Ecumenical Coalition on Third World Tourism.

17. Ibid.

18. Agena, K., *A New Alliance: Multinational Corporations and Private Development Agencies*, New York: Fund for Multinational Corporations, 1986.

19. Stuart Howard, quoted in Gosling, G., 'Cheap labour at the end of a phone line', *The Independent*, 3 July 1995.

20. *EIU Travel and Tourism Analyst*, No. 5, London: Economist Intelligence Unit, 1995.

21. *Transnational Corporations, Services and the Uruguay Round*, op. cit., p. 103.

22. *The Tourism Industry: An International Analysis*, op. cit., p. 198.

23. Ibid., p. 200.

24. Ibid., pp. 185–204.

25. *Working Conditions in Hotels, Restaurants and Similar Establishments*, Geneva: International Labour Organisation, Report V1 (1), 1990.

26. *Conditions of Work in the Hotel, Catering and Tourism Sector*, Geneva: International Labour Organisation, Report 2, 1989.

27. Anne Badger, quoted in *Tourism in Focus*, Winter 1993.

28. Fillmore, M., *Suggested Guidelines for Assessment of the Impact of Tourism on Women*, India: Equitable Tourism Options, 1994.

29. Long, in Sinclair and Stabler, op. cit., p. 207.

30. See P. Bachmann, *Tourism in Kenya: Basic Needs for Whom?*, Berne: Peter Lang, 1988.

31. *Transnational Corporations, Services and the Uruguay Round*, op. cit., p. 105.

32. Information presented at the conference on Tourism and Third World Peoples at Bad Boll, Germany, March 1986.

33. See 'The Gambia tries to cash in on its roots', *Panoscope, PS magazine*, London: Panos Institute, January 1992.

34. *Transnational Corporations, Services and the Uruguay Round*, op. cit., p. 105.

35. Albertina Almeida, quoted in *Tourism in Focus*, Autumn 1995.

36. Haunani-Kay Trask, in a speech at the conference on Tourism and Third World Peoples at Bad Boll, Germany, March 1986.

37. Robert Peake, quoted in *Tourism in Focus*, Spring 1994.

38. Maybin, E., *An Abuse of Innocence: Tourism and Child Prostitution in the Third World*, London: Christian Aid, May 1995.

39. *Services in Asia and the Pacific: Selected Papers*, op. cit., p. 369.

40. See Sexton, S. and Chatterjee, P., 'Fairway to heaven?', *The Guardian*, 17 September 1993.

41. Piercy, S. (ed.), *Ecotourism*, Panos Briefing Paper, January 1995.

42. *World Travel & Tourism Environmental Research Centre, Annual Review 1993*. Oxford: WTTERC, 1993.

43. *World Travel & Tourism Environmental Research Centre, Annual Review 1994*. Oxford: WTTERC, 1994.

44. Ibid.

45. Tricia Barnett, in conversation with the author, November 1995.

46. *The Tourism Industry: An International Analysis*, op. cit., pp. 217–18.

47. See Madeley, J., *Foreign Exploits, Transnationals and Tourism*, London: CIIR, May 1996.

10. Health

1. Eckett, Simon, 'Balancing more for less', *Financial Times*, 16 March 1998.

2. Quoted in 'The drug industry – deceitful, corrupt, ruthless', *Utusan Konsumer* (Penang), Mid-September 1996.

3. *Transnational Corporations in World Development*, New York: United Nations, 1988, pp. 222–3.

4. Chowdhury, Z., *The Politics of Essential Drugs*, London: Zed Books, 1995, p. 58.

5. UNCTAD study quoted in *Essential Drugs Monitor*, No. 17, Geneva: World Health Organisation, 1994.

6. Chowdhury, op. cit., pp. 5–6.

7. Ibid., pp. 1–2.

8. Ibid., p. 3.

9. *Essential Drugs Monitor*, op. cit.

10. O'Brien, T. F., et al. 'Resistance of bacteria to antibacterial agents: report of Task Force 2', *Reviews of Infectious Disease*, Vol. 9 (Supplement 3), May–June 1987, quoted in Chetley, A., *Problem Drugs*, Amsterdam: Health Action International (HAI), 1993.

11. Professor Stuart Levy, quoted in 'Antibiotics: the menace of your medicine chest', *The Observer*, 8 December 1996.

12. Professor Jacques Acar, quoted in *Essential Drugs Monitor*, No. 20, Geneva: World Health Organisation, 1995.

13. 'Antibiotics: the menace of your medicine chest', op. cit.

14. Dr Graham Dukes, quoted in Health Action International (HAI) brochure, op. cit.

15. Dr Graham Dukes, quoted in Chetley, op. cit.

16. Health Action International brochure, Amsterdam: HAI, 1996.

17. Ibid.

18. Chetley, A., op. cit.

19. Henry, J., *The British Medical Association Guide to Medicines and Drugs*, London: Dorling Kindersley, 1991, p. 145.

20. Chetley, op. cit.

21. *Drug Evaluations*, Philadelphia: American Medical Association, W.B. Saunders Co., 1986, p. 841.

22. Chetley, op. cit.

23. Ibid.

24. HAI brochure, op. cit.

25. Cookson, Clive, 'Drug group in bid to wipe out elephantiasis', *Financial Times*, 26 January 1998.

26. *WHO Issues New International Guidelines for Drug Donations*, Geneva: World Health Organisation, Press Release, 30 April 1996.

27. *Vi Menn* (Norwegian weekly magazine), April 1996.

28. Letter to the European Union Presidency, 2 October 1995.

29. Purvis, A., 'The Goodwill Pill mess', *Time*, 29 April 1996.

30. Ibid.

31. HAI Press Release, 15 May 1996.

32. Community Development Medicinal Unit, Press Release, 8 April 1996.

33. 'Expired drugs found in airlift for poor', *The Telegraph* (India), 9 April 1996.

34. *WHO Issues New International Guidelines for Drug Donations*, op. cit.

35. Chowdhury, op. cit., p. 9.

36. Ibid., pp. 47–9.

37. Ibid., p. 63.

38. Ibid., pp. 67–8.

39. Ibid., pp. 73–5.

40. Ibid., p. 87.

41. Ibid., p. 162.

42. Ibid., p. 34.

43. Mirza, Z., 'Non-emergence of Pakistan's national drug policy', *The Lancet*, London: British Medical Association, 13 July 1996.

44. Chetley, A., *A Healthy Business*, London: Zed Books, 1990, p. 73.

45. Stichele, M. V. and Pennartz, P., *Making It Our Business – European NGO Campaigns on Transnational Corporations*, London: CIIR, Briefing, September 1996.

46. Roberto Lopez, quoted in the HAI brochure, op. cit.

11. The corporate persuaders

1. Moody-Stuart, George, talk to the Development Journalists Group in London, April 1997, about his book *Grand Corruption, How Business Bribes Damage Developing Countries*, Oxford: WorldView Publishing, 1997.

2. von Bern, E., *The Infiltration of the UN System by Multinational Corporations*, Zurich: Association pour un Developpement Solidaire, 1978.

3. UNCTC leaflet, DESI E. 130, New York: UNCTC, 1986.

4. Chowdhury, Z., *The Politics of Essential Drugs*, London: Zed Books, 1995, p. 140.

5. *World Investment Report, 1995*, Geneva: UNCTAD, 1995, p. 256.

6. Tran, M., 'G7 does U-turn over Unctad', *South*, August 1996.

7. Watkins, K., 'Global market myths', *Red Pepper*, June 1996, p. 14.

8. Stichele, Myriam Vander, *Towards a World Transnational s' Organisation?*, Amsterdam: Transnational Institute, April 1998, p. 9.

9. Ibid., p. 5.

10. Stichele, Myriam Vander, speech to NGO meting in Geneva, May 1998.

11. Watkins, op. cit.

12. Enron representative addressing a US Congressional Committee, quoted in *The Ecologist*, July/August 1996, p. 179.

13. Richter, Judith, *Engineering of Consent, Uncovering Corporate PR*, Dorset, UK: The Corner House, March 1998.

14. Communications Programmes for Europabio. Leaked strategy document, Burson Marsteller, January 1997.

15. Richter, op. cit.

16. Ibid., from Saunders, E., *Nestlégate, Secret Memo Reveals Corporate Cover-up*, London: Baby Milk Action, 1981. At about the time this was published, I received a call from Mr Saunders's office asking if I would meet him for lunch. I said possibly, but made it clear that it should be a group meeting. The offer of lunch was withdrawn the next day, however, presumably because Nestlé discovered that I would be a most 'inappropriate' contact.

17. Richter, op. cit.

18. Torry, Saundra and Dewar, Helen, 'Big tobacco's ad blitz felt in Senate debate', *The Washington Post*, 17 June 1998.

12. Tackling the power

1. Burns, M. and Zadek, S., *Open Trading Options for Effective Monitoring of Corporate Codes of Conduct*, London: CIIR/New Economics Foundation, March 1997.

2. Coats, S., 'Organisation and Repression', *Multinational Monitor*, June 1995.

3. McMillion, Charles W., 'Misnamed "Growth Bill" would inflict NAFTA's horrors on Africa', *The Ecologist*, July/August 1998.

4. See, for example, 'Monoculture inefficient', in *International Agricultural Development*, July/August 1996.

5. Kneen, B., *Invisible Giant*, London Pluto Press, 1995, p. 208.

6. Hildyard, N., Hines, C. and Lang, T., 'Who Competes', *The Ecologist*, July/August 1996, p. 142.

7. *Purchasing Power*, London: New Economics Foundation, 1998.

8. *Transnational Corporations in World Development*, op. cit., p. 219.

9. Christian Aid leaflet, March 1997.

10. Madden, P. and Orton, L., *The Global Supermarket*, London: Christian Aid, 1996, p. 31.

11. See 'Banana producers take on big traders', *Financial Times*, 19 November 1996.

12. Anne Simpson, interviewed on BBC television, *Newsnight*, 13 May 1997.

13. 'DuPont's Goa Constrictor', *Multinational Monitor*, December 1995, p. 15.

14. Ibid., pp. 9–16.

15. Stichele, M. V. and Pennartz, P., *Making It Our Business – European NGO Campaigns on Transnational Corporations*, London: CIIR, Briefing, September 1996. This briefing includes a number of detailed examples of NGO campaigns and has suggestions for future strategies. A UK-based organisation, New Consumer, collects information on the social and environmental activities of major TNCs and has published material on socially responsible shopping.

16. See, for example, 'Globalising Trade Unions', *Multinational Monitor*, June 1995.

17. See 'Rights and Wrongs', *Financial Times*, 18 March 1997.

18. William M. Dugger, quoted in Korten, D.C., *When Corporations Rule the World*, London: Earthscan, 1995, p. 207.

19. Korten, op. cit., p. 212.

20. Roddick, A., 'A voice for moral choice', *The Guardian*, 30 October 1996.

21. Korten, op. cit., p. 270.

22. Kneen, op. cit., p. 206.

23. Ibid.

Index